The Juju Rules

THE
Juju Rules

Or, How to Win Ballgames
from Your Couch

★

A MEMOIR OF

A FAN OBSESSED

★

Hart Seely

HOUGHTON MIFFLIN HARCOURT
BOSTON   NEW YORK
2012

For information about permission to reproduce selections from this book,
write to Permissions, Houghton Mifflin Harcourt Publishing Company,
215 Park Avenue South, New York, New York 10003.

www.hmhbooks.com

.

Library of Congress Cataloging-in-Publication Data
Seely, Hart, date.
The juju rules : or, how to win ballgames from your couch : a memoir of
a Yankee fan obsessed / Hart Seely.
p. cm.
ISBN 978-0-547-62237-8 (hardback)
1. New York Yankees (Baseball team)—Miscellanea. 2. New York
Yankees (Baseball team)—Humor. I. Title.
GV875.N4S44 2012
796.357'647471—dc23
2011036905

Book design by Victoria Hartman

Printed in the United States of America
DOC 10 9 8 7 6 5 4 3 2 1

Article on page 201 used with the permission of the Associated Press
copyright © 2011. All rights reserved.
Photo on page 269 © Madeline Seely.

To the Secret Yankee Club

and secret Yankees everywhere

★

Contents

★

Acknowledgments

★

The author wishes to thank the following people for their support and encouragement in the writing of this book: Allan Burnett, Justin Chamberlain, Carsten Sabathia, John D. Damon, Phillip D. Coke, Philip J. Hughes, C. Edward Gaudin, E. Scott Hinske, Alfredo Aceves, B. Anthony Bruney, Nicholas Swisher, Melky A. Cabrera, Brett M. Gardner, Susan Canavan, Jorge Rafael (Villeta) Posada, Robinson J. Cano, Bruce Nichols, Ramiro (Gauna) Pena, Dámaso (Sabinon) Marté, Barbara L. Jatkola, David Robertson, Jerry Wayne Hairston Jr., David McCormick, Andrew E. Pettitte, Jose Benjamin (Matta) Molina, M. Charles Teixeira, Francisco Cervelli, Alexander E. Rodriguez, Captain Derek Sanderson Jeter, and the Honorable Reverend Mariano Rivera.

Note: Since its inception in June 2007, the author's alternative Yankee reality website IT IS HIGH! IT IS FAR! IT IS . . . caught (johnsterling .blogspot.com) has generated more than a million page loads.

Most important, since IT IS HIGH! was launched, the Yankees have won 64.7 percent of their games — a rate significantly higher than the franchise's all-time winning percentage of 57.8.

That equals eleven extra wins per season, which I believe is a direct result of the website's surgically targeted juju transmissions.

This writer has faithfully sought to describe the events of his life as accurately as possible, without the distortions of eloquence or wit.

Nevertheless, some readers may chafe at the detailed descriptions, accounts, and other use of play-by-play, which, without the expressed written consent of Major League Baseball, is prohibited.

They should rest assured that all instructions on the assembly of juju weapons have been altered slightly to render them ineffective if used on American soil against the New York Yankees.

A final note: If the book is adapted into a film, the author requests that he be depicted as sleeping with more women — specifically, the nun in chapter 10.

Prologue: When Ari Met Seely

★

True story: In 2003, I personally broke the news to Ari Fleischer — then White House press secretary in the hell-bound administration of George W. Bush — that the Yankees' only decent starter of late, Jose Contreras, alias "the Bronze Titan," had tweaked a gonad and was headed for the disabled list.

"Oh, no," Fleischer said. "He's our only decent starter of late."

Ari had phoned to praise my hilarious op-ed piece in that morning's *New York Times*. After a few spineless pleasantries, we cut to the glaring, red-meat issue of the day: the senior citizen kazoo band that was masquerading as the New York Yankees' starting rotation. History will show that while Fleischer horribly understated the consequences of invading Iraq, his dire assessment of our pitching staff proved to be chillingly dead-on.

I tell this story not to boast about having a hilarious op-ed piece in the *Times,* an event so common that it's beneath mention. I tell it to save a life. *Your life.*

Originally, I planned to model this book on John Grogan's 2005 bestseller, *Marley & Me: Life and Love with the World's Worst Dog,* the inspirational, 300-plus-page tribute to his Labrador retriever, which was later transmogrified into an Owen Wilson movie and a lucrative series of spinoffs, including the children's book *A Very Marley Christmas*. Hell, I've had dogs. Good dogs, each one as loyal and commercially viable as Marley. I quickly conceived a project with the working title "Me & Bullwinkle: Livin' and Lovin' with the World's Most Commercially Viable Dog," only to realize that every writer in America would be sniffing from the same literary kibble. I foresaw the bestseller list:

1. Stephen Hawking, *A Brief History of Tricksie*
2. Mitch Albom, *Tuesdays with Fluffy*
3. Glenn Beck, *Arguing with Poodles: The Continuing Assault by Untrained Lap Dogs on Our Furniture*
4. Barack Obama, *The Audacity of Bo*
5. Jack Canfield and Mark Victor Hansen, *Liv-a-Snaps for the Soul*

That day brought a revelation: *In our lives, baseball players fill the same niche as pets.*

Think about it. Your favorite major leaguer's career has the life span of a beagle. Some players go twenty years. Some get hit by Buicks. You've got your loyal Cal Ripkens, who never tire of fetching the ball, and your rabid Ty Cobbs, who need an iron muzzle and cattle-grade shock collar. Some players simply cannot be trained. You feed them, walk them, rub their tummies, but with the bases loaded and two out, they pee all over the carpet.

Applying the Marley template, I decided to write "Jeet & Me," a delightful book and future motion picture about my amazing adventures with Derek Jeter. For example, there was his courageous 2004 headlong dive into the stands against Boston, his flip play at home plate in the 2001 playoffs, and his heartfelt speech in 2008 after the final game in Yankee Stadium. What about Jeet's game-opening home run against the Mets in the 2000 Subway Series? Or the ball he hit that landed in twelve-year-old Jeffrey Maier's outstretched glove in the 1996 postseason? Or his glorious 3,000th hit, a home run, in

2011? Let's not forget his women: actresses, singers, supermodels, all of whom I often Google. I have so many fond memories of Derek, where would I start? (Of course, I'd store a few holiday chestnuts for "A Very Jeet Christmas.")

There's just one rub: during those inspirational Jeterian moments, I did not exist.

Generally, I have no clue where I was or what I was doing, other than that I was screaming at some cowering, defenseless TV. I was in a bar, or my living room, or hiding behind a couch — frozen like a Bond girl squealing "Look out, James!" — while some pitcher tried to separate Jeet from his sternum. In those situations, I was attempting to channel incalculable amounts of energy into Jeet's astral plane, and I was surely frightening small children, most notably my own. But it's all a thick, frothy blur. I wasn't there. I was just watching on TV.

Good grief. At least with a dog, you get up and run around the yard. To scratch his belly, you don't just lie on the couch and toggle a remote.

Some folks render unto humanity great gifts, such as American League pennants. Others exist to pace the rug, chew their knuckles, and watch. Sadly, I am of the latter species.

I am the wedding guest who leaves the crowded ballroom to monitor scores that scroll across the TV.

I am the father who can recite the Yankees' Double-A pitching rotation at Trenton, but not his children's middle school teachers.

I am one of the reasons so many people hate the Yankees, or at least Yankee fans.

I am that sad soul who is commonly introduced as "the biggest Yankee fan you'll ever meet," which is code for "Whatever you do, *don't* mention the Yankees!"

I was always this way. The Yankees are the ghosts that whisper over my shoulder, the schizophrenic voice of God inside my head. In the shower, I rally the team, like Churchill addressing the collective British soul. Lying in bed, I converse with Derek, share pitching secrets with Mariano, and dispense fatherly advice to Joba.

Some say only Jesus Christ is capable of offering unequivocal love to those he will never know. They never met a Yankee fan.

But it's not always love. Inside me lurks a dark, swaggering presence, a Yankee Mr. Hyde. I cannot control him. I cannot reason with him. He is coarse and insatiable, petty and vindictive, a truly bad sport. He cheers when enemy players get hurt. He forgives the behavior of any Yankee, knowing the only crime is losing. He would sell his soul, if he had one, for a decent bullpen lefty. When we win, he boils with the rapture of one who has been touched by God. And when we lose, he is measuring nearby bridges.

Throughout my life, I have seldom made personal decisions without seeking input from this monster, this fiend, who eyes me so disappointingly in the mirror.

I am not sure whether this book is a celebration of sports or a one-way journey into mental illness. But here goes . . .

True story: I win ballgames for the New York Yankees.

The Juju Rules

1

★

Opening Day

It starts this way. I'm scrunched up on my mother's lap, surrounded by grownups in the flicker from an Admiral console TV, which is the size of my playpen. The image, my earliest memory, survives in black and white, except for the red lipstick smear on Mom's cigarette filter and the front-pocket pack of Pall Malls, which forms a lump in her breast when I cuddle.

They're watching a ballgame. I want to believe it is the epic 1956 World Series between the Yankees and Brooklyn Dodgers, when Yogi Berra not only performs a flying bear hug onto the perfect Don Larsen but also homers twice to win game seven. In a perfect world, it would be Larsen's perfect game, but I honestly cannot say. It could be a meaningless contest against a team nobody gives a whit about, such as Boston.

I am as cute as I will ever be — curly hair, missing tooth, wandering eye — peak toddler foliage. Somebody asks a question, and it doesn't register that the person is addressing me. I burrow into my mom's belly, my safe house, and inhale the warmth of her breasts.

"Harty," she says, "they want to know who you're rooting for."

This washes over me. I have no idea what she means.

But for the first time, I do sense one awesome concept: the universe — that is, the godlike adults who live up above the gray-blue nicotine cloud — awaits *my* opinion. I have the microphone and the podium. I have an audience, though no idea of what to do with it.

So I say the words that someone has planted: "Yang-geez."

The house erupts with laughter and applause. For the first time, I have *killed* a crowd. Mom gives me a squeeze. Instead of snuggling deeper, I turn to acknowledge my fans. They fling back their heads and throw smoke at the ceiling, twiddling the ice in their tumblers, gurgling approval. They love me. Everybody loves me.

Best. Moment. Ever.

It will take years to process what just happened.

Let me tell you about my dad, Hart I. Seely Jr. He was a beery, unfulfilled, small-town cheese. He ran the *Waverly Sun,* the weekly newspaper that his father founded around 1910. Back then, when upstate New York boomed with windowless brick factories and shotgun housing, my grandfather — the original Hart I. Seely — launched a chain of rural papers. He was a beery, *fulfilled,* small-town cheese. He became a vice president of Rotary International and traveled across the country giving motivational speeches to civic boosters. Folks called him "Hart I. — for *I AM!* — Seely." That probably sums him up.

My grandfather died in a car crash near Watkins Glen before I was born. His death forced my dad to come home from working on the railroad, which he loved, to manage the family newspaper, which he loathed.

Today, my dad would be considered repressed, quirky, and effectively self-medicated, his life filled with rites and routines that only he understood.

Each morning, he rushed home from the office to eat lunch while watching *Hollywood Squares,* the first TV show dedicated to the proposition that all men are not created equal: some are celebrities. Dad loved that show, lies and all. He could accept that the stars received their questions in advance, even though it reeked of the scandals that years earlier had nearly gutted America's game show industry. He recognized that the basic rules of morality were suspended in the presence of fame, even the B-list variety, the Florence Hendersons and Robert Q. Lewises, who owed much of their fame to being famous.

What riled him was how the great game of tic-tac-toe had been subverted.

My dad used a stopwatch to determine the exact amount of game play in an average twenty-four-minute *Hollywood Squares*, if one disregarded the time wasted on celebrity–host banter. He calculated that one episode offered less than two minutes of actual game action. This infuriated him. Whenever Rose Marie started yapping with Peter Marshall, Dad would blurt, "Jesus Christ! Let's get this round in!" If, with three minutes left in the show, a contestant picked Paul Lynde, Dad would slam his glass on the desk and yell, "It's over, damn it! We won't have enough time!" He claimed to have written the producers a nasty letter. They never responded.

Throughout his life, my dad raced against time. He'd ram our Ford station wagon across Waverly, touching the brakes only to make them squeal. From the backseat, it was like watching futuristic sequences from Grand Theft Auto. At every stop, he'd fume at the enemy drivers. "Any day now, Lady Bird!" he'd yell. "We're waiting, Lord Buckington!" "Make your move, Queenie!" But when Queenie made her move, he would goose the gas and try to beat her through the intersection. "Okay, Your Highness, you wanted it? You got it!"

In those face-offs, my mom usually sided with Queenie. "Make your *own* move!" she'd bark from the death seat. "Don't blame *her*! *You're* the one using both lanes!"

"Thank you, Louise," he would grumble, squeezing the wheel. "Thank you *so much* for supporting me as a loving wife and . . . *Hey, Helen Keller, you don't see a stop sign?*"

My friends in Little League appreciated Dad's disdain for the pretensions of adulthood. Once, at the annual father-son game, he pulled his shirt out of his pants and staggered around with a hip flask, pantomiming a drunk who was trying to bribe the umpires. He had everyone crying. "Your old man," a teammate said, "he don't give a shit." From a kid, this was the highest compliment to be paid, the Nobel Prize in Parenthood.

Later, when our football team beat Bath High School, Dad's front-page headline boasted, WAVERLY TAKES BATH, COMES OUT CLEAN. When we lost to Thomas Edison High School near Elmira, he wrote, EDISON SHORT-CIRCUITS RED-AND-WHITE'S CHARGE. On one legendary weekend, Dad showcased his carpentry skills to my Cub Scout troop by disassembling a sawhorse and nailing it back together — only to find an extra piece. We never figured out where it came from or where it was supposed to go. It stood in the corner of our garage, a reminder of the mysteries of life that lurked everywhere, even in Waverly, New York.

In football, my father claimed to root for the Dallas Cowboys and Los Angeles Rams, because "they are the cities that killed the Kennedys!" Hearing this, the stunned audience would search his deadpan face for a sign that he was joking and then giggle nervously after none was brokered. But as Dad aged, and as he drank, his punch lines grew louder, though not funnier, and some of the darkest ones ossified into angry political opinions, as if his worldview was being molded by the half-baked zingers of some bad comedy routine. The words he once spoke to provoke shocked reactions now became his core beliefs. I'd hear the whispers: "Whatever you do, don't get him started . . ."

But on this day, in the TV room, as I nuzzle Mom's pack of cigarettes, there is one joke that everyone knows to be absolutely, 100 percent real — which means it is no joke at all: my dad has an all-consuming hatred of the New York Yankees.

It centers his identity. It is his mission statement. He often says he hates the Yankees more than he hates life itself. His favorite team: "APY — Anybody Playing the Yankees." He hates Mickey Mantle. He hates Whitey Ford. He hates Yogi Berra — if such a thought can be imagined. He says, when times look bleak, he thinks of a Yankee loss, and the sun comes out, the roses bloom, and God smiles.

Yes, the God of my father hates Yogi Berra, too.

So on this day, in the moment of my greatest triumph, the Seely clan is gathered, and — who knows, maybe Don Larsen *is* throwing his perfect game. My dad is hunched over and shackled down, the son of the local big fish, stuck in the town he spent his youth vowing to escape. John Fitzgerald Kennedy is alive, Derek Sanderson Jeter is not, and Lawrence Peter Berra has yet to reexperience déjà vu for the first time. When the gallery asks me to name my favorite team, it is not my answer — "Yang-geez" — that moves the applause needle into the red. No, their laughter stems instead from Dad's death mask expression, as he shakes his head, lowers his eyes, blows out his cheeks, and takes a long, hard pull from his glass.

Yeah, somebody coached me. It had to be him. But he didn't foresee the outcome.

This day, for unexplained reasons, I become a lifelong Yankee fan. I'm Peter Parker, bitten by the radioactive spider. From that moment on, every molecule inside me is changed. I become the Yankee boy, the lunatic fan, bent in a direction that ensures that my father and I will always collide — even if, when we hit, we smash into neutrinos.

We will quarrel over lineups. We will fight over balls and strikes. We will argue over whether Roger Maris belongs in the Hall of Fame (he does, by the way), and whether Thurman Munson is better than Carlton Fisk (he wasn't, by the way). At times, we will stop talking altogether. At times, we will tell each other to go to hell.

Today, I realize my father's intentions. He was pushing my buttons, the ones he'd installed, perhaps without knowing it. The Yankees were the one subject that shouldn't matter, the one harmless disagreement where a father and son should always find safe harbor. Who really cared if Munson was better than Fisk? Seriously, *who really cared?*

He just didn't see what was coming.

THE ART OF JUJU

Before he retired from broadcasting in 1996, Phil Rizzuto made it a point never to switch topics during a Yankee rally. He might be re-counting a recent trip to Utica, a story with no remote connection to the game. As long as the Yankees kept hitting, Phil would keep talk-ing about Utica — a stream-of-consciousness filibuster that eventu-ally would include a few lucky restaurants and car dealerships. Later, if the Yankees needed a run, he'd resurrect the Utica trip, just to see if any magic remained in the tank.

"Gotta get back to Utica, White!" he'd yell to his partner, Bill White. "Amazing town! Had a great meal at . . . *Base hit by Murcer!*"

My dad hated Rizzuto. He called him a fool, a laughingstock, a clown — and he prosecuted Phil's every gaffe with the rage of a Salem witch judge. Often, late in a game, Dad would crank down the TV volume and launch a furious, point-by-point rebuttal to everything Rizzuto had said. This usually continued well beyond the postgame show and sometimes deep into the night, unspooling into ever higher magnitudes as I marched up to bed.

Phil's tangents never bothered me. I knew exactly what he was do-ing. He was trying to win us a ballgame. And he was not alone.

I don't watch Yankee games. I work them. I pour myself into each pitch, certain that my movements, my physical and mental actions, have an impact — and that somehow, *I matter.*

I sit one way when the Yankees are at bat, another way when they're in the field. If three Yankees get consecutive base hits, I note where I am and what I am doing. It's instinctive. It's beyond my control. Some region of my brain records stance and whereabouts, then scours the universe for a psychic link to the game, like a police scanner roaming for signals. If I'm in the kitchen, as long as the Yankee hits keep com-ing, I'll stay planted. If I'm on the phone, I'll keep talking — my own private Utica. I never tamper with Yankee success.

Don't get me wrong: I'm not a fool, a laughingstock, or a clown. It takes at least three hits to sell me on a juju position. I agree with the supervillain Auric Goldfinger, who explained to James Bond, "Once is happenstance; twice is coincidence; three times is enemy action."

That was a man who recognized the power of threes. So did the architects of baseball. Three strikes, you're out. Three outs per inning. Three outfielders. Three bases. Nine fielders — three times three. Twenty-seven outs — three times three times three. Babe Ruth wore three. He hit sixty home runs, ten times three, in 1927. Three is the first odd prime number. America put three golf balls on the moon. Bad luck happens in threes. And when the Yankees record three straight hits, it's not happenstance, it's not coincidence, it's not Toronto pitching. Something has flared in the universe, and if you want to win the game, damn it, it's no time to switch chairs.

Listen: I am not a kook.

Friends will tell you I'm a straight thinker, a realist, a regular guy. I don't do hooey. No shaking of beads. No pyramids, no magnets, no crop circles in Area 51. Aside from my father's sawhorse, I have yet to meet a mystery that cannot be explained through third-grade science. I don't believe in UFOs, Bigfoot, or Nessie. I don't even believe that for every drop of rain that falls, a flower grows. Seriously, do the math.

I'm normal. Get it? I drive six miles over the speed limit because the cops can't nail you at six. I keep library books an extra day because they give you a grace period before the overdue fine kicks in. I'm too educated to play the lotto, too disciplined to run off with a floozy, too wily to get caught checking girlie websites at work. I married a great woman and raised *three* great kids. When I walk down the street, people say, "There goes a run-of-the-mill, totally average, regular slob. Just don't get him started on the Yankees."

Because when the Yankees lose, I blame myself. Always have.

Listen: I realize there is *no way* my physical and mental gyrations on a living room couch in upstate New York can affect a ballgame a thousand miles away.

It cannot happen. It does not happen. It will never happen.

But what if, on a certain day, a certain person happens to move a certain way, which sends a certain wave of unknown energy particles —let's call them Rizzutons—through a certain unexplained wormhole, causing a certain 90 mph fastball to hang like a Christmas ornament in the center of a certain batter's wheelhouse?

I'm not saying it happens. I'm just saying that until a few years ago, we called Pluto a planet. We still don't know what electricity is —I don't, anyway—or why extension cords always knot up when left alone, or why elevators stop at certain floors *when there's nobody waiting to step aboard*. Don't call it happenstance. Don't say coincidence. It's direct action. The only question is whether it stems from friend or foe.

In my life as a Yankee fan, I have devised offensive and defensive schemes that should win at least ninety-five games per season. In most years, that clinches a wild card berth. It's not my fault if both Boston and Tampa win ninety-six.

When we're at bat, I confront the TV head-on, eyeballing the screen with a belly-on-fire intensity, my face a heart-attack red and clenched into the kind of zombie grimace commonly linked with disgraced celebrities on the cover of the *National Enquirer*. I bend my knees slightly (good for the back, by the way) and assume the cobra-coiled stance of a mixed-martial-arts fighter.

Because that's what I am. Sort of.

Of course, I do not practice kickboxing on my TV. Such an act would be not only cowardly but also counterproductive. I would lose my direct link to the YES Network, the official Yankee government news agency, and my primary wormhole for Rizzutonic transmissions.

I work between pitches. I pace the room — touching objects, reaching corners, experimenting—always returning to my juju spot, my lotus point, one micromoment before the pitcher begins his windup. No matter how far I roam, I return to my juju spot at the moment of delivery. If I'm a nanosecond late, we have squandered the pitch.

It might be a ball in the dirt. Maybe the Yankee batter will stroke a base hit. Whatever happens, though, he would have done better had I completed my rounds.

On defense, I switch gears, usually pitching directly to the screen. Sometimes I lie bonelessly on the couch, eyes nearly closed, cobralike (I do enjoy cobra analogies), to lull the enemy bats to sleep. This in itself can be draining, especially late at night. At times, I've woken up horrified to learn our bullpen crapped away my hard-earned lead.

The game of baseball affords thinking fans at least twenty-five seconds between pitches — enough time to ponder not just this game but also the disappointment we are to this world, and to ask, for once in our miserable, straight-to-home-video lives, *How can we help our team?*

The answer is juju: an anecdotal science rooted in the theory that every living being has a cosmic purpose, and yours just might involve a couch and a channel changer.

What if I told you the Yankees' twenty-seven world championships resulted not from great players, wise managers, or even the avalanche of money regularly bestowed by its owners — but from the collective juju, the Rizzutonic emissions of twenty million fans, the largest base of sports whack jobs on this planet?

Obviously, I'd be kidding, right?

Seriously, it would be *insane* to believe such nonsense, right?

We all know better . . . *right?*

Because that's what Cubs fans say.

2

★

Off the Wall

I clack into the kitchen of our home, wearing my Kennedy cleats. Seated at the table, smoking a cigarette over a plate of doughnuts, is Dwight D. Eisenhower, the thirty-fourth president of the United States.

I recognize him instantly, because his baby face adorns posters, buttons, and bumper stickers piled throughout our house. He wears a duct-tape-gray suit and tie, and he looks a bit rumpled, as if taken apart and reassembled, like my dad's sawhorse.

"You must be Harty!" he says, sounding more boisterous than a leader of the free world probably should. "Your mom says you're a big Yankee fan."

As I nod, it occurs to me that this is not Dwight D. Eisenhower, but some local political shrub that is running for some local political office. I hear voices in the dining room and peer around the door. Appearing as a robot version of herself, my mom stands before a group of women, reading a speech from a scrap of paper. I see my Cub Scout den mother, the village clerk, and the lunch-line ladies from school, freed from their hairnets and cafeteria whites, wearing fruit hats and parakeet colors, with fake pearl necklaces that match their teeth and eruptions of mascara that today would conjure thoughts of a 1980s techno band.

My mother, as chairperson of the Village of Waverly Republican Party Executive Committee, has molded our family into a veritable strike force for Richard M. Nixon, the great right hope. Upon her subtle signal, I proudly bare the souls of my sneakers, revealing my Kennedy cleats. The ladies applaud. If they were beatniks, they'd snap their fingers.

The cleats represent a Seely tradition. Each fall, my sister and I infiltrate the Democratic Party headquarters on Broad Street, filch a handful of campaign buttons, and pin them to the bottoms of our shoes. For weeks, with every step, we are symbolically torturing our opponents, be it John Kennedy, Adlai Stevenson, or some poor local town official who never did anything to us. It doesn't matter. Within days, his smiling mug has been scraped into a hideous skull, sheared across the pavement as if we were squashing a bug.

This is rookie juju, my introduction to the ways of winning elections and controlling the universe. It comes from my dad, who probably learned it from the inimitable "Hart *I AM!*" With each step, I carry the legacy.

But this is mere politics. I trace my real juju links back to the summer of 1961, when I led the Yankees to my first world championship. That season, whenever the team needed help, I ran to the backyard and threw tennis balls against the garage, imagining myself to be the Yankee pitcher. In my head, Phil Rizzuto called the play-by-play: *Holy cow! Manager Ralph Houk is gonna go with the rookie, this Seely kid, who tossed yesterday's shutout. He's coming in to face the heart of the Tigers' lineup.*

I faced doubters. Although Mel Allen and Red Barber often discussed the special fire and intensity that my nine-year-old presence brought to the Yankee clubhouse, they questioned whether a third grader could hold up in a pennant race. Only Phil believed in me, and I vowed not to disappoint him.

In the backyard, I blew smoke past an overmatched Al Kaline, then froze Rocky Colavito with my sidearm curve. The garage wall cracked, and its concrete base crumbled, but my parents never complained. They liked hearing me out there, rhythmically punishing the clapboards and calling plays in a weird, "I-talk-to-the-dead" monotone. They called it "off the wall," and in more ways than anyone guessed, it was.

The 1961 Yankees might be the greatest baseball team in history. They hit 240 home runs, won the pennant by eight games, and took the World Series in five. That summer, whenever I hustled outside to throw, I returned to find we had taken the lead. The first time, of course, was happenstance. By the third, it became clear that I was triggering the rallies. From then on, whenever Mickey and Yogi faced trouble, I grabbed my mitt and ran to their rescue. They were Timmy, lost in the well, and I was Lassie, coming with a rope.

Of course, the Yankees did not go undefeated. Sometimes, despite my best efforts, we lost the game, leaving me to wonder what went wrong. Did I not concentrate? Did God judge my effort unworthy? At times, I *did* cheat, missing the plate but yelling "Strike three!" anyway, trying to catch God looking. Obviously, it didn't work. He saw through my crapola. In my mind, I could fool Al Kaline, and maybe even Phil Rizzuto, but in the real world of juju, the damage had been done. Against major league hitters, one mistake would cost me dearly.

It took months to refine the power of the garage, a process that evolved in tiny stages.

At first, I believed that the games were actually taking place inside our TV and that, by waving at the screen, I could make a batter blink. I tried to push routine fly balls out of the park, as if using a modern touchscreen computer. My dad complained that he couldn't see his shows through my fingerprints.

"Hands off the glass," he'd bark when I tried to intimidate celebrities on *Hollywood Squares*. "I can't even tell Morey Amsterdam from Charo."

Next came a tarot phase, in which I arranged Topps baseball cards to influence play. If I placed Whitey Ford over the card of an opposing batter, by the laws of reason the hitter should have no chance. If the guy somehow smacked a base hit, the next time he came up, I'd reposition Whitey, like Ralph Houk resetting the outfield. Once, my older sister, Virginia, stormed into the den and savagely kicked my piles. On the next pitch, the Tigers' Norm Cash lined one off the right-field wall. After that, I began hiding cards in couches and heating grates. I later spent years searching for those secret locations, looking for cards that today would hold the sticker value of a new Toyota.

My dad worked his own juju. Each Saturday, he scored NBC's Game of the Week in a huge business ledger that was printed by the *Waverly Sun*. (He also printed fake parking tickets that said, "Thanks for taking up two parking spaces. I had to park a block away, you STUPID IGNORANT BASTARD." Because of the swear words, the cards were highly coveted by my friends, and I used them as currency, like hundred-dollar bills.) The ledgers, heavy as gravestones, seemed to go back to the beginning of time. I could open a book and touch the names of DiMaggio, Mays, and Musial. It was sort of scary, like reading the spells of a sorcerer.

To score his games, Dad used an incredible new invention, the felt-tip pen. He preferred an electric pink-purple, which today might trigger someone's gaydar. He stashed his prized felt-tips in the back of a desk drawer that he must have thought was secret, because it also held copies of *Playboy*. When the coast was clear, I'd unfurl a centerfold and outline the Playmate of the Month on tracing paper with a pink-purple felt-tip. To me, this was wanton debauchery, the equivalent of a weekend in Vegas.

After the Yankees and the Kennedys, only one other topic could tweak my dad's anger: the TV psychologist Dr. Joyce Brothers.

My mother and grandmother considered Dr. Brothers to be an angel sent by God, the most beautiful and talented woman ever to roam the earth. They never missed *Tell Me, Dr. Brothers,* a talk show that, in my dad's opinion, advised women how to murder their husbands without going to jail. He called her "Dr. Hot 'n' Bothered," and whenever she appeared on TV, he would lurk in the doorway, mimicking her words in a mousy falsetto. Once, when she served for a week as guest host of *The Mike Douglas Show,* another Seely house favorite, we ate supper in the den to absorb every precious minute.

Early that week, Mike asked Dr. Brothers how someone could discern a potential mate's true personality. Her reply: *Note the way he drives.*

"Let's kill all the men!" Dad squealed from the doorway.

"We're watching our show," Mom said crisply. "We don't bother you when the game is on."

"Shoot the men, and our problems will go away!"

Had not Dr. Joyce Brothers been a human beacon for family harmony, I believe my mother might have chosen such an option. A few minutes later, after a strident discussion, Dad and I found ourselves in the backyard, playing catch.

"I'm not only pretty, but I'm smart!" he sang, throwing the ball. "Look at me, I'm just like Mrs. Yogi Berra!"

He not only hated Yogi. He even hated Yogi's wife.

To defeat the Yankees, Dad used a pair of wooden drumsticks, which he always kept near. He'd position a *TV Guide* on his lap and drum on it, gathering steam as each Yankee stepped into the box. He'd whisper, just loud enough for me to hear, "First-pitch *strike.*" Then he would start drumming the next pitch.

I tried counter-drumming, pounding on the floor and shouting, "First-pitch *ball!*" It didn't work. He was a grownup, and I was just a kid. What hope did I have of beating an adult at juju? One Saturday afternoon, Dad drummed a complete-game victory over us, with help from Detroit's Frank Lary, the infamous "Yankee Killer." Dad never let up. In the ninth, he was still drumming ninety-five miles an hour, setting us down in order. I was humiliated, shamed, and — most of all — scared. Against those drumsticks, the Yankees were helpless. It was like the Russians having the bomb. I had to act.

The following Saturday, when one of our batters hit a pop-up, I leaped into the air and, just as the ball landed, shouted, "Miss!" The impact of me crashing to the floor did not affect the infielder, but it seriously dislodged the TV's vertical hold.

"Damn it!" Dad yelled. "Never do that! You'll break the TV! Besides, it's too late! Don't you see? The ball is in the air! *He's already out! Understand? It's too late!*"

He was right. When I thought about it later, it was ridiculous to think that you could dislodge a fly ball from a major league fielder's mitt by stomping the floor at the last moment. Everything happened *between* pitches.

That day, my father made a critical blunder. While trying to calm the flustered TV, he banished me to the backyard. I wandered into the garage, picked up a tennis ball, and began throwing it at the wall.

Fastball catches the outside corner! Phil Rizzuto cried. *Kaline flings his bat in frustration, and the Tigers are retired!*

That day, I found my juju. Soon I was "off the wall" every game, and we were the greatest team in history.

JUJU RULES 1 AND 2

DADT

According to a 2009 survey by the Pew Research Center, two out of every three American adults somehow have infused their core religious beliefs with recurring plot lines from *Scooby-Doo, Where Are You!* Sixty-five percent told the pollsters they believe in at least one of what I call the eight-man batting order of Rizzutonic awareness: Reincarnation; Spiritual Energy in Physical Things; Yoga for the Soul; Evil Eyes; Astrology; Talking to Dead Folks; Psychics; and Ghosts.

If America had a church, it could be called Our Lady of the Immaculate Kreskin.

Right now, millions of God-fearing knuckleberries are pacing pentagrams into their living room carpets or waving refrigerator magnets over the pickled head of their uncle Herbie in hopes of fixing the outcomes of state lotteries, GED test scores, and — in the truly saddest cases — vote totals for *American Idol*.

Sadly, few Americans recognize the Rizzutonic powers they *do* possess. Their prayer requests for wealth and fame regularly wind up in the slush pile of the universe, not even warranting impersonal form rejection slips. You can't just march into God's office and ask for a million dollars. He's not your congressman. Besides, he can't just sign off on your latest get-rich-quick scheme. That's no way to run a cosmos.

However, if you lowered your request to, say, a first-pitch strike thrown by Mariano Rivera, who knows what difference you could make?

To those who wish to take up the ancient art of juju, this book offers twenty-seven essential rules, starting with the two most important:

Rule 1: Don't ask anyone what they're doing.
Rule 2: Don't tell anyone what you're doing.

Never try to rationalize juju. Never try to prove it statistically. Never ask why juju works. Never complain when it doesn't. Never confirm it. Never deny it. Never mention it. Never acknowledge it. Never hint about it. Never deny hinting. Do we understand ourselves on whatever it was that we were not discussing?

(By the way, this applies especially to calls from the Pew Research Center. The polltakers will befriend you on the phone and marvel over your keen wit and superior intelligence. Later, to their coworkers, they'll make fun of you. They'll imitate your voice and accent, even give you a lisp. Worst of all, when they publish their findings, the region where you live will look stupid.)

No one will ever understand your juju. No one will ever appreciate your juju contributions. Your job is to win ballgames, not to lose custody in family court. And if your secret does slip out, always pretend you are joking.

Like I'm joking now . . . understand?

Are we clear?

3

★

Swept Away

It wasn't exactly the Bronx, but make no mistake: in 1963, Waverly, New York, was Yankee Country, USA.

The local AM radio station, WATS in Sayre, Pennsylvania, had carried Yankee games for as long as anyone could remember. I probably heard Mel Allen while in the womb. Before I reached age ten, Mickey Mouse had morphed into Mickey Mantle, and Yogi Bear had become — well — take a guess. How could a kid in upstate New York *not* love the Yankees? Each summer brought an endless succession of Yankee games, and most of them quickly blossomed into Yankee victories.

My grandmother rooted hard for the team. In her parlor, she listened to every game, zonked on Lipton tea and sweets. She stocked her kitchen with candy — the uncut, felony-grade stuff, such as Sky Bars and the licorice we called cherry reds. In family slugfests, after everybody finished hammering the Kennedys and Liz Taylor, she and I would discuss the twenty-five-man roster, player by player, even down to Mickey's late-inning defensive replacement in center field, a kid named Ross Moschitto.

"Needs to lay off the breaking ball," she said.

She gleaned such tidbits from Rizzuto, her primary source for

Yankee reality. She understood Phil and trusted him without reservation. She loved how he talked himself into corners to keep a rally alive, and she was the first to point it out to me. She recognized Phil as the guy behind the counter at Kresge's department store, the neighbor who helped rake your leaves, the old friend who visited with a bag of Snickers. She saw into Phil's heart and pronounced him one of us.

"Old Phil," she'd say, "he's such a huckleberry."

During games, my grandmother counted pitches. By making slashes on napkins with a pencil, she kept a running total. Forty years later, the general manager of the Oakland A's, Billy Beane, would inspire a book called *Moneyball,* which outlines the revolutionary strategy of draining your opponent's starter by forcing him to throw too many pitches. My grandmother, who grew up on a farm outside Athens, Pennsylvania, understood this in 1963.

"Whitey's at a hundred ten," she'd say, then lean toward the radio to speak directly to the manager, as only a skilled fan can do. "Ralph, take him out."

That year, I attended fourth grade in a downtown storefront opened by the Waverly Central School District to handle the wave of baby boomers entering the system. It was a controversial move, putting us kids on Broad Street — near the pool parlor and the Tommy's In-Crowd tavern, with Satan's own strobe-lit dance floor. But we loved it. From our front window, we could look out on the fire station, Woolworth's, and Harpers' News Stand — the Times Square of Waverly. I'll never forget the day they hung the Christmas lights. The whole class cheered. That day, we learned no math or history — only how to savor life.

That fall, for the first time, I was publicly marked as a Yankee fan. My teacher, Mrs. Williams, selected me to sit in the back of the classroom and track the World Series on her radio. Back then, with World Series games played in daylight, each October meant an entire week of school devoted to the Yankees and whichever National League team they were playing. Every teacher, janitor, and lunch lady would keep tabs on the game, having bought squares in the wagering pools that were based on final scores. Because the downtown school had no gym or TV room, I would serve as the human conduit of information.

I sat far in the back, at Mrs. Williams's desk, surrounded by her hygiene creams and knickknacks — an unforgettably creepy experience. I could feel traces of her body warmth, breathe her lingering perfume. I wanted to run, but I had a job to do. Hunched over the Philco radio, touching it to improve reception, I felt like a soldier taking updates from the war. And the news was steadily grim: The Dodgers' Sandy Koufax and Don Drysdale were mowing down our troops.

With no access to a garage wall, I ad-libbed juju moves. I switched hands, touched objects, and scribbled over the names of Dodger players. Nothing worked. It was as if the classroom was lined with lead. Mrs. Williams's desk was a black hole for juju emissions, and I couldn't escape, stuck to the radio like a prisoner shackled to the bars of his cell.

Every few minutes, Mrs. Williams — a Yankee fan, by the way — called for an update.

"We're down," I'd say. "But Mantle's up with a runner on!"

The room would buzz. She would turn to the chalkboard. I'd lean harder into the Philco. And then, *strike three* — another zero on the board.

That fall, I learned the art of political spin: Report the slightest shard of good news the moment it happens, and concede defeat only when the bodies start washing up on shore. Boost public spirits by exaggerating whatever ray of hope exists — a two-out walk or a pitching change — and always project victory. Never relent. *Never admit defeat.*

The Dodgers swept us.

I had not believed it possible for the New York Yankees to lose a World Series. Thus, the October of 1963 taught me something else: the treachery of this goddamn world. You could live safe in your home — getting good grades and being polite to grownups — but one day, the very gods you worshiped could be torn from their batting stances, stripped of their jerseys, and desecrated right in your school. The Yankees would not always win. Nothing in life was a sure thing.

I still believed in God. But I would never again trust him.

"Fifteen strikeouts by Sandy Koufax!" my father rejoiced, adding the final felt-tip strokes to his game ledger. His drumsticks, still warm, sat nearby. "Would you believe it? That's a new World Series record!"

It wasn't fair. He had his pen and drumsticks, and I never got to throw one pitch at the garage. Every move at Mrs. Williams's desk backfired. That night, I lay in bed replaying each at bat, knowing the Yankees hadn't failed me. *I'd failed them.*

The final loss was so traumatic that Mel Allen — "the Voice of the Yankees" — could not call the late innings. The network announcers said Mel was ill, but I knew the truth: his world had been shredded. Who could talk? That evening, my father homed in on Mel. He said Mel was "going, going . . . gone to throw up!" He called Mel a coward and picked at the poor man's carcass, until I ran to my bedroom in tears. He and Mom exchanged words. Dad came upstairs to apologize. He stood at the door and asked if I wanted to go outside and play catch, and I said I would never play catch with him again as long as I lived.

And — oh, God — I kept that promise.

Mom took me to my grandmother's house, where she and I sat in the dark parlor, eating cherry reds.

"I can't believe we just let Drysdale shave our hitters," my grandmother said bitterly. "You gotta put their guys down. Know what happens when you score four runs in four games? You get swept."

Swept.

Six weeks later, JFK would be shot, ending my time in Kennedy cleats and inspiring the first half of Dad's future punch line about Los Angeles and Dallas being his favorite cities. My grandmother would never see another Yankee championship.

She lived her final years in a county nursing home near Towanda,

Pennsylvania, blind and bedridden, and beyond the range of Yankee radio broadcasts. When I visited as a teenager, she hungered for news. Had Joe Pepitone made use of his God-given talent? Did Ross Moschitto ever figure out the breaking ball?

"How's old Phil doing?" she'd ask. "He's such a huckleberry."

JUJU RULE 3

Shirts

Throughout history, numerous cults have attempted to cloak, festoon, or even paint themselves with sacred emblems that they believe will amplify their supernatural powers.

Avoid these people.

By all means, wear your team's colors to the game, and yes, scream like a fat lady on a sinking raft. But never kid yourself: by donning some stupid garment, you are not expelling workable juju.

The most potent, weapon-grade Rizzutons are milled by people in their homes, working through their televisions and radios. That's where pennants are won. And in those private war rooms . . .

Rule 3: There is no "lucky" article of clothing.

If a guest shows up in his "lucky shirt," turn him away. He knows nothing about juju. He knows nothing about life.

If *only* it were that easy. A "lucky shirt" . . . yeah, right.

Listen: A shirt that actually improved its wearer's lot would be worth $100 billion on the international black market. Nations would fight wars over it. Such an incredible garment would be sought by the CIA, the oil companies, and aging, pockmarked billionaires whose names cannot be spoken publicly. If such an enchanted frock truly exists — trust me here — it's owned by some Kuwaiti oil prince or ruthless industrial titan, not your unemployed cousin Shep.

Next time some beery dunderhead shows up in his threadbare, ripe-scented, multistained "lucky shirt," rip it off him like a five-dollar chest wax and send the clod home in a bag designed for garden clippings. Don't worry, neither your team nor your fashion sensibilities will suffer.

That said, evidence suggests that some juju-contaminated fabrics, if planted in your home or place of work, *could* pose a threat to you and your loved ones. I hesitate to call them "unlucky shirts," because such "street" definitions cause credible scientists to cringe. The truth is, we're still studying them — pulling on their threads, so to speak. In the meantime, we must be vigilant to the danger.

The most frightening example of a so-called shirt bomb occurred in 2009, when a thwarted terrorist plot stunned the nation. A Redsock operative named Gino Castignoli, working as an undercover laborer on the new Yankee Stadium, attempted to sabotage the ballpark by burying a David Ortiz jersey beneath a future service corridor. This treachery failed only because some anonymous hero blew the whistle. The Yankees quickly halted construction, isolated the threat zone, and jackhammered through two feet of new concrete to extract the cloth. It took five hours. Contractor Frank Gramarossa, after excavating the talismanic shroud, told reporters that most workers on the site were Yankee fans who "were upset it was in there."

The Yankees won the 2009 World Series.

David Ortiz didn't hit a home run that year until May 20.

We don't know whether Gino Castignoli was a mercenary paid through some Redsock slush fund or a lone renegade zealot, seeking to make a name for himself. Under questioning, he pretended to be a union simpleton who'd worked only one day on the stadium project.

Amazingly, there is no record of the jersey ever being subjected to scientific analysis. Questions regarding its juju have been met with stony silence. More troubling were news accounts that the vestment was returned to Redsock Nation in 2009, as a sort of prisoner exchange, so it could be "auctioned off" through the Jimmy Fund charity rather than be secured in a suitable location, such as the Yucca Mountain nuclear waste repository in Nevada. Today, the jersey's whereabouts are unknown.

We do know that anti-Yankee hotheads like Castignoli are forged every day in the schools, churches, and youth organizations of New England. When the subject is beating the Yankees, these monsters have no conscience. They will come into your home, eat your chips and dip, play with your dog — and then bury Kevin Youkilis's underwear in your couch.

Today, the threat looms greater than ever. What if some Redsock dead-ender someday smuggles into Yankee Stadium a backpack containing the cryogenically frozen head of Ted Williams? What then?

We must be prepared. We are living in a dangerous world.

4

★

The Dice of God

By age 14, in 1966, I figured I had witnessed life's full carnival of Yankees, from Mantle and Maris to Dooley and Duke. (That's Dooley Womack and Duke Carmel.) In just five years, my outlook on life had plummeted from the summit of the world to the basement of the American League.

I had survived the Dodgers' humiliation of the Yankees in 1963 only through the certainty that my revenge would be swift and sweet. We would punish the Dodgers so excessively that the people of Los Angeles would wish that Sandy Koufax had never been born. Until now, I'd never owned a shitlist. Now I had one with twenty-five names on it. Each would pay for his insolence. I would never forget, never forgive — never rest until blood vengeance had been rendered.

Nevertheless, the following year Bob Gibson's Cardinals beat us in seven games, an even more agonizing defeat due to the baby-seal brutality of its conclusion. In the ninth inning of the final game, Clete Boyer and Phil Linz homered, mounting our miracle comeback. With a six-run deficit suddenly slashed to two, I felt the tornado of Rizzutons forming, and I spread my arms like Charlton Heston, seeking to part the St. Louis defense. A base runner, that's all we needed. We had our leadoff man, Bobby Richardson, coming to bat. Bobby swung, hit a pop-up, and before the ball began its descent, I was crawling behind the living room couch. (That series would haunt me for decades in the chattering TV presence of Tim McCarver, Gibson's personal catcher, whom I believe still hates the Yankees on at least a subconscious level due to the permanent passions aroused in 1964.)

And the worst was yet to come.

In 1965, for the first time in forty years, the Yankees — with Mickey Mantle, Roger Maris, Whitey Ford, and Elston Howard — lost more games than they won. They accomplished this horror after firing Yogi Berra as manager and buying the Cardinals' leader, Johnny Keane. (Before free agency, we could only raid other teams' managers.) At one point, my social studies teacher asked the class in a quiz: *What baseball team has just fallen ten games out of first?* He looked directly at me, smirking. I lowered my head. Ten games out. It wasn't even June.

I felt ashamed, incompetent — disgraced. I had backed America's one sure winner, the greatest dynasty in professional sports, and it had promptly slipped in the shower and broken its hip. A Phillies kid would get sympathy. Not the Yankee kid. Grownups crossed Broad Street to offer an elbow of their repressed anti-Yankee rage. "Hey, little Harty Seely, how's your team doing? Ha ha. Well, too bad, maybe next year. Ha ha."

Keep in mind that I missed the Yankee dynasties of the 1940s and 1950s. I wasn't around to rub Joe D. and Marilyn into their noses. I never razzed one Brooklyn backer about Bobby Thompson's home run in 1951, or taunted an Indians fan for whatever he had done to become an Indians fan. But they didn't care. Their lifelong enemy, the mighty Bronx Bombers, lay dead in the road, and they lined up to kick the carcass — or better yet, the team's nearest fan.

This happened during the hellhole of puberty, the time of my first:

1. Crush on a girl (Stacy)
2. Schoolyard butt kicking by a bully (Harold)

3. Glimpse of a baseball hurtling toward me and changing direction in midflight (Dave Owens)
4. Realization that I would never — as long as I lived — hit such a pitch

Back in fourth grade, I lived in the comfortable delusion that I would someday play for the Yankees. By seventh grade, I knew the reality: Some boys already had beards and sounded like Tony the Tiger. *They* were the future Yankees. I was a future Yankee fan.

Of course, the 1965 Yankees played so raggedly that I figured they must be disappointments to their fathers. The basic laws of nature seemed to have gone askew. Everybody knew the Yankees were supposed to always have a star center fielder. Now we just kept churning bodies, waiting for the next Mickey Mantle to float down from the clouds. I expected it to be Tom Tresh, because of the alliteration thing. Then Roger Repoz and — well — Billy Bryan and Frank Fernandez. I finally gave up on wordplay and targeted Tony Solaita, who'd hit 51 homers in the minors. Nothing. One by one, they came, they hit .225, and they disappeared. No Mickeys. We even tried Joe Pepitone in center.

In 1966, we finished last. How could the Yankees — just five seasons removed from the greatest team ever — finish last? I refused to accept it.

Every day after school, I marched up to my room, closed the door, and immersed myself in an alternative-reality dice game called APBA Baseball. In it, every major leaguer was issued his own three-column card of numbers. The APBA print ads featured testimonials from people who claimed to play entire seasons and achieve statistical results remarkably similar to real life. To do so, they must have played fifteen hundred games — each one lasting about twenty minutes. Some serious social interaction issues, eh? Nevertheless, I imagined them to be the coolest adults on the planet. Each winter, when APBA issued the new cards, I vowed to re-create the previous season and become next year's official dice-rolling spokesman.

I scored hundreds of APBA games but won no testimonial contract, because my results never remotely resembled those of the real world. In my league, the Yankees had a friend at the top. Playing in "Seely Stadium," the 1966 Yankees won every APBA pennant, challenge match, and World Series, thanks to yours truly: God.

Unlike a certain Deity Who Shall Remain Nameless, I took an active part in Yankee games, especially in the ninth inning. There, I observed one minor rule change: if the dice didn't fall our way, I picked them up, dropped them back in the shaker, and rolled again. If that didn't work, I turned one die on its side and — *bam!* — the 56, a pop fly, became a 66, a home run.

With my assistance, the pitiful Yankees scored the greatest comebacks in sports history. Down by eight? No sweat. Their miracle rallies left my sold-out crowds in awe.

I also achieved payback. Don Drysdale didn't shave my batters. Instead, he and Koufax suffered punishing defeats, battered into submission. Once, Bob Gibson never even retired a Yankee, dispatched to the showers with six runs plated and the imaginary crowd throwing turnips. All-star lineups fell to that tenth-place Yankee team. And the more my Yankees won, the more I wondered why God let our real team fall apart. Didn't he care? Wasn't he watching?

Then one night, an actual miracle did visit Seely Stadium. We were down in the ninth with the weak-hitting Jake Gibbs at bat. The dice rolled a 66. For most hitters, 66 was a home run. For Gibbs, a catcher with no power, it just meant a second roll. I set the dice in the shaker and let them go: another 66 — *a game-winning, walk-off grand slam.*

I had not intervened. The cards and dice had done it on their own. It was a true miracle, the greatest comeback in my APBA history.

I had witnessed something incredible, an event that I might never see again. Unfortunately, I had nobody to tell. That night, the future Yankees were out playing ball or chasing their future Yankee wives. That night, I realized I could never re-create a full APBA season and become a dice-rolling testimonial. I tore down Seely Stadium, replacing it with a record player and an album by a band called the Doors.

And that girl I had the crush on, Stacy? I never did work up the courage to tell her. Too scared to roll the dice.

JUJU RULE 4

Furniture

During a typical game, the skilled jujuist will hold or touch a wide range of household items, seeking to gauge what power they possess and whose side they're on. Occasionally, you'll find a shy or spiteful object, one that wants no part of being handled. *Move on! Don't antagonize it!* Perhaps later, it will come out of its shell and feel more receptive to your good-faith advances. Nevertheless, if that coffee mug just gave up a three-run, walk-off home run to Dustin Pedroia, maybe the bastard needs to understand just how a three-run, walk-off home run feels.

Rule 4: Unless you remind an unresponsive juju charm that you mean business, it will not respect you.

Let's consider how one great juju master, the late manager Billy Martin, dealt with inanimate objects — in this case, umpires. Whenever a close call hurt his team, Billy would sprint from the dugout and assume his signature juju lotus stance: mouth positioned directly across from his target, at a preferred distance of two to four inches. From there, Billy would spew a foamy, tobacco-spiced spray, which, at times, included words. Billy would kick dirt. He would throw his cap. He would rage about injustice. It didn't matter.

Billy knew the ump would not change his decision. He was setting the table for the next close call.

That is what you must do with the objects in your zone. Be prepared to confront every nearby appliance, stick of furniture, and replaceable keepsake. Periodically, call one out and make an example of it for all to see. Berate it. Slap it around. "Accidentally" drop it on the floor. Hold it upside down over a toilet or out the window of a seven-story building. It will get the message.

(*Note:* Don't be cowed by the size of that refrigerator, which outweighs you by nine hundred pounds. Pull its plug, and suddenly somebody doesn't look so tough anymore! One way to humiliate it: whip it with its own power cord. Slash the sides facing the wall, and you will leave no telltale scars.)

(*Secondary note:* After the torture session, be sure to return the plug to its electric socket.)

Let everybody watch. Challenge a chair to make a move. Lamps don't like being strobed. Fancy pilsner glasses hate being picked up with a finger jabbed down their throats, like a trout on a hook. (I draw the line at waterboarding; that's just evil.) Give the living room a glimpse of your inner Christopher Walken (*Yankee fan, by the way*), and you will never face juju unrest.

My personal rule: If the Yankees lose, the door should expect to be slammed.

Remember, no matter how tough that inanimate object thinks it is, you have one huge advantage: you are alive.

(*Note:* I advise against the use of fire. In June 2007, following a disastrous outing, Yankee bullpen cog Scott Proctor pulled out a can of charcoal lighter fluid and torched his glove, hat, and uniform. Proctor told reporters he was exorcising his bad luck, claiming it had always worked in the past. Well, it didn't this time. Proctor continued to get lit up, and four weeks later, we dealt his fiery act to the Los Angeles Dodgers.)

As a final note, I don't suggest wasting time with voodoo dolls. In the late 1980s, with the Yankees mired in a thirteen-year slump, a mysterious woman stitched for me a voodoo doll of the person on whom I blamed all worldly pain: George Steinbrenner.

I'm not proud of the things I did to that doll. But trust me: if voodoo worked, "the Boss" would have never seen 1990.

5

★

Bobby, Mickey, and the Duke

In quiet, tree-lined Waverly—where the dads mowed lawns and the moms were known for their potato salad—I lived a sheltered baseball life. I knew fans of the Mets, Dodgers, Giants, Pirates, and Phillies, and the back alleys teemed with Yankee haters. But to my knowledge, no Soviet spy, illegal alien, or Redsock supporter ever set foot in our town. Like Yeti and Bigfoot, I'd heard tales about such creatures but never expected to meet one.

At Hobart College—a private school in Geneva, New York, derided then as "Camp Ho-Ho" and today as "Hogwarts"—my eyes were pried open to the looming red menace. There I spent four yeasty, bohemian years, each full of experiences I would not trade, even if it meant remembering them.

Nevertheless, during that period, 1971 to 1974, the Yankees did everything they could to play themselves out of my life. In their best season, they finished fifteen games out. Our lone beacon of light, the heroic Bobby Murcer, languished in a lineup that included Jerry Kenney, Ray Barker, and Jake Gibbs, the dice-roll miracle of Seely Stadium. If not for Bobby, I might have hung up my Yankee cleats.

At Hobart, I encountered not just Redsock fans but also an armor-piercing weapon that they wielded with abandon: sarcasm. The harshest practitioner was Foley, a cynical, Massachusetts-born wiseass whose opinions about the Yankees respected no human boundaries. Although he claimed to root for Boston, I think Foley's favorite team was my dad's: Anybody Playing the Yankees.

With my team twenty-five games out, I accepted verbal abuse on matters relating to an Al Closter or a Len Boehmer. At times, I joined the revelry. Why defend Dooley Womack after he blows a three-run lead? Nevertheless, I drew the line at Bobby. Every time Murcer strode to the plate, he carried my thirty-six-ounce heart in his hands, and I would go tongue-tied with rage when Foley fired off a round.

"Look, everybody! It's *the next Mickey Mantle!*"

"Bobby . . . You . . . He *good!*" I'd yell.

Foley would let a pitch go, allowing everyone to savor my stupidity.

"C'mon, we need a hit . . . *Mickey!*"

"Better'n you!"

"Look, everybody . . . *Mickey Charles Murcer!*"

At that point, I would stomp out of the room. I could kick the walls and scream at traffic, but I had no response to Foley's snide attacks. Dad had thrown much at me — drumsticks, Rizzuto, Koufax — but sarcasm was the knuckleball I'd never seen. Fortunately, Bobby Murcer became an all-star center fielder, forcing Foley to confront his own darkest fear: he *might* be the next Mantle! Bobby's hitting pulled me through freshman year. After that, Foley never got in a shot without taking a sarcastic broadside in return.

"Look, it's *the next Mickey Mantle!*"

"No, it's Danny Cater, who you stole from us — *for Sparky Lyle.*"

"He's not . . . You, upt . . . *Shuddup!*"

Foley and I dueled farcically for four years, a lost period when neither team was worth defending, unless it was done sarcastically.

Then there was Spry, a downstate hippie/jock, who rooted against the Yankees as his personal means of sticking it to Richard Nixon. Spry wrote sports columns for the campus newspaper that were choked with obscenities. He was the first person I ever heard say the word "motherfucker," and he probably said it six times in ten seconds. A former Yankee fan who had renounced the team on moral grounds, Spry would launch into anti-Yankee tirades that were beyond my ability to rebut or re-create. In them, the Yankees were not only Nixon but also Kissinger, Watergate, Agent Orange, and Tang. Once Spry began a ten- to fifteen-minute screed, he would round up every injustice, every inequality, everything wrong throughout world history and fling it into the turtleneck-squeezed kisser of George Steinbrenner. If you tried to intervene, he would spout some John Lennon–based insult —you were "a rocking-horse person eating marshmallow pies"—and you had to walk away. My only tactical advantage was that he and Foley could never work together. Once Spry fired up a rant, nobody —not even a fellow Redsock traveler—could wedge in a word.

I had Yankee allies. In a pitched battle, my Long Island roommate, Whale, could be counted on for a few surgical cracks about Carl Yastrzemski's country-club work ethic. And Hank, from Syracuse, could unleash his own furious hell rants, although they always came several hours too late—sometimes several days late—and they inevitably ended with him saying, "Aww, screw it. We suck!"

With your team fifteen games out, what else could you say?

My greatest nemesis, though, was the Duke, a former Hobart offensive lineman from Newburyport, Massachusetts, whose nickname came from his amazing ability to exude aristocratic grace while blotto. Periodically, the Duke would stuff himself into a borrowed Hobart blazer and crash the nearest alumni shindig, making a beeline for the open bar. Presently, you'd see the Duke engaged in rapt conversation with some red-cheeked fusspot, blathering impromptu politics, his eyes narrowed to embryonic slits, and every seam in his jacket screaming. His pockets bulged with cocktail weenies as he loudly shook the ice in his tumbler to signal for a fresher-upper. He would be the last to leave, charming the cleanup crew as he poured himself a traveler.

For three hours each day, the Duke and I unloaded trucks at the

UPS hub on the north side of Geneva. That meant for three hours, I endured what could charitably be described as his Redsock hallucinations. In them, the Duke painted an alternative reality where Tony Conigliaro never took a bean ball, Jim Lonborg never wrecked his knee on the ski slopes, and the DiMaggio brothers — Dominic and Joe — traded teams. He gleefully calculated the home run records that Yaz would set if he played in a "minor league bandbox like Yankee Stadium." He lived baseball fantasies beyond anything my loaded APBA dice ever conjured.

The Duke was the first Redsock fan I ever dueled, straight up, in juju. It happened during spring break of junior year, when our UPS jobs required us to stay a week on the otherwise deserted campus. The National Hockey League playoffs were under way, pitting my New York Rangers against his Boston Bruins. Early on, we brokered a deal: After each game, the loser had to verbally admit defeat. If the Rangers lost, I would have to stand on the front porch and yell, "All hail the Bruins!"

One might think this a minor concession. But each night, in front of the TV, we waged constant war for possession of the "lucky chair."

Of course, there was no lucky chair. The designation simply belonged to whichever chair one of us held while his team had the lead. If the Rangers were winning and I went to the bathroom, I would return to find the Duke perched in my seat, smirking with pride. I had only one option: physically take it back.

All night, we grappled over that elusive juju chair, stopping only when one of us yelped or someone on TV scored a goal. We never fought. We never grew angry. It never grew personal. If one guy tweaked an elbow, everything halted, and the chair reverted to previous custody, sort of a Robert's Rules of Order for juju. But we fought three-hour wars, collapsing the armrests and opening huge wounds in the upholstery.

My Rangers lost to Bobby Orr and company, and I performed my act of public humiliation. But I won some of those chair battles, and the Duke never reveled in my agony. Our roommates returned to find a house full of exposed springs and gutted cushions. They were lucky the TV worked.

In the spring of 2009, Foley returned to Hobart to receive one of those obnoxious alumni achievement awards that rich donors have a tendency to get. He had become a big, sarcastic cheese at the University of Florida's athletic department. I could imagine him saying to somebody from Florida State, "Whoa, look, it's *the next Bobby Bowden!*" He hadn't changed. I made an amusing quip about David Ortiz's urine glowing in the dark, and he started yipping and snapping about A-Rod's ladies.

In 2007, Spry, who had become a successful capitalist, developed an aggressive form of pancreatic cancer. The news devastated his friends. That summer, about twenty of us gathered for a reunion. He came in severe pain. He brought me photographs from a recent visit to Fenway, a jab to my ribs. Despite his weakened state, Spry ginned up a few anti-Yankee rants, obscenities and all. They were magnificent.

Months later, Hank and I drove to Philadelphia, basically to say goodbye. By then, Spry's mind was cloudy with painkillers, and he drifted in and out of conversations. He had lost interest in many things, yet he still spoke passionately about the upcoming Redsock season, which he would not live to see.

Spry even summoned up a rant. I cannot rebut it or re-create it, but it generally went like this: No matter where he ended up — be it heaven or hell — he would always, always, *always* hate the New York Yankees, but he would always, always, *always* cherish the memories of doing it.

Weeks later, he took his final breath, listening to John Lennon and surrounded by family.

And to this day, when the Yankees (or any other New York team) win big, my phone inevitably rings, and on the other end is a regal voice from somewhere, hovering, I suspect, over pockets jammed with cocktail weenies and a tumbler being skillfully shaken. "Congratulations," the Duke will say. "All hail the Yankees!"

JUJU RULE 5

Your Partner

Our last rule outlined the occasional need to beat a sneering toaster or to embed that smart-aleck smart phone in the nearest drywall. Urgent, unexpected violence is an efficient disciplinary tool for the inanimate item that doesn't want to play ball. But one home appliance must always be respected.

Rule 5: Never abuse your TV.

Don't hit her. Don't unplug her. Don't twist her knobs, hide her channel changer, or scar her private areas with hot silverware. Only a coward does such things. Moreover, do not subject your TV to verbal threats or ridicule. It's not her fault that your team lost. She's doing the best she can.

No ballgame was ever won by hurting the warm-circuited companion with whom you have chosen to share life's most intimate moments. Nevertheless, a raw undercurrent of TV hatred, against both flat screens and consoles, runs through American society. Too many viewers blame their TV for the quality of the program or the strength of their team's rotation. This is wrong. Even in high definition, your TV cannot turn a Steve Trout into a Catfish Hunter.

Listen: Unless you prefer watching games on the radio or through a magnifying glass on your phone, she's all you've got. Treat her like a lady.

I sense some readers reacting indignantly to these words. "What?" you say. "Me, hurt my TV?"

Oh, no; not *you*. *You* would *never* do such a thing. On the contrary, you pamper her with copper-flanged input jacks and the fanciest channel packages money can buy. When she's dark, you brighten her. When she's dusty, you massage her face with a soft cloth. You spend whatever it takes to put the hottest new shows on her screen every night. You keep her juiced up with electricity, gorged and ready to tend to your primal needs. You turn her on; you turn her off. You may even keep a sister of hers up in the bedroom, or a third cousin mounted over the bar down in your basement playpen. Oh, no . . . *you* would *never* hurt your TV — not *you*. She's not just some cheap date. She's your best friend.

Reader, have you watched yourself lately? When the game goes sour, when A-Rod strands the tying run, do you make foul gestures toward your plasma partner? Do you yell insults, mute her volume, and then run off to some flashy, satellite-fed, big-screen TV in a bar?

Too often, we don't see ourselves as our television does. Remember, the louder you shout, the less your set will listen. At a certain point, she may tune you out altogether. If that happens, your juju season is over.

6

★

The Two-Second Threshold

On the day that I theoretically reached adulthood, I woke up in my dormitory room amid mounds of clothes, beer cans, pizza cartons, unjacketed record albums, and former furniture cushions, with a buddy snoring on the couch, a raging barn fire for a forehead, and — somewhere in the compost heap — my college cap and gown. My parents stood in the doorway, clutching trash bags. It was 1974, graduation day at Hobart, and I was preparing to do what I had spent the last four years promising myself I would never do: go home.

I returned to my childhood bedroom and slept in my childhood bed, beneath a framed promotional glossy of second baseman Horace "Hoss" Clarke, the emerging symbol of Yankee mediocrity. (His claim to fame: twice leading the American League in total at bats.) The picture, a gas station freebie snagged by my dad, summed up my new outlook: the best years — my beer keg and Yankee dynasty years — were over, and I now faced a stems-and-seeds future of Rich Coggins, Otto Velez, and the forty-hour workweek. Each day, my mom made my bed, and I wondered if I would ever escape it.

I stayed in Waverly two years. I won't call them the worst of my life, but they were certainly the most lost and devoid of hope. I never dated, not once — a fact my parents steadfastly refused to mention, like teammates keeping silent about your no-hitter. I had partied through college, never imagining the hangover. So there I was — same bed, same bedroom, the site of the former Seely Stadium — a twenty-two-year-old male Eleanor Rigby, except it was Hoss Clarke's face that was kept in the jar by the door, grinning at me beneath the Hitler mustache and devil's horns, which I drew with one of Dad's prized electric pink-purple markers.

That fall, I found a job reading the news at WATS, the radio station just across the border in Sayre, Pennsylvania. I worked six nights a week, from 3:00 P.M. to midnight, a schedule that put a sizable crimp in my social life. Every night, I cued up the national anthem, flicked out the lights, locked the door, and sprinted across the East Side Bridge to the nearest bar, just in time for the West Coast game. On a good night, I'd stay there until dawn.

I was hired at the station through family connections, despite my lack of broadcast training. A friend once said I delivered news like a kindergarten teacher reading *Goodnight Moon*. ("An Athens man died last night when his car turned allllll the way over . . .") My screw-ups regularly traumatized the staff. I broke equipment, erased tapes, and botched newscasts in ways that were new to a seventy-year-old industry. George Thomas, the program director, continually scrambled to undo my latest mistake.

The owner hired me in the moronic belief that an automated radio station was idiot-proof. WATS recently had replaced live deejays with a temperamental computer that was roughly the size of the Waverly High School offensive line. Every newscast, commercial, and public service announcement — every human voice, that is — was recorded on cassettes and played by the automated system, which was to be treated like Barbra Streisand.

Maybe that's what caused my problems: I refused to curtsy in the computer diva's presence, or to back out of the room, fawning praise for Her Royal Highness. For reasons I will never know, the electronic system at WATS loathed me. It worked fine for others, befriending them, clicking its heels. But when I stepped into the studio, I could feel the system recoiling from my touch. I would follow the exact same procedures as everyone else, but the computer would choose not to work.

I knew what was going on, but I kept quiet. No one would believe me. They would take Barbra Streisand's word over mine. I wasn't going to let her have the satisfaction of beating me in a duel. But in private moments, I told the computer exactly how I felt: she was an asshole.

I had grown up listening to WATS and its cast of locally inbred radio personalities. One jock in particular loved to call the area "Pennsyltucky," a phrase that even today haunts me. The soundtrack of my youth had spun from those turntables. But the new automated style sounded otherworldly, like a conversation between Prozac-happy zombies.

Female voice: Time check, two thirty.
Program director: High school football, tonight at eight.
Me: The Sayre Sons of Italy will hold a potluck supper Thursday at the post on Desmond Street. The public is invited.
Female voice: The time? Two thirty-one.

Across the Penn-York Valley, people wondered what the hell was going on. How could four announcers share a microphone all day and never once acknowledge one another? We never conversed, never kidded, never argued. Did we hate one another? Were we sequestered in soundproof booths, like contestants on game shows? Were we reading from scripts with guns pressed to our heads? The greatest mystery surrounded the mature, deep-throated lady who only gave the time. What did she look like? Was she married? How could a woman display such superhuman self-control? And if aroused, what might such a dynamo of discipline be like in bed? We called her "the Minute Maid." When I described her as "one *fine* piece of audio," eyes widened. What time did she get off work?

Every Friday night, the station shut down Barbra Streisand and went live, broadcasting high school sports to the area's rabid audience, which consisted mostly of former high school athletes and cheerleaders. The annual Waverly-Sayre football game drew bigger crowds than the two villages' combined populations, and the weekly Ingersoll-Rand Company paychecks that were wagered on each outcome amounted to a redistribution of wealth that would have tickled Karl Marx. Brawls and the defacing of school property were cherished homecoming traditions. Authorities halted the 1970 game in the fourth quarter after fans in both bleacher sections ran onto the field to dispute a pass-interference penalty. Waverly lost the game, but we went home clucking over the fat lips we had delivered in the brawl. That night, we had kept the juju chair.

In our radio broadcasts, I served as acolyte to the station's play-by-play superstar, a newspaperman named Gene Paluzzi. A World War II vet, Gene had hustled for everything he'd ever achieved, and he seldom held back an opinion, no matter who stood in its crosshairs. In his weekly column, writing as "Gino the Italian," he treated every issue before the Sayre Borough Council with a level of suspicion worthy of the Watergate break-in. People bought the paper just to see who was on Gino's shitlist. At the station, Gene was called "Buckets," as in "buckets of bull," but I loved the guy.

"No matter what you may have heard about me, I do not hate the Yankees," Gene once announced as we traveled to a game in Elmira Heights. "I'm simply stating that there is no concrete reason why a Pennsylvania-based station should run the games of a New York–based baseball team. It's that simple."

Gene claimed the station should carry Phillies games because Sayre was geographically closer to Philadelphia than New York City (by five miles, if you adhered to his routes). Every year, he pitched the station management to drop the Yankees and pick up the Phillies. He might as well have been calling for legalized man-boy love. Regardless of the standings, this was Yankee territory. So instead of trying to convert me, Gene offered an alternative pitch.

"If the Yankees aren't in it, just consider the Phillies, that's all I'm saying," he explained. "If people ask, 'Who's your second team?' say 'The Phillies.' That's all. Watch a game now and then, just to see the National League style of play. You know, the Phillies aren't like the Dodgers or the Cardinals: we've never hurt you."

That night, driving to Elmira, Gene grew so animated about the Phillies that he went past our two highway exits, and we almost missed the opening kickoff. I was screaming, begging him to hurry, but Gene never broke a sweat. We hooked up the phone line with seconds to go, and nobody — except George, who was throwing cassettes back at the station — ever knew.

That winter, with Gene's support, I ascended to the role of play-by-play announcer for high school basketball. This prompted my dad to spring into a career-counseling mode.

Long before, he had identified Phil Rizzuto as the living embodiment of everything wrong with mass communication. He had documented Phil's worst atrocities, and now, whenever I dropped by — usually lugging my laundry — he rushed to his desk and tore through mounds of paper looking for his notes.

There was the game during which Phil had spent three innings recounting a lunch in New Jersey. He had mentioned the restaurant ("A free promo! Disgusting!" Dad thundered), the meal ("Food always tastes good when you don't pay!"), and the waitress ("Of course she's nice! Celebrities always tip!").

"Wait! Here's another one!" Dad would shout, chasing me into the driveway. "Seventh inning, two outs, tying run at the plate! He's talking about Tony Curtis! *Who the hell cares about Tony Curtis!*"

Well . . .

"Tony Curtis?" my grandmother said, suddenly roused from her nursing home bed. "Phil's hanging out with Tony Curtis?"

Despite my dad's critiques, Phil was onto something. For a few hours each day, coinciding with a ballgame, he simply reported the meanderings of his life. If Phil found a dollar on the sidewalk, he would ask the world who had lost it. And if Phil said he ate a decent burger at Joe's, who could doubt that Joe's served a decent burger?

Twenty years later, Oprah Winfrey would redefine the modern day-time TV personality by doing the same thing—talking intimately about her life. The difference? She didn't bother with a game.

But Dad laid down the law: "I don't ever want to hear you talking about where you ate lunch!"

"Great meal last night at Yanuzzi's," Gene Paluzzi would say half-way through the pregame show. "The ziti there is fabulous. Best you'll find in the state of Pennsyltucky."

Gene offered one rule of broadcasting: when calling play-by-play, always linger two seconds behind the action. Process what's happening, then describe it after that cool, two-second delay—the way the TV networks bleep out obscenities at the Oscars. The listeners wouldn't know. Just imagine yourself a detective tailing a car, staying two vehicles behind. That way, you won't say something stupid.

This I could not do. I shouted games in a streaming, helium frenzy, which folks mimicked when they thought I didn't hear. I'd start calmly, maintaining the two-second event threshold through the opening minutes of the first quarter, then—*gabbagabbagabba*. By halftime, I'd be hoarse from wailing, words exploding from my breast almost simultaneously with the game action, if not in advance of it.

George, the program director, once said I sounded like a deaf person preaching in a religious revival tent—*if* he suffered from Tourette's syndrome and was reporting the crash of the *Hindenburg*. Some people, referring to the way I bellowed, began calling me Engelbert (as in Humperdinck). The other joke going around was that when I yelled "Whooooooah, yeahhhhh!" I was getting oral sex under the press table.

I developed an unfortunate catch phrase: "long and lanky." Figuring basketball players should be "long and lanky," I used the words whenever the circuitry between my headphones shorted out. After a while, it turned into a verbal tic. I described short, dumpy coaches as "long and lanky." I called shots "long and lanky." In a diner, a waitress once said, "Here are your eggs, just the way you like 'em: long and lanky."

As the Pennsylvania high school sectionals neared, the pace of my announcing grew even more frantic. Games descended into manic, roller-coaster ejaculations of spit and adrenaline. I called shots before they hit the rim. I barked players' names before they touched the ball. And in the third quarter of the final game, I sliced the threshold too thin on one Athens player, whose name I will never forget: Kevin Hunt.

"Pass! Dribble! Shot! *Kunt!*"

Had I just kept blathering, the c word might have washed over the listening audience like static in a storm. Unfortunately, upon hearing myself speak the unspeakable, I turned into stone. I sat numb, unable to talk, unable to breathe, certain that everybody in the gym, players and coaches included, had heard my obscenity — the worst word anyone could utter in 1975. My arms lost sensation. I thought I was having a heart attack. The ball changed hands. I couldn't track it. Finally, after about ten seconds — a lifetime in live radio — I tried again to say the name:

"*Keee-ahhhhvinnnn . . . Heee-oo-aunnt.*"

At that point, Gene sprayed coffee onto his notes. I sounded like a voice-distorted anonymous source on *60 Minutes*. For the rest of the game, whenever Kevin Hunt scored, Gene leaned over and piped in, "Bucket by Kevin Hunt!"

I cannot remember who won. I recall only the ride home, shivering in the car because my clothes were soaked with sweat. Gene was driving, trying to piece me back together. He praised my passion. He praised my diligence. He said I was improving. He said nobody listened closely to radio anyway. He never mentioned Kevin Hunt. He said not to worry about anything. The trick was always to keep thinking about the next game. That was what mattered — the next game. That's how we left it.

Amazingly, the next day at the station, nobody said a word. Maybe Gene had laid down the law. Maybe it was George's doing. Maybe the owner had never heard, because I'm sure nobody ever told him. They pretended nothing happened.

But come Monday, the waitress smiled and said, "Hello, *Keaeeeeeevvvvvvvven!*"

That night, as we drove home from the game, I thought my life was over. I would be fired. My dad would be furious. My mom would be tossed from the GOP. And I would be the town laughingstock, the fool, the clown. Gene kept saying, *No, no, no . . . Life is not an all-or-nothing ride.*

"Hey," he said, "everybody has a bad stretch now and then. Even the Yankees!"

JUJU RULE 6

God

I never blame God for a Yankee loss, even to Cleveland. When dealing with the Supreme Being of the Universe, it's generally wise to be a good sport.

Go ahead and boo Javier Vazquez after he serves up the 2004 American League Championship Series–ending grand slam to Johnny Damon, effectively concluding an eighty-six-year period of Yankee world harmony, along with your personal sense of well-being. But never boo God (or Mariano Rivera).

That said, I personally find it hard to believe that God carved New York Harbor into North America's jagged eastern seaboard just so the Yankees, a hundred millennia later, could serve as slap-hitting also-rans in the American League East. Clearly, God has his reasons for everything that happens. He created Johnny Damon. He created Javier Vazquez. Let's give him the benefit of the doubt. He's *God*. He knows what he's doing, for God's sake.

Some of you may be thinking: *All this talk of Rizzutons and juju ignores the power of prayer. To win ballgames, shouldn't one's first steps be through the front door of a church?*

No. Absolutely, without question, no.

Rule 6: Never ask God to choose sides in a sporting event.

That means no prayer candles, rosary beads, kosher hot dogs, bows to Mecca, animal sacrifices, or handling of poisonous snakes. This rule applies to all Uppercase Deities — God, Jesus, Allah, Gaea, Buddha, even L. Ron Hubbard, if you're a Hollywood celebrity.

Simply stated, asking God to fix a ballgame is like asking Bruce Springsteen and the E Street Band to perform "Hot Cross Buns." You're insulting him. By rights, he should smash his guitar and walk off the stage.

Nevertheless, if you absolutely *must* beseech God (some folks won't eat breakfast without beseeching him), here's my advice. The night before the game, praise him extra heavily — extra sauce, extra cheese, double-extra exaltation: "Yea unto Thee . . . Thou art great, really great, and I'm not just saying that . . . Thou art super-great . . ."

Remember: God is *always* great, but in your humble opinion, he's having a career year. (By the way, you must say this even if an earthquake just annihilated fifty thousand people. Pretend you haven't heard the news.)

Next, ask for world peace.

Yes, you read correctly. *World peace.* God respects lowly creations who beseech him on behalf of world peace. It shows class. It shows that your puny, selfish, troglodyte head is screwed onto the right moral threads. Pray for an end to hunger, poverty, disease, war, and so on — the whole doomsday list. If you run out of social ills, put in a word for the dolphins. (Considering how we've polluted the oceans, they've been pretty good sports.)

Remember: You are Billy Martin, setting the table.

Now — after beseeching on behalf of cultures that none of us would know of if not for Madonna's maternal desire to adopt — mention a sick friend who would get a long-overdue boost *if the Yankees play well tomorrow.*

Say nothing more. God will get the message. He's very smart.

During locker-room invocations, you'll never hear a professional cleric ask God to win the game — not even at Notre Dame, where the team priest privately wants to see Michigan State stomped into a bloody paste. On the record, he'll keep his sadistic and sick impulses to himself and say, "O Lord, let us feed everybody and end human suffering, and while we're at it, please protect these young competitors *on both teams . . .*"

He is Father Billy, setting the table.

Remember: Whatever your religion, to God it's still just a game. And the last thing he needs is a point-shaving scandal.

7

★

Rudy May Not

Despite the periodic pleas of Gene Paluzzi, WATS in Sayre, Pennsylvania, had cast its permanent lot with the Yankees Radio Network. The station aired not only every Yankee game but every Yankee pregame, postgame, exhibition game, postseason game, and Special Edition whatever, all in their Yankee entirety. It squeezed out every second of Yankee airtime like a desert nomad wringing drops of water from a cactus root.

That was fine with me. In fact, the upcoming summer of 1975 loomed as a paid vacation. Five days a week, I would work the station's soundboard, sneakers planted on desk, eating cherry reds, and eyeing the comely students of the nearby Robert Packer Hospital School of Nursing from my catbird seat over downtown Sayre — paid to monitor Yankee games.

Let me repeat those golden words: *paid to monitor Yankee games.*

Unfortunately, the team was recovering from another lean season. We had traded Bobby Murcer to San Francisco, ending his quest to carry on the Mantle legacy. With Yankee Stadium undergoing renovation, we'd play home games at Shea, the Mets' haunted dumping grounds, where drainage pipes would wreck the knee of our young center fielder, Elliott Maddox. From my broadcast window, I foresaw tough times ahead for team and country.

Near our house in Waverly, a boulder held the names of three young men I'd personally known who had gone to Vietnam and never come home. The rock wasn't big enough to list everybody who had returned bent or disillusioned. Each night on TV, we watched the slow-motion implosion of Richard Nixon, which my dad refused to accept. Whenever I mentioned Watergate, he changed the subject to the Yankee bullpen or Paul Lynde's latest one-liner on *Hollywood Squares*.

Having coaxed me through college, my mom and dad had hoped to hang up their cleats and retire from parenthood. But now they followed my budding career at WATS around the clock, living and dying on my every word. Whenever I turned on the microphone, I knew they were out there, praying I wouldn't mess up another newscast.

"People say nasty things," my mother said. "I just say, 'Turn to another station.'"

Of course, that was the problem of living in Waverly, New York: there was no other radio station.

Shortly before Christmas, in a swirl of publicity, the Yankees signed Catfish Hunter, the premier free agent on the market. For the first time in my Yankee fan life, we added a great player without having to surrender three or four future stars — deals that usually unleashed a series of events that ended with George Steinbrenner canning the manager. At last, we found a deal that couldn't backfire: we just bought the player outright.

Best of all was its message: we had finally gamed the system. Yankee lawyers talked Yankee judges into killing the contractual clause that bound non-Yankees to non-Yankee teams. From now on, the richest franchise — us — controlled the APBA dice. It was capitalism. It was Machiavellianism. It was sweet. We could resurrect the Yankees, and then — who knows — maybe America. No more Nixon, no more war, no more inscriptions on that lonely boulder. No more third place.

And *I* would run the soundboard, *paid to monitor Yankee games.*

That winter, George Thomas assigned me to produce a series of promos for the upcoming season. "Keep them simple," the program director stressed. "Just say, 'Yankee baseball, coming this spring!' Or, 'Coming this spring, Yankee baseball!' Nothing complex."

In the station's automated format, each promo would play hundreds of times. Thus, each one needed to be formless, humorless — indistinguishable from the rest.

For the first time at WATS, I said no. I viewed these Yankee promos as my canvas, my art form, the work I was born to do. Okay, I'd botched a few newscasts, erased a couple of master tapes, and maybe said the c word on the public airwaves — but now I would give back. I would produce a hundred promos, each one a tribute to Yankee ingenuity. From Elmira to Binghamton, listeners would buzz about those hilarious Yankee promos on that tiny station out in Pennsyltucky. My artistic soul burned with the challenge. This was my Yankee rock opera, my Yankee epic poem, my Yankee Stations of the Cross.

"You're making this more complicated than it needs to be," George said.

I bristled. Already I was drafting promo slogans around the clock, even waking up at night to jot down revelations.

We've hooked a big one! Reel in Catfish Hunter, on WATS!

When boating in our lakes and ponds, tune us in, for Bobby Bonds!

Rudy May — or he may not! Find out this spring, on WATS!

"Rudy May?" George asked.

"Lefty starter. Yankee fans will love our meticulous attention to detail."

"No."

"How about, 'Rudy *may* just be a Yankee, but — '"

"Forget it."

One by one, George scrapped my rhymes, my metaphors, the parables I'd aimed at true Yankee fans — my people.

"Just do ten versions of 'Yankee baseball, coming soon!'" he said. "We don't need '101 Yankee Fricking Dalmatians.'"

I grimaced. He might as well have kicked me in the groin. In many ways, this was a free speech issue. I was trying to unite my tribe, speaking for an indigenous Yankee fan way of life. Now the radio station was seeking to silence our collective voice, to undermine our oral traditions.

"You're making this way too complicated," George said.

"I'm trying to lead the way from mediocrity."

"This is a one-hour job."

"This is a once-in-a-lifetime opportunity."

"You're overthinking this."

"You're not thinking this over!" I countered. "Are we men or pre-recorded male suitors of the Minute Maid?"

My crack about the time-check lady caught George off-guard. We compromised: I could record nine generic promos and one short "art house" piece, which would air just once a day and, thus, stay fresh in Barbra Streisand's can.

Over the next week, I whittled down my list to one perfect ten-second spot, a one-liner with more artistic layers than a Bob Dylan protest song. Adding to the effect would be my delivery, each word piped with a cool, impish tweak of sarcasm.

"All we say is: If the Yankees don't win this season, it won't be because every game isn't heard on WATS Radio!"

Genius. That was the only way to describe it. The piece defied conventionality. I read it a hundred times to perfect the cadence, to merge its humor and truth. It was smart, quick, edgy — and for the first time since merging Kevin Hunt into one syllable, I pondered a long and successful radio career. When I heard the final cut, I laughed out loud. I imagined the Penn-York Valley united by one voice, one person who dared to rise above the automated drone: me. I imagined those young Robert Packer Hospital School of Nursing students thinking, *The hell with trying to bag a doctor. I'll seduce that radio announcer.*

With George on vacation, I put the promo in its carousel on Thursday, welcomed the college intern who would babysit Barbra, and set off on a rare three-day weekend — seventy-two hours of self-congratulatory bow taking.

By late Sunday afternoon, I found myself in a bar outside Waverly, drinking with several old high school friends. They'd been star athletes — the future Yankees of my seventh grade. They now worked construction or ran machinery at Ingersoll-Rand — with free weekends, new trucks, hot girlfriends, stomachs like cobblestones, and salaries three times my weekly pay. I was driving my grandmother's Ford Falcon, making $320 a month, and lugging a jelly doughnut on each hip. But this day, I reveled in my newly achieved B-list fame. With each utterance, my celebrity voice — my James Earl Jones voice — resonated across the tavern.

"You on the radio, right?" a craggy old guy finally inquired. His face resembled a callused foot, with one tiny eye and one big-toe eye.

"Hart Seely, WATS assistant director of news and sports," I said modestly.

"Yeaaaah," he said. "I know you."

I sipped and rearranged the coins in front of my drink.

"Yeaaaah," he said, his big eye glowing. "I know you."

"I do news, sports . . . *Yankee promos.*"

"Yeaaaah. You're the fuggin' moron."

He elongated "mo-rahn" as if it were the name of a batter stepping up to the plate.

I laughed graciously. Obviously, he was kidding. One of the trappings of my new fame would be to accept the gentle ribbing of fans. It would mean something for them to make me laugh.

"Yeaaaah," he said. "If I hear you say 'Ain't gonna be our fault if the Yankees don't win the pennant' one more fuggin' time, I'll strangle somebody! You hear, *I'll strangle somebody!*"

"Jeez Krice!" a lady chimed in. "This is *him*?"

"How many times do you gotta say that?" the bartender grumbled. "Don't you ever get tired? Do they *make* you say it?"

"Three times in ten minutes!" someone yelled. "Buddy, what the hell is wrong with you? You think that's funny?"

"Fuggin' *mo-rahn.*"

I tried to explain that I wasn't the fuggin' mo-rahn. The computer was the fuggin' mo-rahn. I merely recorded a promo, and apparently it was running more often than intended. The computer had messed up, not me.

"Jeez Krice, it wasn't funny the first time," the woman said.

"Someday I hope that time-clock lady tells you to shut the hell up."

A silence tiptoed across the bar, until someone asked, "Is she married?"

The next day, I learned the reason behind their fury. Somehow, I — or "Funny Girl," the computer — managed to insert the promo cassette in the wrong carousel tray. Instead of twice a week, my "art house" piece ran three times an hour. Every twenty minutes for two excruciating days, my hometown heard me deliver the same exact joke, with the same exact inflections, with the same exact overindulgent sense of irony and glee, as if speaking the words for the first time.

Every twenty minutes.

"People can be mean," my mother said. "All they have to do is turn it off."

JUJU RULE 7

Noise

Egged on by stadium organists whose hottest new songs were learned directly from 8-track tapes, baseball fans jubilantly shout, "Let's go Mets!," "Roil them Royals!," "Mar them Marlins!," or whatever Rally Monkey–inspired catch phrase has temporarily weaned them from self-awareness.

Baseball craves blind obedience from its fans. The scoreboard says, "CLAP!" People clap. The scoreboard says, "NOISE!" They make noise. If the scoreboard said, "BA-AH-AH!" we know what they would do.

On command, these goodhearted sheep — sorry, I mean *fans* —

wave promotional hankies (made in China and featuring TV news catch phrases or the logos of evil corporations) and cheer the local mascot—be it the Phillie Phanatic, the San Diego Chicken, Mr. Met, Bernie Brewer, the Mariner Moose, Rosie Red, Billy the Marlin, or Wally the Green Monster. This *Sesame Street* ensemble of seven-foot-tall carnival kewpies, animated by borderline personalities that no parent would ever let near his or her young children, is Major League Baseball's attempt to manufacture stadium juju.

But stadium juju is like stadium food: at the time, it tastes good, but the next day it turns up in the loss column.

(By the way, Redsock fans have their own special cheer: "Yan-kees suck!" They chant it not only at ballgames but also during wedding receptions, bar mitzvahs, beauty pageants, Christmas tree lightings, fire drills, convenience store openings, meals, and, in some cases, I suspect, the moment of ejaculation. In 2004, HBO aired *The Curse of the Bambino,* a documentary narrated by actor Ben *"I would rather utter the words 'I worship you, Satan,' than 'My favorite baseball team is the New York Yankees'"* Affleck. In it, a crowd celebrating the New England Patriots' Super Bowl victory spontaneously breaks into "Yan-kees suck!" It's a Disney moment.)

There is no law against going to the game and screaming your lungs into a two-pack-a-day cigarette burn. The concept of crowd noise as the home team's "tenth man" harks back to the old-time lynch mob, a tradition of public spirit through which modern communities periodically attempt to re-create the Old West. Occasionally, crowds do spook an opposing player, especially one just up from Batavia. But don't confuse noisemaking with juju.

Rule 7: In juju, a whisper is as effective as a shout.

This also holds true for booing, hissing, and shrieking hate-filled obscenities or barbed taunts, such as "Damn, Papi, those pills sure can shrink a penis!" or "Hey, A-Rod, it must be hard fielding a grounder while studying yourself in the mirror!" However witty we think they are, our verbal attempts to distract opposing players usually fail. Short of running shirtless onto the field with your teenage son and physically attacking the first-base coach (as two White Sox rooters did in 2002), few fans ever get to create an actual game-changing distraction. Yelling just doesn't cut it.

To the pro athlete, cheering — especially *organized* cheering — is factory noise. They don't hear it. Nor do they notice JumboTron diversions, such as the video appearance of the Los Angeles Angels' famous Rally Monkey. To actually intimidate an opponent, the Angels would be better served by unleashing a live monkey. *That* would be a distraction.

Sadly, inept juju practitioners often end up screaming like background singers in a bad Hall & Oates tribute band. Not only do they fail to help their team, but they undermine the thinking fan, who *is* influencing play.

That could be you, without having to strain your vocal cords. Think: What were you discussing just before that home run? What happened while you went to the bathroom? If the hits keep coming, shouldn't you keep remembering Utica?

Remember: Whatever you yell, the players are not listening. But the juju gods hear everything.

8

★

Yankee Love

It is June 1976, with Bicentennial fever reaching full intensity. As the July Fourth holiday nears, the hype has become apocalyptic, like two Super Bowls and a celebrity murder trial every day. I am blasting along in a red Ford Maverick, howling with Bruce Springsteen (*Yankee fan, by the way*), who is beamed from a Rochester, New York, FM station where the oh-so-cool announcers take great pains not to sound like announcers. I'm hurtling through a confusion of highway called "the Can of Worms." Bruce finishes "Born to Run" with his signature wail, which I — a broken hero on my last-chance power drive — empty both lungs to match.

After leaving just enough dead air to prove that he isn't any run-of-the-mill deejay, the FM voice reads last night's scoreboard. He says the Yankees — *his* Yankees — won again and lead the American League East.

This is my revelatory Yankee moment.

The Yankees are in first place?

Thus ends the first brief period in my life when I cannot instantly recite what the Yankees have done in the past six hours. It is as if I've awoken from a Yankee coma. It dawns on me that manager Billy Martin must have performed a miracle and that maybe this time the spring training hype was true: we are no longer baseball's version of the Bay City Rollers.

Yankees in first? Where was I?

The answer: Pennsyltucky. For two years, I had listened to not just every stinking Yankee game, but every stinking Yankee pregame, postgame, and Special Edition whatever — all in their stinking Yankee entirety. The previous October, when we finished twelve games out, I heard stinking Yankee games in my sleep. I couldn't take another Yankee inning, another Yankee loss.

Back at WATS, I'd tracked games five days a week, and then, on my days off, I'd listened to games while taking long drives in the country. I'd absorbed so many of Rizzuto's ruminations — on cannolis, golf outings, and *The Bridge on the River Kwai* (his favorite movie) — that Phil had become the voice that interpreted my world. He was Socrates to my Plato, Anne Sullivan to my Helen Keller, Charles Bukowski to my Tom Waits. In his talks with Bill White (Phil called him just "White"), Rizzuto expounded on basic elements of the human condition:

Existentialism. "Was talking to myself there a little while, White, and I was very uninteresting, so I brought you in."

Geography. "Ever been to Concord? Great place. Everything up there is named Walden. Great poet."

Culture. "A lot of money in that chess, I'll tell you that. But it's not a spectator sport."

White was an unlikely candidate to own space in my head. He'd played for the 1964 Cardinals, which had beat us in seven, cost Yogi his job, and launched our eleven-year trek through the deserts of Horace Clarke. Early on, my grandmother had predicted White's Bronx career would end as soon as Clete Boyer, her favorite Yankee, cut an audition tape. "He's St. Louis," she groused. "If he needs a job, let *them* put him on." But over the years, as White became Phil's conduit for truth, my grandmother came to adore him.

Weekends, I would kill afternoons just driving and listening to them chatter. One Sunday, while snaking along the Susquehanna River, I heard Phil launch a bizarre seminar on fishing. As he jabbered, it became apparent that he knew nothing about the subject but that White knew quite a bit. Another announcer would have taken over the conversation. Not White. He let Phil steer the car. We were just along for the ride.

That day, I experienced three punch-in-the-nose revelations:

1. Phil's genius as a broadcaster was in the way he didn't sound like a broadcaster.
2. Phil's tangents would make interesting freeform poetry.
3. I had no future in radio.

The last one hurt. I was wasting my time. My contemporaries were making money, launching careers, and hooking up — while I was perpetually cruising the back roads between the towns of White and Rizzuto, listening to the Yankees kick away another summer. I vowed to leave Sayre.

But first, I had one last great radio botch to deliver. It came that spring. I drove forty miles into Pennsylvania to call Athens's quest for a high school baseball championship. I arrived early at the field and set up the equipment — according to procedure. I called George to check the phone feed and synchronize our watches — according to procedure. Because I was outside the WATS listening range and could not monitor the broadcast, I waited until precisely 4:05:30 P.M. and started calling the game — *exactly* according to procedure.

For the first three innings, I delivered a textbook play-by-play performance. I painted the game with artistic brushstrokes of verbs, nouns, and adjectives, despite a recurring distraction. Every few batters, a scrawny farm urchin would poke at my shoulder. Being the consummate pro, I would wave him away. Finally, between innings, I spun around, cut the mike, and hissed, *"What the hell do you want?"*

"J̄ou from Sayre?" he asked.

"Yeah. What?"

"J̄ou know they cain't hear you?"

A pipe bomb went off in my stomach. I glanced at the transmitter cord, which dangled loose from its plug. In a nuclear panic, George had called a pay phone near the field. The poor kid kept answering. I plugged in the cord, yelled, "George, here we go!" and resumed talking, as if nothing had happened. Back at the station, I pretended to be shocked — *shocked!* — to learn we had experienced technical difficulties.

George covered for me. We blamed Barbra Streisand.

But I was done. Unlike the oh-so-cool deejays, I didn't sound like an announcer, *because I would never be one.* I told George I had to leave. To others, I claimed to have gotten the Minute Maid pregnant. They would never hear her give the time without a twinge of sadness for her personal strife.

From there, I began a series of minimum wage jobs, designed to punish myself. I sorted library books, flagged cars, and worked as a temp. Then one day I announced that I was moving to Rochester to stay with Jocko, one of my best friends from high school.

Actually, I went for a woman. I'd visited him for a New Year's Eve party and, at the crack of midnight, found an attractive young nurse thrusting her tongue down my throat like a Roto-Rooter technician on an emergency call. Unfortunately, a few minutes later she was on her hands and knees, vomiting into a snowbank. Bad love omen? Yeah. Still, it was the closest I'd been in a while.

I found work in an army surplus warehouse run by the Bachman brothers, two cigar-chomping lugs who taunted employees, paid in cash, never bothered to learn my name, and yet were amazingly lovable. They owned a junkyard of discarded military debris, most of it destined for scrap. You needed a map to navigate the twenty-foot-high mountains of gun barrels or tank treads. All day, I lifted and sorted steel. My arms grew as hard as carrots while I pumped iron in the sun, listening to the FM non-deejays, never taxing my mind beyond an inventory count.

I rented an efficiency apartment that was too efficient for even a coffee table, and I hung out at Jocko's house, where he lived with a loose collection of friends from college. None of them followed the Yankees, and he had lost touch with the team, too. Eleven years of mediocrity did that to a fan. Thus, my arrival filled a void. With the Yankees in first, we resurrected each other as fans.

Every night, we watched Yankee games on WPIX, using Springsteen records as supplementary juju. To launch a rally, we set the needle on "Born to Score a Run." To close a game, we played "10-Inning Freeze-Out."

We also hit the bars, this being an era in American history when drunk driving was a skill rather than a crime. But we spent most nights in a houseful of young women who lived with Jocko's longtime girlfriend, Olivia. (To protect the innocent, I've changed her name.)

She was bookish, slender, and decidedly nonathletic, with Gloria Steinem glasses that made her eyes seem the size of golf balls. She quoted poems by Rilke, whom Jocko and I derisively called "Rendell Rilke." He called it her "child-of-nature, friend-of-man" thing. They had dated since college.

I brought to Rochester a new persona: sensitive, underachieving future literary figure. I was writing my great American novel, about a mental institution that offered baseball as therapy. I had a radical concept: baseball as a metaphor for life. Three outs, three meals. Four bases, four seasons. Nine players, nine planets. Pitcher-catcher, man-woman. Yes, I was insufferable.

In high school, Jocko had been the king of Waverly: class president, National Honor Society, Most Popular Student, and star quarterback. He still owned the school record for longest run from scrimmage —

ninety-six yards — a feat made possible because I, a lowly offensive guard, stuck out my foot and tripped a blitzing all-state linebacker. He and Olivia had been together so long that they seemed married. Everyone assumed that their wedding was just a matter of time. But up close, you saw the grinding of tectonic plates moving in opposite directions.

That July, the upstate New York recession cost Jocko his job, forcing him onto unemployment. At first, he exulted in the lifestyle of sleeping late, playing pickup basketball, and watching the Yankee game every night with a twelve-pack and me. But it soon got old. He fell into a fidgety, T-shirt–and–sweatpants funk, with nothing to do but doubt his worth and wait for the next pregame show. Back in Waverly, I'd been the guy who'd watched scores scroll across the TV while others danced and enjoyed life. As Jocko's spirits lagged, the Yankees became *his* topic, *his* reality. He became me, and it was a role I was happy to relinquish.

Around that time, a strange thing happened: Olivia took up the cause of Yankee bashing. Every night, she picked a fight. She'd claim Carlton Fisk was better than Thurman Munson, or she'd make a war-like crack about Bobby Murcer. She found my buttons and pushed them, whenever she could.

Of course, the Yankees won my duels for me. We had Chris Chambliss, Willie Randolph, and Thurman Munson — the captain, whom I had raised from a minor league puppy. One night, we escorted a contingent of nurses to a Rochester Red Wings Triple-A game and watched a kid named Cal Ripken play third base. On the ride home, Olivia and I argued furiously over whether he was any good. Jocko couldn't get in a word.

A few days later, he came to me with a lost look. He and Olivia were drifting apart. He thought they were done as a couple.

"No," I said. "You love each other. Stay together. If I were you, I would never let her go, never!"

He vowed to try. But next time I saw Olivia, she and I quickly locked into a Yankee crossfire, tuning out everyone else.

Every few weeks, I drove to Waverly for treatment of a bone spur. Mom would be waiting with a box of laundry soap — I always brought dirty clothes — and a bag of cherry reds, along with the questions she tried not to ask. Dad would burst from the den, clutching a sheet of notes like a rabid raccoon.

"Two outs in the eighth, bases loaded, tie game, and guess what Phil is talking about? Water wings! *Inflatable water wings!*"

As October neared, Jocko and I suspended all nonessential activity — work, food, and procreation — to commit ourselves to the playoffs. We faced the Royals, a team of emerging stars that nonetheless represented the traditional Yankee killing grounds of Kansas City.

We laughed through game one, as their slap-hitting third baseman George Brett, a famous hemorrhoid sufferer, made two critical throwing errors. We blew game two, thanks to an implosion by Yankee reliever Dick "Dirt" Tidrow, but took the third game behind Dock Ellis (who is today mostly remembered for throwing a no-hitter while on LSD). In game four, KC's bullpen leviathan, Doug Bird, shut us down for nearly five innings, even though Jocko and I nearly wrecked the turntable stylus from playing "Born to Score a Run."

Next came the deciding game five. We fell behind early, after their big first baseman, John Mayberry, homered, but we rallied to take a three-run lead into the eighth. Brett came up with two men on base. To honor his discomfort, we fanned our butts with Springsteen albums.

Brett hit a three-run shot. We sat. Tie game.

In the ninth, Chambliss hit his now iconic home run, crashing through a wall of fans to reach the dugout. We gathered the ladies and went out on the town, setting our rotation for Cincinnati's Big Red Machine.

From my recollection, the lone positive aspect of the 1976 World Series was its brevity. In game one, Joe Morgan homered before we dipped a chip. In game two, we collapsed in the ninth when our shortstop, Fred "Chicken" Stanley (we called him "Plucky") threw the ball away. In game three, Cincinnati beat us like a tambourine for nine innings, while third baseman Pete Rose dared us to hit a ball at him. In game four, for the first time, we actually led. Then they buried us. That night, Jocko doused his Yankee cap with lighter fluid and flicked a match. The damn thing smoldered, belched a few toxic fumes, and died. Just like the Yankees.

The next night, with no more baseball, Jocko and I sat in his dark living room, talking to each other's silhouettes. He said he and Olivia were done. He had tried everything. He asked what he should do. I hemmed and hawed. We ended up discussing whether the Yankees would sign Reggie Jackson.

I went back to my apartment. A few minutes later, there was a knock on the door. It was Olivia.

From there, everything spun on its own momentum. For the next few weeks, Olivia and I met secretly, whenever we could. For eight hours a day, while sorting steel, I made imaginary speeches to Jocko. I talked about love and friendship and sacrifice, and I added baseball themes. Then at night, in his presence, the golden phrases that resonated over the scrap piles refused to come. We would talk about how Munson didn't get enough credit, or whether Billy Martin was right for the team. Later, I realized that Jocko, asking for advice that night, had really just been asking me to come clean about my feelings for his girlfriend. He knew where everything was going. I could tell the truth to those piles of gun barrels, but I lost my resolve everywhere else.

The night Jocko found us together resulted in a surprising lack of fireworks. I think by then the explosives had been drained from everyone. He and Olivia went off to talk, to have a "final" conversation. I couldn't look at anyone. I felt too ashamed. I sat up all night, waiting for a call.

The next day at work, I ran a thousand conversations in my mind. I was like the computer that plays chess, rating every conceivable move with every possible piece. I worked up speeches full of gut-wrenching guilt, hope, sadness, anger — everything. The steel cried. I would tell Jocko the hard truth: I was in love with his girlfriend; we would marry and raise kids, live happily ever after. He needed to make peace with it. Life was strange. Who could predict love? I drove home, ate, showered, and headed to his house.

I found them on the couch, listening to Springsteen. I saw the flush in Olivia's face, and my heart dropped through the floor. We exchanged small talk for a few minutes, and then I said I had to be somewhere. They didn't object. I drove home and set my alarm for 4:00 A.M. Before dawn, I drove past Jocko's house, just to see for myself what I knew would be there.

Her car, still parked out front.

For the next week, I worked, came home, and stayed in my apartment, refusing to answer the phone. It rang constantly, sometimes ten or twenty rings. I was sure it was Olivia, or Jocko, and I steeled myself not to answer. I paced and willed the phone to stop. It felt good not to answer the phone. I imagined them wanting desperately to talk to me, but I would not let them.

It turned out to be my mom, calling to say my bone spur doctor's appointment had been postponed.

At the warehouse, the Bachman brothers were scaling back for the winter. They said I was welcome to stay, but they wondered why a guy with a college degree wanted to hang around such a place. It was the first time I realized they knew anything about me.

Eventually, Jocko and I sat down to talk. He asked how deeply I was in love with Olivia. I said I had no idea what love was or how you measured it.

"If you ever figure it out, put it in your book," he said.

Then one evening, I heard a knock on the door. I let Olivia in, and for a long while, we just stood there. She said she was leaving town to take a civil service job in Buffalo. Before she left, she had a question: That night when Jocko had found us, why hadn't I come after her? Why had I let her go? Why had I abandoned her?

I had imagined a million scenarios, written a million speeches — but I hadn't seen that one coming.

I gave the Bachman brothers my notice, determined to leave Rochester before she did. They cursed me but salted my last pay envelope with a few extra bucks. As I said, they were amazingly lovable.

A few days later, I shook Jocko's hand and vowed to see him at the World Series next year. I watched him shrink in my rearview mirror — he wore that ridiculous charred Yankee cap — and I drove home to Waverly, to sleep in my childhood bed next to the picture of Horace Clarke.

My dad said nothing about the Reds' sweep. He must have remembered how badly I reacted to Sandy Koufax. One night, I stayed up late and drank beer with him, watching *The Tonight Show* with Johnny Carson. Full of joy, I think, from the return of his only son, Dad pulled out his drumsticks and pounded along to Doc Severinsen and the NBC Orchestra. I drummed on the floor, and we laughed ourselves silly at the hot new comic, Steve Martin, who Dad insisted must be smoking pot.

Jocko stayed in Rochester and married a great lady. I guess you could say he finally found that happily-ever-after. No matter how far apart we drift, he and I stay in touch. We have Waverly. We have the longest run from scrimmage on record. And we have the Yankees. We both know any Yankee news that has occurred in the past six hours. We never talk about Olivia.

For months, I made mental speeches to her. In them, I said that it was not her fault, that I'd always feel sad for how everything had played out. I told her I never meant to let her go that night; I was trying to read her mind, trying to do what was right. I didn't know. I was a rookie.

Listen: Love never goes away. It just becomes obscured, like a plant that disappears behind new growth in a garden. After a while, you forget it's there. But its roots always remain deep in the ground.

Years later, I bumped into Olivia at a wedding. Upon seeing me, she started in on the Yankees. We began to argue, just like old times. We raged at each other about Cal Ripken. Then I went into the bar to watch the game. She stayed in the ballroom and danced.

JUJU RULE 8

WMD

Some fans who regularly beat up inanimate objects aren't really trying to help their teams. They just like to hurt things.

Avoid these people. They mock juju. They laugh at the idea of a David Ortiz jersey buried in Yankee Stadium, or of fans who selflessly change seats to spark a rally. They think a catastrophic juju event cannot happen on American sporting soil. They refuse to accept the hard, anecdotal evidence.

On that note, let's ponder the most powerful juju event in recent history. It occurred on October 5, 2007, at approximately 10:36 P.M., EST, with an epicenter traced to the shoreline of Lake Erie, between the mouth of the Cuyahoga River and the eastern ridge of Cleveland. That night, the temperature hovered around 80 degrees, hot and hazy, with the wind blowing in from the north at around seven miles per hour. No anomalies were measured in the earth's magnetic field. There were no reports of unidentified aircraft.

The Yankees led the Indians 1–0 in game two of the American League Division Series. Needing only six more outs, New York sent to the mound Joba Chamberlain, an emerging force of nature, while the great Mariano Rivera began warming up in the bullpen. By all known theorems of baseball, the Yankees had won the game.

Working from my home, in tandem with millions of fans across the Yankee jujuverse, I had melted the Indians' bats like paraffin. Together, we had the Cleveland players talking to themselves in languages that disappeared ten thousand years ago.

For eight innings, I'd used an ever-changing, impromptu Jazzercise of juju moves — lamp rubs, jumping jacks, finger flutters — never lapsing into a pattern the enemy could decipher. I could feel the whiplash crackle of Rizzutons shooting into my TV, and as each Cleveland batter swung and missed, my juju grew in size, until it had become almost painfully engorged. By the time Joba emerged from the bullpen, I was ready to attack a recliner. I swaggered and strutted with the boldness of a college security guard with his Taser pressed to the neck of a wiseass grad student.

That. Game. Was. Ours.

Then, from the moonless sky, a gazillion tiny winged creatures descended upon Jacobs Field. It was like a demon cloud in a Harry Potter movie. Joba flailed helplessly at the buzzing swarm, and an overmatched Yankee trainer jogged out with a can of bug spray. For all the good it did, he might as well have brought Old Spice deodorant.

That night, despite the millions of Yankee fans transmitting juju, nobody knew what in hell to do.

We had a scheme for their lefty hitters.

We had a strategy for their bullpen.

We had no tactic for biblical plagues.

Rule 8: Always have a backup plan.

That night, the global Yankees Entertainment and Sports (YES) Network collapsed into a chaos of terror and wild pitches. My hotline rang from outposts across North America. One of my greatest juju technicians, a now retired New York City banker who goes by the secret Yankee nickname of "Alphonso," phoned in a toddler-like state of agitation. He seemed to be speaking in tongues. Alphonso could not even verbalize his strongest incantation, which merely required him to say, "The game is over. I am turning off the TV and going to bed." He could not enunciate the words. He was too cowed, too overwhelmed, to fight back.

Cleveland tied the game without recording one base hit. We lost in the eleventh, a defeat that cost us the division series and opened the floodgates for Boston to win the 2007 World Series, its second world championship in four years.

That night, somebody, somewhere, opened a serious can of Aleister Crowley on us.

We still don't know how they did it. My guess is that Cleveland operatives — probably with direction from Boston — detonated a small-scale juju bomb made from enriched Rizzutonic particles that had been collected for years, perhaps as far back as the early 1980s Indians era of Bob Owchinko and "Super Joe" Charboneau.

We never had a chance.

Listen: Each of us must maintain an emergency juju reserve, which we pray is never needed. We face a stark reality: The government will not protect us; the Yankees are far too unpopular. Nor will big corporations intervene; they fear the controversy we would bring. This Yankee defense arsenal must come from concerned individuals, everyday citizens, thinking fans . . . *like you.*

How can we do this?

Let me pose an example: It's mid-May, and you're standing in your kitchen, waving a commemorative Yankee saltshaker at the TV. As a result, Robbie Cano lashes a two-out, upper-deck, walk-off grand slam. You have just identified an off-the-charts nuclear juju hot spot — by far the most potent location in your home. *What should you do?*

a. Run about the house, fluttering your hands and blathering to everybody you know, especially our enemies, so they can ridicule you, bury in your couch a Kleenex used by David Ortiz, and, if possible, steal your Yankee saltshaker and torture it, seeking to turn it against us.

b. Stand there, waving said saltshaker, dumbly watching TV for the rest of the season, because you believe it will cause every Yankee batter to hit a home run, and the team will never lose again.

c. Calmly pretend nothing happened; note precise time and body placement; relocate saltshaker to a secure place, keeping encrypted records to ensure a perfect re-creation of said event in the postseason, or whenever necessary.

If you answered "a" or "b," congratulations: you are a Cubs fan.

Save your thunderbolts for the next plague of locusts. Our enemies are saving theirs.

9

★

The Yankee Crier

After leaving Rochester, I bit my lip and returned to radio.

I moved to Binghamton to read news for an AM station whose programming format was called "The Songs from Your Life." Considering the advanced age of our audience, it should have been called "The Sores from Your Bed." Here I was, a twenty-five-year-old Springsteen die-hard trapped in a playlist Alcatraz of Perry Como and Jerry Vale. On the rare occasion when WENE touched the 1970s, it was for a dollop of Helen Reddy or Debby Boone, the musical equivalents of creamed corn in an assisted-living cafeteria. Between the commercials for funeral parlors and stool softeners, I reported car crashes, drug arrests, and shootings — whatever it took to keep the oldsters terrified.

One morning, I reported that Lynyrd Skynyrd's plane had crashed. Minutes later, a woman called the news line, sobbing hysterically. It took a while to coax intelligible words. Finally, I figured out the source of her despair. She thought I'd said the Lennon Sisters.

Half our audience no longer drove. The other half was starting to accept Beatles music. If a young woman at a party learned where I worked, she instinctively assumed I'd had a chin tuck and was wearing a wig. The more mail I received from senior centers, the more I felt like a suck-up Young Republican, barely a notch below the scammers who sold "you can't be turned down" life insurance. Every morning, when I heard the deejay play his weeper anthem — "The Men in My Little Girl's Life," by Mike Douglas — I would stare into the blackness of my coffee as if it were Nietzsche's abyss.

But one bright light shone upon me: Billy's team.

We had signed Reggie — adding him to Thurman, Catfish, Willie, Chambliss, and Roy White. This was 1977, a season later memorialized in the book and ESPN miniseries *The Bronx Is Burning*, so titled because both the Yankees and the country seemed to be exploding. It was a year of racial tensions, the murderous "Son of Sam," Billy's liquor cabinet, and the Bicentennial party hangover. I watched it unfold at the Stadium.

The Stadium was one of those darkness-at-noon bars with pocket-comb cardboard dispensers, giant jars of Polish sausages, and a dusty mirror that protected the regulars from getting an honest glimpse of themselves. It took its name from the days when Binghamton had been home to a Yankee farm club, seasoning the likes of Whitey, Thurman, and Joe Pepitone. The walls held framed glossies of ex-prospects who had vanished into the firmament. One booth was autographed by former New York Football Giants running back Ron Johnson. There I would meet "the Dog Man" and "the Yankee Crier."

The Dog Man was a Hobart friend who two months earlier had nearly died in a car-train collision. Surgeons had pieced him back together, but his mind was still a hurricane. At Hobart, he'd been one of the smartest guys in the room. Now he was moody and jumbled in thought. Once, he had been a lock for law school. Now he pondered the skilled trades. But the Dog Man had one great point in his favor: he was damn grateful to be alive, and he celebrated every sunset, every Big Mac, and every cold beer that slid his way. Me? I was keeping shot glasses of Drano. We counterbalanced each other, sharing two obsessions: Springsteen and the Yankees.

We developed a secret language of Springsteen lyrics.

"Hey, Spanish Johnny," he'd say on the phone, "you wanna make a little easy money tonight?"

"It's a town full of losers," I'd reply.

"Show a little faith!"

And so on. Generally, the call of the Dog Man would lure me from work on my baseball novel. The Stadium, located within walking distance, made a perfect watering hole. It was racially mixed, too cheap to discriminate. When a game came on, whites and blacks stood together. It was a Yankee bar.

The Yankee Crier read news for a competing radio station, which meant that at first, we didn't get along. You didn't make any friends jousting for position at news conferences. Moreover, I hated that his FM station played album cuts from emerging bands — the Eagles, Fleetwood Mac, and Pink Floyd (the Perry Comos and Jerry Vales of today). His colleagues played thirty-minute "rock blocks," punctuated by ads for head shops and far trendier bars than the Stadium. At the Crier's station, nobody gave a hang about last night's pot arrests, because the on-air personalities either pretended to be stoned or actually were. I listened all the time and imagined the women I'd meet if only I worked there, rather than in an Andrews Sisters torture chamber that was still tracking its way through Prohibition.

The Crier possessed two superhuman talents. He could cram sixty seconds of ad copy into a thirty-second spot — "aWHOPPER-aWHALER-andsoftdrink-foraDOLLAR!" — without fainting, and he could, at any time, conjure up a heart-stirring story about the Yankees. But there was one catch: he always cried.

"So it's Old-Timers' Day, and they've announced Mickey and Joe, and then Bob Sheppard says, 'Ladies and gentlemen, please welcome a special guest.' And I'm thinking, *No, it can't be! He said he'd never return!* But there he is! It's him! There's silence across the stadium. Nobody believes it. Then, suddenly, the whole place is screaming . . . *Because there he is!* The all-time single-season home run champion! And what does he do? *I'll tell you what he does!* He covers his face, and he drops to his knees! This man who hit sixty-one home runs in a single season, this man, Roger Maris, *drops to his knees . . . and he weeps! You hear me? He weeps!*"

By this time, the Crier would have dropped to his own knees, bawling like Meryl Streep. We would lift him to his stool, the beet-red cheeks streaked with tears, his face twitching like a VCR on fast-forward. Every Yankee fan within a ten-foot radius would be whimpering, hugging, reborn.

"Wind up wounded, and not even dead," the Dog Man would say.

Two innings later, the Crier would relaunch. It might start as a complaint about backup catching and evolve into a re-creation of Yogi's awkward childhood.

Every story would send him dangling from the table, deep into a Yankee *Rigoletto.* "And then . . . stepping to the plate . . . from the mean streets of Puerto Rico, it's *him . . .* Otto Velez . . . *the man they said could not hit a major league curve!*"

"Cut loose like a deuce," the Dog Man would add.

That fall, as the pennant race raged, the Crier and the Dog Man phoned me every night, too agitated to sleep. The Crier would drive to a newsstand, buy the next day's tabloids, and read me the latest crises: Billy was to be fired. Reggie had ripped Thurman. Mickey Rivers wanted a raise. Each emergency pushed him closer to despair. He'd pace his house, ranting into the mouthpiece, roiling to a climax, then sob and hang up. It was like a demented form of Yankee phone sex, with tears instead of the orgasm. And when the Crier was done, I would collapse into a chair, wiping my eyes with a shirtsleeve, too fired up to sleep and too exhausted to write.

Seconds after I'd hang up, the phone would ring.

"We gotta get out while we're young," the Dog Man would say.

We cried and recited Springsteen lyrics into October, when I watched the World Series alone, from the floor of my apartment. My best pennant race juju had been pushups, so I lay in front of the TV and did them between pitches, dozens at a time, until my arms shook. It worked. Moments after Reggie hit his third home run to seal our victory over the Dodgers — a vengeance fourteen years in the making — I crashed to the floor, exhausted, and the phone rang.

"*The fireworks are hailin' over little Eden tonight!*" the Dog Man yelled.

"We're gonna play some pool," I said. "Skip some school."

"Act real cool."

"Stay out all night."

"Just kinda feel all right!"

We met at the Stadium, my arms still burning. I could barely lift a glass.

The Crier left radio and took a job with the state tax department. I can imagine him going over somebody's audit, weeping, as he recounts Don Mattingly's final at bat.

Now and then I get a postcard from the Dog Man, lately from somewhere in Delaware. He never married. He became a video technician, and he stayed sort of crazy. Once he spent fifteen cold hours on the roof of Giants Stadium so that he could sneak into a Springsteen concert. The Dog Man's postcards still come in Bruce-ese, though the lines hold a tinge of sadness. "*The poets down here don't write nothing at all*" . . . "*Walk tall, or better don't walk at all*" . . . "*Maybe we ain't that young anymore*" . . .

Now and then, as I'm fumbling with the radio dial, I catch Mike Douglas singing "The Men in My Little Girl's Life." It hits me like a bucket of water. I think of the Stadium, the Lennon Sisters, and the Crier's story of Roger Maris weeping at home plate. I think of my own little girl, all grown-up, and I throw tears every single time (*God, I am so pathetic*), every single time.

Over the years, I've recounted the stories of that summer to those who were there, and in full disclosure, I must note that they recall one detail slightly differently. They say that the Yankee Crier was never the first one in our group to burst into tears. He was always just reacting to me.

JUJU RULE 9

The Tet

Growing up, I recall no blood feud with Boston. The Redsock teams of Frank Malzone and Gary Geiger never sent me scurrying to the garage wall. In high school, it was the fearsome Baltimore Orioles, with Boog Powell and the Robinsons, Frank and Brooks, that sent me trudging up to my room in despair. In college, the Oakland juggernauts of Reggie Jackson and Catfish Hunter, our future pets, routinely ate my lunch. Yes, I swapped hairy eyeballs with a few Boston hotheads, but Redsock fans seeking to taste my humiliation usually settled for cold leftovers.

Not until 1975, with the arrival of Jim Rice, did Boston — the team, rather than its fans — capture my attention. I cannot remember the Yankees ever retiring the Redsock shortstop, Rick Burleson, with runners on base. But Fred Lynn tanked, and Carl Yastrzemski ossified, and for the next eight years, I lived in fear of losing to Kansas City.

Yankees vs. Royals, 1976 to 1983: now *that* was a rivalry.

In the late 1980s, Boston won three division titles, while we fielded a Tijuana donkey show lineup of Alvaro Espinoza, Kevin Maas, and Mel Hall — a man today remembered for bringing a gun into the Yankee clubhouse, walking his pet cougars on the streets of Manhattan, and being convicted for sexual abuse of a minor in 2009. In 1990, we finished last, *dead last,* beached and belly-up, the *Exxon Valdez* of baseball.

If Boston happened to collapse every October, it wasn't my fault.

But in 1991, during the darkest days of Yankee fanhood, Bostonians started blaming us for everything that ever went wrong.

The previous year, *Boston Globe* sportswriter Dan Shaughnessy published *The Curse of the Bambino,* an accusatory manifesto that laid the Redsocks' whole sorry-ass history on our kitchen table. It was our fault they hadn't won since 1918. It was our fault that Boston had committed baseball's "original sin" — the sale of Babe Ruth. We were the fast-talking New Yawk shysters, the slippery traffickers in human flesh, who'd wheedled the bighearted Bambino from those God-fearing Pilgrims, the same way we'd stolen Manhattan from the Indians, John Lennon from the Beatles, and salted bagels from the Jews.

From then on, we were the Great Satan, the Evil Empire, the Dark Lord Sauron, Rupert Murdoch, chickenpox — take your pick — while Redsock Nation reveled in its glorious, "Bruce Willis on the asteroid" martyrdom. Overnight, Redsock Nation proclaimed itself to be our archrivals, even if this was news to us. We had been unwittingly eating off their dinner plate for seventy years, and now they wanted a food fight.

Suddenly, we faced a virulent strain of Redsock fan, often without discernible ties to New England. You'd find them in remote villages across Pennsylvania and upstate New York, traditional Yankee strongholds. They transcended profiling. They might hate the Kennedys, loathe Harvard, and cheer if Nantucket sank into the sea. Yet there they were, in the bars of Elmira and Scranton, ringing in the New Year with drunken choruses of "Yan-kees suck!"

By the year 2000, these newly hatched Yankee hate groups had begun to coalesce around the Redsock ideology. Young recruits — lured to Massachusetts by its booming software industry — made pilgrimages to Boston, funneling money to the team through purchases of swag. Inspired by the so-called "curse," Shaughnessy's radical followers began producing Rizzutons, greasing the skids of secret Redsock operations, much as the CIA had once bankrolled the mujahideen of Afghanistan.

Their army grew virally, while we sat back and did nothing. We thought ourselves invulnerable.

But what was coming was not some one-night whammy bomb, fired from a floating lab in Lake Erie. In the American League Championship Series of 2004, we faced the Tet Offensive of juju. We were hopelessly outgunned.

Rule 9: *Juju requires overwhelming strength in numbers.*

Publicly, Redsock Nation will dispute the existence of juju. That's like North Korea denying its nuclear program. For decades, Boston fans courted every dark element that might slither out of a Black Sabbath lyric, as long as it might heal Nomar Garciaparra's troubled hamstring. One fan planted a Redsock cap on top of Mount Everest. One tried to raise Babe Ruth's piano from the bottom of a lake. I personally know a fan who drove two hours to Cooperstown, donned a Boston cap, and ran three laps counterclockwise around the National Baseball Hall of Fame. *Three times: enemy action.*

And what did we do? Did we recruit Sherpas to sabotage the Everest expedition? Send depth charges to destroy Ruth's piano? Drive to Cooperstown and run clockwise laps?

No. We lay on our embroidered Yankee pillows, secure in the delusion that no Redsock player could harm us and that Boston's claims to cultural relevance would forever be limited to Sam Adams and Ally McBeal.

In 2004, our world changed. Boston rallied from a three-game deficit to crush the Yankees in the AL Championship Series. In game seven, I remember going to the bathroom and hearing Johnny Damon — the bearded, evil Redsock version — clobber that game-breaking grand slam off Javier Vazquez, ending the world as I knew it.

Today, to restore past dynasties, the Yankees have only one option. It does not involve money, farm system, scouting, or free agents. We need to find new sources of juju.

Our quest increasingly looks to Third World nations, where rural cultures are sitting on vast underground deposits — reservoirs that for generations were used by shamans and village healers to control the weather and ward off disease. What a waste. They could have been winning baseball games.

In its raw, anecdotal form, Third World juju appears to be far more powerful than anything produced in industrialized societies, even with our advanced methods of embellishment. These lost cultures are the future of baseball.

Importing juju is a tricky business, but it's hardly new. For half a century, Latino players have thrived in the major leagues via juju sent from their own remote towns and villages, where kinfolk gathered around shortwave radios to work the games. But as their home economies flourished, Latino juju began to grow stale and brittle. Today, baseball scouts comb distant mountains in Venezuela and Africa for sources of pristine juju, just waiting to ignite rallies.

Why is this juju so powerful? I believe that after the industrial revolution, humanity lost much of the original psychic powers that helped it survive the glaciers and giant boars. We ceded to machines our superiority over nature, while maintaining spiritual links only to our greatest passions — such as Yankee baseball. Another blow came with the invention of the TV remote. Once humankind could change channels without leaving the couch, our juju shrank noticeably.

The Rizzutonic emissions of our brawny, cave-dwelling ancestors far exceeded anything today's balding, socks-and-sandal-clad juju masters can muster. Juju-wise, we have become a race of channel-hopping weenies.

But there *is* hope. In the winter of 2009–2010, the Yankees launched an unprecedented world outreach program. The team toured its newly won World Series trophy throughout the Pacific Rim, visiting far-flung localities where most of the population would think the syllables "der-ek jee-ter" represented a seafood casserole. This trip was no exotic paid vacation for the Yankee brass disguised as a tax write-off. It was an expedition into uncharted areas, a trek into the heart of darkness, seeking to find and exploit the richest veins of juju on the planet.

If we can teach these cultures baseball, hook them on Yankee pride, offer cheap rates on Yankee swag and YES Network cable programming, we can siphon off their weather-controlling juju and boost the team, maybe by as much as ten extra victories per season.

Some Yankee fans say we should assassinate or depose foreign leaders if they appear to be siding with the wrong teams. I disagree.

We must win the support of the people. Without it, their juju will win no ballgames.

My motto: *No wars for juju!* Instead, if we can capture the hearts and minds (and juju) of 600 million new fans, we can once again make the game of baseball safe for Yankee children.

10

★

The Hoosier Show Lounge Massacre

●

I am hanging from a ceiling beam above the strobe-lit dance floor of Bob and Zip's Hoosier Show Lounge in New Albany, Indiana. On a wide-screen projector TV — one of those miniature drive-in theaters that is the rage — the Yankees are massacring Boston. Yes, *the* massacre. It is Saturday, September 9, 1978, and I have been massacring the Redsocks for two hours. I am hoarse, overheated, and soaked in sweat, and my lungs ache. Dangling from the rafters, I am yelling, "GAHHHHHH!"

You may be wondering how I got here.

At this moment, *I* am wondering how I got here.

Ten months earlier, I again quit radio. I woke up one day in Binghamton to realize I was drinking a six-pack a night and earning the wages of a Burger King drive-through-window attendant. My life had become a pointless succession of deadlines, each one a lead pipe to the head. And it would never change. Every May, Syracuse University's S. I. Newhouse School of Public Communications belched a new crop of budding broadcast personalities, like ink from a giant squid, filling the local airwaves with big-voiced gerbils who would happily work for a résumé line and a business card. As a result, the labor conditions of radio stations rivaled those of overseas sweatshops. At least in Asia, you could filch a pair of Nikes. Here, they'd frisk you for ballpoint pens.

One day, I interviewed a recruiter from VISTA — the U.S. government's Volunteers in Service to America program — and before the radio segment aired, I'd given notice and volunteered. I told friends I was done "picking cotton for the Man."

In truth, I was a basket case. I had developed another secret crush on a buddy's girlfriend. Every time we saw each other, we flirted just a bit more, sometimes even talking Yankee baseball. Before déjà vu happened all over again, I vowed to leave Binghamton or finally leap off that bridge.

I couldn't tell anybody. I just watched her and pined. The more her fiancé urged me to stay, the more desperate I became to run. So I fled to VISTA, my French Foreign Legion, and left for Somewhere, Anywhere — the netherworlds of Indiana, well beyond the solar system of Yankee baseball. I planned never to return.

As a VISTA volunteer, I was assigned to become an organizer for a consortium of neighborhood groups in Indianapolis. I spent a week in Chicago, training at a tiny outpost for ex-hippies called the Midwest Academy. They taught the Saul Alinsky art of rabble-rousing, which made organizing look like a frat party. You made a speech, played a little guitar, stirred up people, pointed to some hapless politico — then stood back and let the spittle fly. Unfortunately, our VISTA group mostly sat around singing Holly Near anthems and complaining about the lack of heat in the office. After six months, we finally organized something — a protest against VISTA, for wasting our time. As a result, the bureaucracy vengefully dispersed us to all corners of Indiana. I wound up in New Albany, across the Ohio River from Louisville, Kentucky, ordered to chill out for my remaining time, then go home and never come back.

Through a sponsor, I found free lodging in the attic of St. Mary's Church, near downtown New Albany. I set up a bed and makeshift nightstand next to a ventilation window about ten feet below the bell tower. I slept surrounded by seriously creepy statues of Mary, Joseph, and the Yuletide manger gang. I tried covering them with blankets, but it just multiplied the terror effect. I absolutely dreaded climbing up there after dark, but the rent was right — zero — and, frankly, I had nowhere else to go.

The most paranoid and sleepless night of my life took place there, after I watched a little-known movie by a regional filmmaker named John Carpenter. It was called *Halloween*. That night, I slept with a baseball bat.

On the next floor down, volunteer counselors staffed the twenty-four-hour crisis hotline. At first, they freaked out at the sound of me staggering up the creaky stairs late at night, because the church was locked and supposed to be empty. Also, they couldn't fathom what kind of psychopath could be living up in the dark spaces between the Crucifixion statues and the boxes of bingo equipment. Eventually, they came to know me as a relatively harmless VISTA volunteer — and "the Yankees fan."

I received $140 in food stamps per month and a $65 weekly paycheck. Back in Indianapolis, where I'd shared rent on a two-bedroom apartment, I had lived in mac-and-cheese poverty. But here, in my rent-free attic of horrors, I had $65 a week to burn on unbridled decadence. So every night, I drank beers at Bob and Zip's until the final baseball scores crawled across the elevated TV's news ticker, then padded up the church stairs in my socks, hoping the hotline counselor on duty didn't call the cops. I needed to get through four months.

That summer, the collapse of the mighty Yankees became a national amusement. Billy was gone, Catfish was hurt, Reggie was whining, and *Sports Illustrated* ran a picture of Thurman Munson standing in right field, arms extended, as if begging for a bullet. At one point in July, we sat fourteen games out — no hope in sight, which summed up my life quite well.

With few daily responsibilities, I killed mornings at the library, tracking the Yankees through the New York tabloids. Nobody in basketball-obsessed Indiana gave a squirt about the American League pennant race, although one friend mentioned a nun in a nearby parish who was said to be a die-hard Yankee fan. He added that she was rather attractive. *Great,* I thought. *I finally meet a good-looking Yankee babe, and she gets hot on color glossies of the pope.* I vowed to say hi — or, amen — if our paths crossed during last call at Bob and Zip's.

I feel compelled to note that this was the disco era, a dank and hollow stretch in American history, remembered now for the invention of "quasar" lights and two-for-one drink specials. I despised disco music and would love to say that I rejected every superficial, glitter-ball, twinkle-toed moment of it. Truth is, once every few weeks, feeling some lizard mating urge, I would don shiny shoes and a paisley shirt and descend into the basement of Bob and Zip's — the Hoosier Show Lounge — a hellhole of smoke and head-thumping rhythm. I would suck in my gut and take off my glasses, which meant worrying that my eyes were crossed. I would find a corner, watch the gene pools mingle, guzzle beer upon beer, and — like Thurman in that photograph — wish for a quick death. By the time I wobbled home, glasses on and gut unclenched, I was a candidate for the crisis hotline.

As Boston's lead dwindled, I began regaling friends with news from back east. I'd burst into the crisis center to announce that the Yankees had gained another game. *Down to five . . . then four . . . then three.* Nobody cared, but I persisted. I retold the Yankee Crier's greatest tales until the counselors, who had heard every sob story ever told, wiped their eyes just to get rid of me. I called myself a Yankee missionary, saving heathen Hoosier souls from an eternity without a World Series victory. I read newspaper articles in a booming baritone, imitating a Bible school headmaster. I'll never forget one story that began, "In the American League East, the cat has nearly caught the mouse . . ."

"We are the cat!" I proclaimed. "This weekend, Boston is the mouse! If you get a long-distance hotline call from Boston, don't worry; it's just the Redsocks, having a crisis."

That Saturday, I arrived at Bob and Zip's around noon. After being told the upstairs TV carried *only* college football, I marched down to the empty Hoosier Show Lounge, figured out how to bring NBC's Game of the Week up on the projector screen, dragged a straight-back chair in front of it, and — using passive-resistance techniques learned at the Jane Fonda hippie academy in Chicago — issued a grand personal declaration: *I would not be moved.*

I ordered beers, two at a time. That day, if there had been a pitch count for Stroh's, I would have exceeded my 140-gulp limit by the fifth inning. Down in the black-lighted, ill-vented Hoosier Show Lounge, I mooned, I threw the evil eye, I delivered imaginary pitches and swung invisible bats, and I bounced off the paneling like Ricochet Rabbit. In the fourth inning, I spooked the Redsocks' ace, Dennis Eckersley, into a public unraveling reminiscent of Jerry Lewis in the original *Nutty Professor.* We scored seven runs. I installed a hitch in Carlton Fisk's swing and planted clouds in the steely mind of Redsock manager Don Zimmer. I threw nine shutout innings, thanks to nonstop beer service from Bob, or maybe it was Zip.

Around 4:00 P.M., my friends arrived. Actually, they drank a while in the bar before hearing a commotion downstairs. Later, one said that when he first descended into the Hoosier Show Lounge, until his eyes adjusted to the darkness, he couldn't see my hands clutching the rafters and thought I was levitating. I was kicking like a baby in a bouncer. I appeared to be yodeling. The staff was circling. The game had ended, and God-fearing people wanted to change the channel, but when anybody approached, I snarled like a pit bull guarding his chow dish.

From that day on, at Bob and Zip's Hoosier Show Lounge, I had a name. I was "Crazy Yankees Fan." Upon seeing me, Bob — or maybe it was Zip — would say, "Hey, there he is, Crazy Yankees Fan!" He would motion for me to do my "Crazy Yankees Fan Dance," a mix of Goose Gossage's huffing and Mick Jagger's chicken flap. He would punch up "Bat Out of Hell" — a song I loathed — and shout, "Go to it, Crazy Yankees Fan! Back where you're from, Meat Loaf is the toast of the town!"

(*Note:* Most Indiana folks never bothered to discern the rather extensive cultural differences between upstate and downstate New York.)

(*Secondary note:* Meat Loaf is a Yankee fan, by the way.)

I spent the last nights of the season at Bob and Zip's, watching scores crawl across the tube. But when the season boiled down to one playoff game — Us against Them, at Fenway — I retreated to my attic with Mary, Joseph, and the Wise Men. I could not bear to watch in the presence of strangers. A counselor, recognizing a looming crisis, loaned me a small TV. That afternoon, as I set it up in the attic, the temperature probably reached 110. Moreover, I was sick with the flu.

Raining sweat upon the floor, I flailed away at my juju lotus positions. At times, my head throbbed so fiercely that I had to lie down, close my eyes, and just hope the juju gods felt sorry for me. Moments after Bucky Dent's home run cleared the Green Monster, I heard banging sounds. Downstairs, at the hotline, they were beating on the radiator.

When the game ended, when Graig Nettles squeezed the final pop-fly out, the pipes again began clanging, but I could not stomp a reply. I fell onto the bed sideways, letting the window fan blow directly onto my head. I lay that way all night. I didn't go to Bob and Zip's. I didn't eat. Not only was I sick and drained, but I feared that, by celebrating, I would overstep my juju bounds.

And I wondered . . . *Sympathy juju?*

A Yankee fan from New Jersey once told me that he had experienced long-term love affairs that did not equal the emotional intensity of that one game. I understood what he meant. If it's true that poltergeists are psychic forces unleashed by human trauma, a part of me is still flinging statues at night in that attic. I still see that ball leap off Bucky Dent's bat and feel myself rising with it. I still see Nettles squeezing Yastrzemski's pop-up and still feel myself falling into bed, paralyzed, euphoric, exhausted.

Two weeks later, we beat the Dodgers in the World Series. The following morning, I sat in the library, devouring the New York papers. It was like sexual foreplay: I stroked the headlines, then entered the story with a long moan. As I set down a *Daily News,* a stunning young woman in a nun's habit snatched it and began to coo. I asked if she was a Yankee fan. She crossed herself and laughed.

It was *her*—the Yankee nun, by far the most beautiful woman I had seen in Indiana. For the rest of the morning, we talked Yankees —everything from Nettles's coolness to our theories behind "Dirt" Tidrow's nickname. We covered the regular season, the playoff game, the World Series, and the farm clubs. She knew her Yankees. She called Thurman Munson "Herman Munster," a line I'd never heard. She had errands to run, but we lingered an hour in the parking lot. I could have talked all day. I sensed that she could have, too. At one point, I thought of just saying, *Hey, wanna marry me?* Had I done it, I know she would have said yes.

We vowed to meet the next day.

That night, at Bob and Zip's, someone played "Bat Out of Hell," and I climbed onto a corner booth and did my Crazy Yankees Fan Dance for my minions, the goodhearted people of New Albany in the great Hoosier state of Indiana. I huffed and flapped as I had never done before (nor have since).

The Yankees were champions of the world, and I had found God.

The next day, I was standing outside the library when they unlocked the doors. I sat in the periodicals room, perched with the tabloids. After a while, I moved toward the front desk. Then I stood outside, pretending to read a book. She didn't show. The day after that, I did it again. She didn't show. That week, I lived in the periodicals room, rehearsing lines about "Thurman Munster." Nothing. I drove loops around the nearby parish school, stalking the playgrounds like a pedophile, hoping to bump into her casually and claim it was mere happenstance.

She didn't show.

I asked my friend. A week later, he got back to me. She had left Indiana. Something had happened. Apparently, during a daily service, she had found herself distracted thinking about the Yankees. She told friends that she considered herself unfaithful to the church and could not continue being a nun. Evidently, she had been wavering for weeks, but something recent — the World Series, everybody figured — had pushed her over the edge.

I never saw her again.

JUJU RULE 10

Sympathy

Some fans expel a lot of energy trying to make the juju gods feel sorry for them. Every postgame encounter turns into a heartbreaking violin solo, a trip to the Department of Complaints and Lamentations to wail about life's latest indignity: the Internet is out, the George Foreman Quesadilla Maker arrived dented, the prized rookie shortstop can't hit lefties. And once the bleating begins — well, where does it stop? Their job stinks, their shoes pinch, and their spouse just added a new chin — number three, if you're scoring at home — and that's why they've stopped transmitting juju during ballgames.

Like a plaintiff wearing a neck brace on *Judge Judy,* they seek gales of sympathy from the juju gods and, of course, a settlement. How about letting that lithe, speedy second baseman swell to the size of a Freightliner truck, hit 50 home runs, and lead the team to a pennant? If that happens, they'll overlook the nasty, spreading skin rash and their lack of health insurance.

They think the world owes them a World Series ring as compensation for every storm that ever pissed hailstones onto their sad, "Send in the Clowns" lives.

Avoid these people. They know nothing about pain. They know nothing about life.

Rule 10: Avoid sympathy juju.

Listen: The juju gods are not the heartless beings depicted by Elizabethan novelists and Chicago sportswriters. But like crisis hotline counselors, they have heard every excuse, shy of tanning-bed-induced dementia, for why you decided to watch *Girls Gone Wild:*

Tampa instead of the ballgame. Claiming the dog ate your channel changer won't cut it. And don't even think about ginning up some story about work or family obligations; you'll cost your center fielder a kneecap.

Nevertheless, the real reason sympathy juju is such a dangerous game is this: *It might work.*

In fact, the juju gods *do* relate to our crapola lives, especially those of us stuck in dead-end careers or climates that annually receive 180 inches of snow. Unlike the Uppercase Deities — God, Allah, etc. — who plan tornadoes, earthquakes, and celebrity scandals, the juju gods are stuck calling balls and strikes. It means working nights, weekends, and holidays. They must answer their own phones, work in tight cubicles, and wear ties or pantsuits. Worst of all, they regularly must see us in our underwear, digging at the spaces between our toes, as we work games from our couches and easy chairs. They witness things no Bigtime Deity would ever want to imagine, much less create.

So if you're down on life — yeah, the juju gods will listen. Suffer hard enough, and who knows? Maybe they'll toss you a bone. Flooded-out New Orleans won the 2010 Super Bowl. Industry-dead Detroit took the 2008 Stanley Cup. Japan, tortured by a tsunami and nuclear power plant disaster, won the 2011 Women's World Cup in soccer. (*Note:* Big mistake. They should have held out for the 2012 Olympics.) Boston shambled around in its neck brace for eighty-six years, and Judge Judy Juju finally saw it their way — probably just to clear the dockets.

But how far can you play that sympathy card? A bout of poison ivy might lift your Dodgers into first place on June 15, but can you still be scratching in October? After a while, you'll end up dwelling on phantom aches and pains, and that could carry over to the team. You grow used to suffering. It becomes your way of life.

Some fans become so addicted to sympathy that they can't fully celebrate the Fourth of July unless their team is twelve games out, the manager's been fired, and their herpes is flaring like an attack of fire ants. When a happy, first-place Yankee fan floats by, they want to lash out with their signature "life is hell" complaint: *The Yankees buy pennants!*

Okay. Fine. Let's deal with this now.

In 2011, the Yankees' payroll exceeded $202 million — more than twice what was spent on teams such as the Mariners, Astros, Rockies, Braves, Orioles, Brewers, Reds, Royals, Rays, Blue Jays, Nationals, Indians, Diamondbacks, Rangers, Marlins, Athletics, Padres, and Pirates. Yeah, that's almost everybody. Not only that, but in a few cases, we spent *four* times as much as they did. We threw more onto our infield than they spent on their entire team.

Long ago, I pondered this glaring, troubling, unspeakable injustice and came to a moral conclusion: *I don't care.*

Listen: I *do* pine over life's inequality. Everybody deserves a hot meal. Every kid should have a chance to run for president. Every family needs broadband. No whale should die for one extra, needless thimble of blubber. Call me conservative. Call me liberal. Call me Ishmael. I don't care. Whether it's "We Shall Overcome" or the theme from *Fox & Friends,* hand me the lyrics, and I'll sing. (I also recycle.)

But once and for all: *If the Yankees buy pennants, it is because other teams sell them.*

When, in 480 B.C., the million-man Persian army marched into view, did the three hundred Spartans at Thermopylae complain to the media about the opposition's high payroll?

Does Pizza Hut whine that Domino's and Little Caesars spend too much on ingredients?

When a Hollywood blockbuster soars over budget, does Ben *"I would rather utter the words 'I worship you, Satan,' than 'My favorite baseball team is the New York Yankees'"* Affleck support a salary cap on actors?

No. War is war, pizza is pizza, movies are movies, and billionaire owners who *don't* try to buy pennants are just scheming tightwads in cheap suits.

Who are these small-market owners, anyway? Let's consider the late Carl Pohlad, beloved former scion of the Minnesota Twins. Before his death in 2009 at age ninety-three, Pohlad ranked 102nd on the Forbes 400, with an estimated worth of $2.6 billion. That could fund a James Cameron movie. Nevertheless, in 2007, when it came to shelling out a few thin dimes to keep star Twins center fielder Torii Hunter — *Oh! Mercy!* — Carl showed up broke and barefoot. And a year later, when the contract came due for Twins ace Johan Santana — *Oh! Mercy!* — Carl's tin cup began rattling. He couldn't afford to pay the kind of salaries those greedy players demanded.

Know why free agents fled Minnesota in the mid-2000s? The reason wasn't the size of the market. It wasn't poor fan loyalty. They jumped ship because beloved billionaire Carl Pohlad was a scheming tightwad in a cheap suit, who didn't want to spend money on base-ball. Now that he's moved on to that Platinum Club in the sky, Twins fans can recall him as a *dead,* scheming tightwad.

How about David Glass, former CEO of Walmart, the world's largest public corporation, and principal owner of the Kansas City Royals? When David throws a birthday party for his wife, do you think he serves 99-cent clam dip from the distressed aisle at ALDI? If he takes his family on a winter vacation to — oh, let's say Syracuse, New York — do you think he loads the kids into the Truckster and drives thirty hours? Well, in 2010, when Royals ace Zack Greinke neared free agency — *Oh! Mercy!* — David Glass showed his empty pockets, recited a few lines from *David Copperfield,* and dealt the guy to Milwaukee.

By the way, *Forbes* that year estimated Glass's annual take from the Royals at $20 million. That beats what Roy Halladay earned in 2010, after thirteen seasons and more than 150 wins.

Reader, these are billionaires pretending to be millionaires so that we will feel sorry for them. And when the team is losing, the owner always plays the same card: *It's not my fault. The Yankees stole our dog.*

The sympathy card: Great for billionaires, lousy for juju.

11

★

Thurman

Gorged and radiant from my World Series triumph, I returned east in late 1978 and groveled my way into a job. I became a reporter for the *Binghamton Press & Sun-Bulletin*, working at the two-man bureau in Norwich, a tranquil city of seven thousand, surrounded by hills full of white people with guns. I covered car crashes, pot arrests, and barn fires, typing my stories into a state-of-the-art word processor that resembled a microwave oven grafted to a keyboard.

The town was home to Norwich Pharmaceuticals (the creator of Pepto-Bismol) and Clarence Rappleyea, the GOP minority leader of the New York State Assembly. On a regular basis, I rewrote press releases about some new antidepressant or shoveled what my editor called "crap from Rapp." Eventually, I came to specialize in profiles that, if made into a regular feature, would have been titled "Today's Local Piece of Work." I wrote about a redneck member of the Posse Comitatus who wore his side arm to school board meetings, and a dairy farmer whose feisty heifers — veritable bovine bra burners — jumped fences and terrorized the meek, less liberated cattle. I wrote about the animal control officer's war on raccoons, and one judge's zero-tolerance crackdown on drivers who squealed their tires on Main Street. Then there was Tracy Vroman, a little girl who lost her arms in a farm accident and had one limb reattached at the Norwich hospital. I visited her family that night in the emergency room. Until then, I had never tried to write while crying.

I worked with a veteran reporter named Jim Wright, who moonlighted as the Chenango County volunteer fire coordinator. He'd worked thirteen years in the Norwich bureau and knew the bones in every local closet, woodshed, and trailer park. More important, Wright knew how to deal with editors, whom he loathed. One favorite tactic: he seldom bothered to use punctuation or capital letters, even with proper names. "Give 'em something to edit," he'd say. "Otherwise, they'll own you."

Nobody owned Jim Wright. Once, he wrote a scathing article about a local bigwig, who promptly declared that he and his fellow bigwigs would boycott the Norwich Elks Club if Wright was in the joint. Jim responded by going every night and laying claim to the center barstool, like Paul Lynde on *Hollywood Squares*. The bigwig caved. One election day, Jim hijacked me for a tour of "polling places," which quickly became the Elks Club. I woke up on the bureau floor, terrified that I'd missed my 10:00 P.M. deadline. No problem. Jim had filed both our stories. The editors in Binghamton never knew, though one did ask if my shift key was broken.

At the paper, we were "Wright and Rewrite."

One other thing about Jim: He hated the Yankees — in particular, Thurman Munson. He spent hours mulling over new and creative ways to provoke an argument.

"You hear about Munson?" he'd say. "Out six weeks with a hernia. He tried to lift Carlton Fisk's spikes."

"You hear about Munson? The Buddhists won't let him in their temple. They say he's no Yogi."

"You hear about Munson? Reggie got a candy bar, so they gave him one: Chunky."

Bad jokes. Horrible jokes. What else did you do at the Norwich Elks Club? We sparred all day: Munson vs. Fisk, George vs. Billy, Reggie vs. the world.

By now, I had perfected the art of jousting with father figures about the Yankees. Wright loved to push my buttons after a Yankee loss. But when we won, he knew I'd come gunning for him.

One Thursday afternoon in 1979, the phone rang in the bureau. Jim was on the line.

"You hear about Munson?" he said.

"Okay, yeah, hit me. What now?"

"I'm sorry . . ."

Thurman had died in a plane crash while visiting family in Ohio.

I laughed for a long, uncomfortable period, accusing Jim of overplaying the joke. Then it sank in: the Yankees were real people, and sometimes real things happened to them. Thurman Munson was gone, and he wouldn't be back in two weeks. Soon I was walking the streets in a daze, trying to process not only the tragedy but also — shamefully — who would catch for us now and whether we should pull off a quick trade.

When I returned, the office phone was ringing. Spry called from Maryland. The Duke checked in from Massachusetts. Jocko phoned from Rochester. For the next few hours, I fielded calls from Yankee lovers and haters scattered across the country. We all needed to talk.

"There's a darkness on the edge of town," the Dog Man said.

That night, our editor told us to write tight. The next day's front page would be devoted to Thurman Munson, who had played in Binghamton. The headline read, MUNSON IS KILLED: YANKEE CAPTAIN, 32, DIES IN PLANE CRASH; WAS FORMER TRIPLET. The page hangs on the wall above me now.

Hank, my college friend, called from Syracuse. We quickly decided that Friday night's game would be an event for the ages, a piece of Yankee world history. We needed to grieve together. I would file my stories early and try to reach Syracuse by game time.

Friday evening, as I sped across the hills of Madison County, I almost didn't recognize Phil Rizzuto's voice on the pregame show. He spoke in a feeble, old man's groan. Now and then, he choked on a word, and it dawned on me that Phil was crying.

Halfway through his talk, Rizzuto halted. After a few moments of dead air, he recited a prayer for Thurman, and then he said this: "You know, they say time heals all wounds. And I don't quite agree with that a hundred percent. It gets you to cope with wounds. You carry them the rest of your life."

I dined that night with Hank and his fiancée, Marge, along with her jewelry business partner, a tall, big-boned midwesterner named Janice. She had huge, expressive eyes and hair that changed color in the light, from Bass to Molson to Killian's. For months, I had watched her from a distance, knowing she was out of my league.

You know the scene in the movie where the regular schmuck encounters the beauty? Every actor plays it differently. Dustin Hoffman (*Yankee fan, by the way*) sucks on his teeth, Richard Gere (*ditto*) flicks his eyebrows, Jack Nicholson (*yep*) flashes his eyes, and Brad Pitt (*you guessed it*) grins — because, well, Brad Pitt cannot play a regular schmuck.

First time I saw Janice, I just pivoted on a heel and shielded my face, like Quasimodo. I didn't want her to catch me staring. There was no sense wasting anybody's time by trying to flirt. I would keep a distance and at least maintain my dignity.

We watched the game in a bar. For the national anthem, the Yankees sent out only eight players. Thurman's replacement, a catcher named Brad Gulden, remained in the dugout. As the players took their positions, the stadium went quiet. So did the bar. On TV, fans were weeping. In Syracuse, people wiped away tears. Sitting in a booth, I disintegrated into a blubbering Yankee fool.

I droned on about how Thurman was my favorite Yankee, how I'd followed him throughout the minors, how my dad hated him, how my mom loved his name, how someone once called him "Herman Munster," how Jim Wright picked on him, how he was the one Yankee I would want to catch me if I were falling off a bridge.

I recalled driving home from Indiana the previous October, during the playoffs. We were down by a run in the eighth against Kansas City, the tying run on base, with Thurman coming to bat. For miles, the AM radio signal in my car had been dying, the play-by-play slowly bleeding into music. If I kept driving, I'd lose reception altogether. And if I lost the sound, we would lose the game. With no other option, I pulled onto the shoulder of the interstate and parked. I sat hunched over the dashboard, windows closed, while tractor-trailers whizzed by, lifting the car in their wake. The Royals brought in Doug Bird, their dreaded bullpen leviathan, who had always killed us. My heart sank. On the third pitch, Thurman — who almost never hit home runs — slammed one into the left-center-field bullpen, the deepest part of Yankee Stadium. I sat in my car screaming, pounding on the wheel. If I'd been in George Steinbrenner's box, I could have no clearer memory of that home run, which I have never seen.

Now, sitting in Syracuse, I blathered on about how ballplayers weren't supposed to die, how you take for granted they will always be there, and I fell into a morbid funk. I recall nothing of that game, only those eight Yankees standing at their positions, the world having stopped.

But I do remember something else. I recall noticing that Janice was watching me, locked in, nodding her head, smiling, wiping her eyes. And I remember wondering, *Wow, could I have a chance?*

JUJU RULE 11

The Lookaway

We have already discussed the need for a civil defense system, sort of a world juju militia that could respond to gnat infestations or losing streaks. But in a pennant race, every Yankee man, woman, and child fan must pitch in however they can. We cannot expect to win championships with the entire Rizzutonic burden shouldered by a heroic few and their beleaguered families.

On that note, let me teach you a juju move that you can perform anywhere — at the office, in a bar, or even beneath your bedcovers.

The "Lookaway," sometimes called "the Coward's Juju," stems from the natural human dread of watching loved ones be humiliated. It is neither physically difficult nor mentally challenging. Second graders can do it. In fact, they might have invented it.

Here's how the Lookaway works.

Concentrate on the TV image, lock onto the ball, and clear your mind of all thoughts. Free yourself from any earthly inhibitions and carnal intentions. *Become the ball.*

Now, as the pitcher winds up and throws . . . *look away!*

No, this is not the juju world's version of a shoulder-held missile launcher. It's closer to a water pistol. If you need a walk-off grand slam, a Lookaway-driven ball won't make it out of the infield. But on a night when the juju gods are distracted or impaired — as is often the case — you could steal a base hit, and maybe a ballgame.

I once met a New York Football Giants fan who swore he won the 1991 Super Bowl by using the Lookaway. With seconds remaining, Buffalo Bills placekicker Scott Norwood prepared for a game-winning forty-seven-yard field goal. As Norwood strode into the ball, my friend jerked his eyes to the left of his TV screen — pulling the kick wide right. (*Note:* He was watching from an end-zone camera, hence the left-right difference.) He had become one with the ball, and when he averted his eyes, it followed.

I've achieved mixed results with the Lookaway. When the Yankees are in the field, I'll drop my head, using a sinker to induce a double-play grounder. When they're at bat, I'll fling my head sideways, hoping to pull a line drive into the corner. Generally, this works better with a star player than with a rookie up from Triple A. Then again, so does all juju.

The Lookaway is a safe, nonconfrontational move for the beginner. No one will accuse you of conjuring Satan or demand that you replace his or her favorite vase. But remember three basic rules:

1. When flinging your head, be mindful of nearby colleagues. *Do not hurl your skull toward anyone who may be planning a*

Lookaway in the opposite direction! (Sports concussions are an increasing concern.)

2. When throwing your head, be mindful of nearby body parts. *Avoid peering into inappropriate spaces!* (Sports concussions are an increasing concern.)

3. If you experience neck pain, dizziness, blurred vision, menstrual cramps, ringing in the ears, tremors, urinary troubles, vivid dreams, hair loss, or suicidal thoughts, stop using the Lookaway immediately. (*Note:* Do not seek medical attention. You do not want to have to explain the Lookaway to a physician.)

The Lookaway represents a fine entry-level juju gyration. But remember:

Rule 11: *No one move should define your juju.*

A complete game demands three hundred to four hundred pitches. The thinking fan must constantly mix up his or her assortment and show command of many moves.

Use the Lookaway on every pitch, and not only will you get hammered, but you will miss the game. You might as well be listening to the radio.

12

★

George Brett

In the summer of 1980, I quit the *Binghamton Press* and moved to Syracuse to live with Janice. For months, we had dated and spent weekends together, despite being separated by a ninety-minute drive that, during an upstate New York winter, could take an entire day. I didn't care. Not even blizzards could keep me away. For the first time in my life, I was in love and at peace with it.

Each Friday, I brought to work a duffel bag and a packed cooler, preparations designed to shave about ten precious minutes off my drive. I would file my last story; climb into my Maverick, with its hiccupping 8-track player; and reach the Chenango County line before the coupler on the office's dial-up modem had cooled. Via shortcuts, I shrank that drive to seventy minutes, careening down serpentine hills like Indiana Jones on a runaway monorail.

What had captured me, finally, was Janice's laugh. It is like watching a flower open in time-lapse photography. At first, she fights it. Her face vibrates, then tightens, and her teeth clench. For a moment, the People's Republic of Janice successfully quashes the insurrection. She maintains composure, posture, and dignity. Then, *ka-boom:* Krakatoa, east of Java. Her head flies back, her eyes close, her body convulses, and an elephant hoot belches up from somewhere south of her hips.

In my last moments on earth, if I can hold on to the image of Janice laughing, it will sustain me wherever I go.

For reasons I will never understand, I could scratch an ear and make her laugh. I didn't have to speak. I didn't have to say something witty. I made that woman into my personal sitcom studio audience. I could burp at breakfast, and she'd spray Cheerios.

And once Janice started to laugh, she owned me. To the clown, is not the crowd all that matters?

Before I moved in, Janice had been warned about me. George W. Bush, twenty-three years later, should have had the depth of intelligence on Saddam's arsenal that Hank and Marge provided about my deviant past. Janice had heard Hank tell stories of our days at Hobart, along with sordid secondhand reports from Binghamton and Indiana, and she herself had witnessed examples of my Yankee bipolarity. She hadn't yet seen me jab needles into a Steinbrenner doll (that would come later), but she knew the risks of throwing in with a guy who arrived with a framed newspaper account of Thurman Munson's death.

Nevertheless, for our first summer, I pulled off the kind of subterfuge worthy of the Greeks outside the walls of ancient Troy. For three months, I shed that Yankee monkey on my back. I washed dishes. I vacuumed floors. I shrugged off tough losses. (*No problem; we'll win tomorrow.*) In bars and restaurants, I'd monitor the game over Janice's shoulder, without her suspecting. I once snuck a radio earphone into a Syracuse Symphony concert. (It was a tight pennant race, I should stress.) Janice didn't notice, though the blue-haired gorgon to my left harrumphed all night. Redsock fan, I figured.

During games, I'd tidy the house while pacing my juju circle. In a pinch, I'd jokingly demand my "game chair," and she'd play along, enjoying a whimsical Streisand-Redford moment. I locked Mr. Hyde in the attic or the shower, taking pains to appear lucid and feign interest in life. And she bought it! She thought my juju addiction was a joke. (Which, of course, it was . . . or is. We know this . . . right? It's a joke . . . ha ha . . . right?) And she would laugh.

Excuse me while I close my eyes and say those words again: *Janice would laugh.* In a pinch, I could make her laugh.

Also, I hadn't lost my touch for groveling. I found a job at the *Syracuse Herald-Journal,* basically because two veteran editors, Jerry Cooley and Bob Haskell, recognized my grandfather's name. They had started their careers long before at the *Waverly Sun.* Family connections: the white man's affirmative action. Although I was pushing thirty, I was still my father's son — actually, my grandfather's grandson.

That summer, we worked long, demanding hours — me, trying to prove myself; Hank, on his way to becoming a doctor; and Janice and Marge, devoting seven days a week to their jewelry-making business, their noses literally pressed to grindstones.

That year, we fulfilled our obligations as productive U.S. citizens.

As did the Yankees. They won 103 games. Reggie hit 41 homers, Goose saved 33 games, and thirty-seven-year-old Tommy John — after a brand-new type of elbow surgery — went 22–9.

Happiest summer of my life.

As the playoffs neared, Hank and I looked forward to the annual pummeling of the Royals. For three postseasons, we had danced over their supine bodies, and now we chuckled in anticipation of another chance to watch their five-foot-five shortstop, "Little Freddie" Patek, grieve in the dugout. Yes, it was time to grill some Kansas City strip steaks. It was October — the month for crisp apples, spongy leaf piles, and a fresh Royals beat-down!

Moreover, this would be Janice's first Yankee world championship. Having grown up outside St. Louis, she fondly recalled her father's love for Bob Gibson and "Stan the Man" — small-market memories that I assured her would pale in comparison to Yankee celebrations. She would learn how Yankee victories outshone lesser life events, such as weddings and births. Our souls would rejoice. I would shower her with lavish gifts, such as — well — a Yankee hat and maybe a Yankee giant foam finger. This would be her first Yankee *ring,* I noted slyly. The good life was near.

Then the playoffs began.

We lost game one after blowing a two-run lead, basically because the Royals' mean-spirited, grudge-holding, Yankee castoff starting pitcher, Larry Gura, hated Billy Martin's guts, and nobody on our milquetoast pitching staff had the stones to knock George Brett onto his hemorrhoid-cream-buttered butt.

"No problem," I told Janice. "We'll win tomorrow."

Nevertheless, for game two, I moved a small TV into an upstairs room, where I could enjoy a bit more privacy. I'd felt a slight negative juju vibe downstairs. At one point, with the Yankees losing 7–2 in the eighth, Janice had suggested that we see what was on another channel. I held my temper. I calmly responded that, yes, even though we were losing and, yes, even though I might have spoken harshly of the Yankees and said the game was over, I still preferred to watch, so I could be certain of the final outcome. I maintained a warm gentlemanly composure.

Now, upstairs, in my makeshift juju pod, I wouldn't have to ask her to sit still, and nobody would have to miss their precious TV movie starring Ben Gazzara (*Yankee fan, by the way*). Besides, I'd suspected in recent weeks, as the Yankees floundered, that the living room might be a juju dead zone. Now I was sure of it.

We lost game two after Willie Randolph was thrown out at home plate when our third-base coach, Mike Ferraro, mistakenly waved him on. George Steinbrenner, on national TV, lip-synched an obscenity that left the network announcers shocked and appalled. In my house, I supplied a human voice to George's muted word.

A minute later, Janice wandered up to ask what the score was, whether I was okay, and what had been banging against the wall.

The score? Yes, I could tell her the score. But, actually, I had a better idea. She could keep tabs on the score via *the downstairs television.* The announcers *would tell her* the score. That was *their job.* Then she wouldn't have to *walk up the stairs and ask the score*. By learning to keep score, she would never have to *depend on the charity of others*. She would be *empowered*. Wasn't that what the women of today wanted? *Empowerment?* Millions of fans did it that way. Only a few fans walked up steep sets of stairs to fetch a score. And what did she mean, "banging against the wall"? *Nothing had been banging against the wall. AND YES, I WAS FINE. THANKS FOR ASKING.*

She studied me for a moment, then belly-laughed, as if to file this away as another precious, Rod McKuen postcard-from-manhood moment. She pivoted and marched downstairs. She didn't return. She watched the final innings on her TV, while I fruitlessly fired Rizzutons into my game set. We lost.

She didn't ask when game three was on.

In the seventh inning of that contest, we led by a run, when my old pal George Brett crushed a pitch from Goose Gossage so hard that the ball soared out of the TV and put a mulligan divot in the wall of my upstairs juju room. Frankly, I was glad. The wall deserved it. The whole room did. In fact, I was preparing to take off my belt and teach the room a valuable lesson about respect, when I heard Janice's footsteps at the bottom of the stairs. She hesitated for several seconds, then climbed the steps slowly, like a ghost in an old English movie. When she arrived, I was flexing pain from my swollen knuckles, while the room stood knock-kneed in its shame and embarrassment. Janice eyed the gouge in the wall, studied my flushed cheeks, and offered the expression of a young woman who just realized the hitchhiker has a hook for a hand.

"Now you're acting crazy," she said, with no hint of a laugh. "This is just a game."

I cannot record my full response here. I remember mere flashes. I do recall that one component of my speech was the expletive (#) mouthed by Steinbrenner in game two. I used several variations on the expression. I remember thinking, perhaps aloud, that she should stay out of my #ing room. I remember wondering, perhaps aloud, if she had #ing ruined everything. I remember thinking, perhaps aloud, that she #ing didn't understand and that, #, maybe she never would, and that I was going the # out and might #ing not come the # back, and I was unbe#ing-lievably #ed! And #-#-#!

I stormed out, punching walls, slamming doors, revving the car like Mario Andretti, and spraying gravel in the driveway. I drove to the closest bar and watched the final, wretched innings with Hank, as the Yankees were swept, while the bar, the city, and the entire world reveled in our humiliation.

One downside of being a Yankee fan: When we lose, don't expect sympathy.

I didn't go home until early morning, flopping into bed with beer and disgrace oozing from every pore. Janice lay wide-awake. She wasn't smiling.

"I'm sorry your team lost," she said. "But don't ever do that again."

THE SCIENCE OF JUJU

Many respectable scientists place juju in the same category as superstition, dogma, and magical thinking. Some even deny its existence altogether. They call it a waste of time — a symptom of lazy intellectual development, if not a fundamental lack of human intelligence.

They are, of course, Yankee fans — lying to cover their tracks. With twenty-seven world championships, they see no reason to share their secrets with the world.

Publicly, these ivory-tower critics refuse to accept anecdotal evidence. They say eyewitness accounts of juju are flawed and oral histories carry no empirical credibility. (Of course, their opinions about anecdotal evidence change in divorce court, when they want to tell everybody about catching their spouse with the grad assistant in the monkey lab. Oral accounts sure do the trick then, don't they?) These "scientists" reject accounts of juju in holy books, literary memoirs, poetry collections, and even their own texts on quantum physics.

Yes, you read correctly. In fact, let's start with quantum physics.

The first study of atom-level juju interaction dates back to 1927 (when Babe Ruth hit his 60 home runs). That year, theoretical physicist Werner Heisenberg's uncertainty principle changed the future of quantum mechanics. The cagey German showed that the more closely you measure one atomic particle, the less precisely you can measure its polar opposite. In other words, every particle — even down to the atomic level — *is affected by the act of being watched.*

Thus evolved the "observer's paradox" — the rule that no matter how hard we try to remain neutral, *the act of watching something changes it.* This exists from the molecular level all the way up to human behavior, where the effects are far more pronounced.

Question: If a laboratory experiment is affected by the act of watching, why isn't a baseball game?

Most people would answer that distance plays a role. If you watch from a thousand miles away, you'll have no impact. Unfortunately, cutting-edge experiments have shown that, at the atomic level, distance does not matter. In fact, it does not exist. Even when separated by miles, positive and negative particles maintain incredibly powerful attractions. Move one, and its counterpart — far away — reacts accordingly.

The laws of physics, or the laws of juju? The differences are increasingly murky.

And then there is the matter of Heisenberg's modern heir, a scientist named Vladimir Shpunt. According to news accounts, between 2004 and 2008 the Los Angeles Dodgers paid Shpunt, a Russian physicist, to watch games on his TV set in Massachusetts and transmit beams of positive energy to the team. Dodgers owner Frank McCourt had hired the seventy-one-year-old Russian émigré to stare into the television and increase his blood pressure on behalf of the Los Angeles players. *Shpunt was selling Rizzutons.*

What do we know about the mystery man who calls himself Vladimir Shpunt? According to the *Los Angeles Times,* he once worked at the same Russian scientific academy as Zhores Alferov, winner of the Nobel Prize in Physics in 2000. At one point, when Shpunt sought entrance to the United States, Alferov wrote a letter on his behalf, describing him as an "eminent scientist" and "outstanding inventor." While in Russia, Shpunt had claimed to have discovered a scientific therapy that directs energy toward sick human cells. Interestingly, his grandfather in Russia had been a village healer.

When he came to America, Shpunt reportedly knew nothing about the game of baseball. Nevertheless, he claimed to be able to improve the Dodgers' winning record by 10 to 15 percent — making him more valuable than a fifth starter.

News of the Dodgers' cash-for-juju deal leaked out in 2010, during a juicy divorce between McCourt and his wife, Jamie. Her lawyer, Bert Fields, told the *Los Angeles Times* that Frank McCourt had paid Shpunt a stipend, plus a bonus of "certainly six figures and even higher," which fluctuated depending on how many games the Dodgers won.

With the help of Shpunt's transmissions, the Dodgers reached the postseason three times in five years. They won no championship, I believe, due to the team's passion-challenged fan base.

But two questions remain: What does Vladimir Shpunt know? Have the Russians cracked the juju genome?

For decades, scientists have sought to create synthetic juju, a blend of physical, chemical, and spiritual procedures that could guarantee supremacy in every sport except bowling. (For reasons believed to be linked to footwear and hair tonic, juju does not seem to work in bowling alleys.) What they produced instead were anabolic steroids, human growth hormone, and other performance-enhancing drugs (PEDs).

Despite the barnlike size of modern football players, no sport more than baseball has battled the taint of PEDs. Nevertheless, for more than a century, secreted away in every championship clubhouse has been the most potent power elixir of all — entirely composed of juju.

The placebo. The sugar pill.

Technically, the placebo won't increase your width, strength, or speed. Technically, it can't cure shingles, enhance erections, or lessen pain. Technically, it doesn't do a goddamn thing.

All of which adds to the scientific mystery of why the placebo works.

In medical studies, positive responses to fake drugs have been measured as high as 62 percent. That puts them in league with some of the "happy pills" hawked to viewers every night during the network news.

But the placebo comes with a warning label: for it to work, the doctor — the giver — must effectively lie and convince the patient that it is a real drug. And as we know, lying is unethical.

Thus the downside of the placebo: eventually, somebody always rats it out. "Grampa, wonderful news! That pill was just sugar! See? Sugar! You're okay! *Nothing is wrong with you!*"

The shock of such an embarrassing revelation leaves Grampa with no dignified option except to quickly deteriorate and die.

In America, the key to success is simple: *believe in the snake oil you sell.*

Placebos require consumers to believe as well. That's why placebos don't work on Alzheimer's patients. They keep *forgetting* to believe.

Baseball is a sport of believing. Know how to always get the pitch you want? *Want the next pitch.*

What was Boston's "Curse of the Bambino" other than a Reverse Rizzutonic placebo, prescribed each fall by Redsock Nation cynics? The players swallowed it whole. At a certain point, Boston fans even hungered to believe in a curse. It beat the idea of losses that held no meaning whatsoever.

So . . . another question: What if ballplayers — the most gullible looncakes in America — happened to believe the juju of an entire nation was behind them? What if they believed that twenty million like-minded whacktoids were pacing their homes, punching walls, and twisting their spines like toffee — all for them?

Reader, I do not believe in superstition, dogma, or magical thinking. But I *do* believe in believing. And if I'm right, the team with the most juju fans — with the most concentrated dosages of pure, uncut, felony-grade placebo — will win the most world championships.

Did I mention that the Yankees have twenty-seven?

13

★

The Ultimate Yankee Fan

In the spring of 1982, I was living in a state of stygian torment, still mourning the events of the previous October. We'd blown a two-game World Series lead, losing four straight to the Dodgers, our worst collapse since the Big Red Machine killed our American Bicentennial. Our most solid hit came after the final out, when George Steinbrenner punched an elevator while trying to leave Yankee Stadium. (*Note:* I have no doubt the elevator said something snide, bringing it on.)

The impact seemed to affect not just George's knuckles but also his head. That winter, he signed speedy Dave Collins and Jerry Mumphrey and dubbed them "Steinbrenner's Striders." He vowed to play "National League–style baseball" with a lineup of Slappy the Clowns. So doomed was this plan that our chief nemesis, KC manager Whitey Herzog, publicly pitied us, saying Babe Ruth would be spinning in his grave. In Rochester, Jocko—who'd torched his last Yankee cap—tore the "NY" off his replacement and sewed it back on, upside down, like an American flag in distress. In dire Yankee times, you do not want to be Jocko's ball cap.

Our country seemed to be twisting in a cold, dry wind. We had an actor as president, inflation hit 13 percent, Britain and Argentina waged war over a rock full of penguins, and now the Yankees—"the worst team money can buy" — planned to bunt their way to the pennant. We had once ruled the world. Then again, so had Portugal.

"Glory days," the Dog Man said, calling from Jersey.

Even my dad quit harping on us, the Yankees being too pathetic to belittle. Seeing me, he would scurry off for his notes, the Rizzuto rebuttal points he'd been compiling, and then disappear. I would find him sitting at his desk amid piles of papers, fumbling to remember where things were. He would shake his head, and we would stare at each other.

"I'm sorry about Munson," he would say, as if the catcher's death happened yesterday instead of nearly three years ago.

He would place a hand on my shoulder, and we would observe a moment of silence. No vinegar. No anger. A respectful moment. It almost seemed that he missed Thurman more than I did. My mom and sister expressed concern. Dad was doing a lot of puttering lately. He never railed about Rizzuto anymore. He never drummed. I didn't think twice. He was just being economical. Why waste bile on a fifth-place team?

That spring, a friend in Syracuse announced that "the Ultimate Yankee Fan" was visiting from Manhattan and I absolutely had to meet him. He predicted we would become great friends, lifetime soul mates. It was like a computer date. I found myself nervous, fearful about making a bad impression. I almost wore aftershave.

We set it up for a fern bar near Syracuse University. Not wanting to be late, I arrived an hour early. I drank beer and watched the Yankees blow a game, thanks to our newly acquired disaster — designated hitter "Big John" Mayberry, formerly of Kansas City.

We had traded three prospects for Big John, who was thirty-three, eight years past virility, and death to every rally his weenie bat touched. Mayberry had engineered another perfect day: oh-for-four. As a Royal, he had killed us. As a Yankee, he was doing the same. I spent the hour thinking up nasty witticisms about the guy, the way pundits do before going on TV. I'd decided henceforth to call him "Maybe," as in *Maybe we should shoot him!*

And then there he was . . . the Ultimate Yankee Fan. He looked to be in his early thirties. Tall, lean, and tanned like a newly minted penny, he had a jaw like a box of Wheaties and a wife who could flip letters on a game show. He wore a dark blue blazer with a Yankee insignia over his heart, as if he'd been awarded the Yankee Medal of Honor. He carried himself like a TV preacher, full of swagger, money, and polished teeth, although he also looked quite at home with a swizzle stick. In his presence, I felt unwashed and homeschooled. I wore old jeans and a plaid flannel shirt that would have been more fashionable on a turnip truck.

All my life, I'd viewed the Yankiverse as a harmonic utopia of peace and equality. If a guy wore the "NY," that's all I needed to know. He could be a peasant or a billionaire, a liberal or a conservative — I didn't care. We were pulling the same dogsled. Unless he was a rodeo clown or a reporter for the *National Enquirer,* I didn't want to hear about his boring, insignificant life.

"So," the Ultimate Yankee Fan said, "I hear you're the *Ultimate Yankee Fan.* How did we do today?"

This rattled me on four levels.

1. I never viewed myself as the Ultimate Yankee Fan. I considered myself a solid, knowledgeable, mainstream Yankee fan. Maybe a cut above average. Not ultimate.
2. I thought *he* was the Ultimate Yankee Fan.
3. I detected a demeaning tone in the way he said "*Ultimate* Yankee Fan."
4. He didn't know the score? What the hell? His car had no radio?

Also, he obviously couldn't read faces. I was scowling, muttering, practically bleeding from both nostrils over the latest Yankee debacle — and, of course, Big John.

"We lost," I grumbled. "Thanks to . . . *Mayberry.*"

I spoke his name in the hateful voice of a political attack ad.

"Good hitter," the Ultimate Yankee Fan said. "He'll come around."

My knees buckled. I took a hard drink. *He'll come around? What was he thinking?*

I said sarcastically that it sure was *smart* to trade for *Big John*, because we needed *young, up-and-coming* players.

"Absolutely!" he agreed. "I do like our team."

I halted my drink. I had been joking, of course. How could anyone consider John Mayberry a young player? How could anyone like this team? Who was this idiot? I stared into his lifeless eyes — doll eyes, dead eyes, button eyes — and wondered what kind of brain clump I was facing.

"How old is Big John?" I asked, nicely.

"John's a good guy," he said. "I've met him."

"Oh?" I said. "How old is he?"

"He comes over during BP, talks to people. Good guy."

"How old is Big John?"

"We have season tickets, so you get to meet the players."

"How old is Big John?"

"He'll rev it up. You'll see."

"How old is Big John?"

The Ultimate Yankee Fan took a long drink, then crunched a chunk of ice between his teeth and stared into the empty space that happened to coincide with my face.

"I go to fifty games a year," he said. "You?"

I studied my sneakers. I wasn't about to tell him that I'd never been to a Yankee game; that my entire Yankee fan life had consisted of radio, television, and newspapers; that I considered the streets of New York City as dangerous as a nest of cobras. No way I was going to tell him *that*.

"How old is Big John?" I asked, defiantly.

"Been to many games this year?"

"How old is Big John?"

"How many games?"

"Thirty-three," I said.

"Thirty-three? That's a lot of games."

"Big John is thirty-three."

The Ultimate Yankee Fan studied me through the bottom of his glass.

"That may be."

"May . . . be?" I said. *"Maybe we should shoot him!"*

Collateral conversations halted. The Ultimate Yankee Fan's wife touched his shoulder, as if she were turning over a consonant. The Ultimate Yankee Fan set down his glass and deftly motioned to the bartender for a refill.

"That may be," he said, glancing at me dismissively. "Or it may be that you don't know a goddamn thing about baseball."

If the bar had had a piano player, he would have stopped, closed the top, and run for cover. I felt every eye in the place turn my way. Every muscle in my body wanted to lunge forward and strangle this smug, fraudulent, fart-faced cluck and his emaciated, clown-haired, vampire wife.

But I didn't. I kept it together. I smiled, swallowed my drink, took a long breath, counted to three, and set down my glass without shattering it. No hysterics. No decibels. If peace required a Gandhi, then I would be Gandhi. I would rise above pettiness. This man might be of a different stripe and timbre, but he was a fellow Yankee fan. We were spiritual comrades. We wore the same internal uniform. Besides, the team could use the money from his fifty games per year. He might help buy us a pitcher someday. Yes, I would stay cool and calm, just as I expected Yankee batters to hang in against a hard-throwing pitcher.

"Indeed," I said. "And it may be . . ."

Then I snapped.

"It may be . . . that if you want Mayberry, maybe he's all yours! Okay? You want him? You got him! *He's yours!* Okay? *Maybe from now on, you OWN him!* Understand? *He's all yours!"*

His eyes flashed with fear.

"And you know what?" I said. *"Maybe this team is yours! This season is yours!* Whatever happens, it's on you! Got it? I wash my hands of this Yankee team! From now on, they're dead to me! You hear? *Dead to me!* From now on, maybe whatever happens, *it's all on you!*"

"Look, I'm sorry, I—"

"*Enjoy your Mayberry!*" I shouted. "*He's yours, all yours! And we shall see . . . what we shall see!*"

I pivoted crisply and walked out. No curses. No drink tossed in his face. I wouldn't have wasted the dregs in my glass on his shaved and cocoa-buttered pork-chop cheeks. I wouldn't have spat in his mouth if he were dying of thirst. I simply marched away.

That day, my season ended. As far as the Yankees were concerned, I was cutting them off. For the rest of the summer, if a Yankee came to bat with runners on base, I'd lean back and laugh. I would salute the TV and think, *You are on your own, Yankees! If you need help, go over during batting practice and talk drivel to the sugar daddy in the front row!*

I never paced a circle. I never broke a pencil. Not one pushup, not one obscenity. No Lookaways, no lotuses, no nothing. I cursed the Yankees, and I reveled in each Yankee loss.

That year, Mayberry hit 8 home runs for us. *Eight.* He batted .209. *Two-oh-nine.* The Yankees burned through three managers and finished fifth, sixteen games out. And I loved every minute.

Looking back, though, I may have overdone it. We did not reach the postseason for thirteen years.

I never again saw the Ultimate Yankee Fan. I suspect he avoided Syracuse, fearful that our paths would cross. He knew what he did, but I wonder if he realized the consequences.

JUJU RULE 12

World Series

To break a losing streak, Billy Martin once drew his Yankee batting order from a hat. It worked. We won the game. Sportswriters hailed it a masterful ploy to relieve the pressure on a certain overly contemplative slugger ("Hamlet on the Hudson," as the great sportswriter Red Smith had taken to calling Reggie). They were wrong, of course. Billy wasn't easing the pressure on anybody. He was doing juju.

Throughout his life, Billy constantly kicked dirt on the shoes of the juju gods, seeking to sway their next call. Like every juju master, Martin developed his own signature move: he would punch somebody.

Billy fought Tommy Lasorda, Jimmy Piersall, Dave Boswell, Ed Whitson, Twins traveling secretary Howard Fox, Rangers traveling secretary Burt Hawkins (he didn't like traveling secretaries), a Tigers fan named Jack Sears, a sportswriter named Ray Hagar, a cabdriver who claimed soccer was better than baseball, two bouncers in a topless bar, and numerous bar denizens, the most famous of whom was a food distributor named Joseph Cooper, whom sportswriters loved to call "the marshmallow salesman."

At one point, in 1957, the Yankees traded Billy after a fight in the Copacabana nightclub, which supposedly started after rednecks made slurs about Sammy Davis Jr. They nearly fired him after a fight on national TV, when he confronted Reggie. And these are just the fights that made the papers. In the privacy of his home and office, Billy fought even more desperate wars.

"I'm getting smarter," he told reporters in 1982. "I finally punched something that couldn't sue me." (Billy had broken a finger while hitting the furniture.)

Make no mistake: Billy Martin started fights. Once, rather than merely tagging Clint Courtney on a play at second, he punched him in the head, nearly starting a riot. On his 1972 Topps baseball card, as manager of the Tigers, Billy flipped the world his middle finger. He antagonized George Steinbrenner into firing him five times. He died preparing for his sixth managerial incarnation. It happened early on Christmas morning, 1989. His vehicle crashed into a ravine while he was riding home from a bar.

You'd think a guy who'd flipped off the world, fought half the bar population of North America, was nicknamed "the Brat," and died after a Christmas Eve binge would not attract many mourners. But people mobbed Billy's funeral. More than thirty-five hundred stood outside in the cold, unable to fit inside St. Patrick's Cathedral in New York. Even Richard Nixon attended.

Billy was buried in Hawthorne, New York, near the graves of Babe Ruth and Lou Gehrig. He got that final call.

Billy Martin understood a fundamental fact of juju: at times, one must lay everything on the line — conscience, immortal soul, material possessions, personal hygiene — the whole picnic, ants and all. You must hold nothing back, regardless of the consequences.

Juju moments happen four hundred times a day, before every Yankee pitch, from April to November.

Rule 12: In juju, every game is the World Series.

Want to sit back, clap politely, and browse a seed catalog? Watch golf.

The thinking Yankee fan never rests. This does not mean you must perform nine innings of high-impact aerobics. But if your signature juju move is to lie on the couch and eat nacho chips, damn it, be prepared to lie *hard* and eat *a lot* of chips. The game is not a salsa-tasting event. *Chew, swallow, eat!*

Still, some moments do call for a direct appeal to the juju gods on duty. For weeks, your calls may have gone straight to voice mail. The team has suffered brutal losses, the kind that can strain relations between you and your TV. It's time for an intervention. Billy would punch the nearest traveling secretary, but you're not him. Your best bet is the move known as "charging the mound." Here's how it works.

You launch from a distant room in the house. Take a few deep breaths. Contemplate your season. Ponder your team. Think about the messages the juju gods need to hear.

Maybe they haven't been themselves lately. They've neglected their duties. Their numbers are off. They've been making careless mistakes. Are they distracted? Are they drinking? Are they favoring another team? If you're unsure, make something up.

Then *go!* Fire yourself like a missile into the TV room. Cover ground quickly. You want the TV caught off-guard. In full view of the furniture, the walls, and the other home entertainment components, you want the juju gods to feel the heat of your passion.

Now touch the TV — *gently*. If you do it correctly, you will feel and hear tiny static crackling sounds along her screen. This is not juju. (Frankly, I don't know what it is.) But in this moment, *you will have the juju gods on the line.*

As the Yankee pitcher prepares to throw, whisper, "First-pitch strike."

Guaranteed first-pitch strike . . . *if you do it correctly.*

Listen: Nobody's perfect in baseball or juju. In fact, there are times when everything seems to fall short. But before you let A-Rod ground into a double play to end a miserable, one-for-fourteen postseason, you owe it to your TV, the juju gods, and yourself to be heard.

Stage an intervention. Yell at the umpire. Pull your batting order from a hat. *Do the unexpected.*

You don't need to start a fight. Just don't go down without one.

14

★

Damned Fool

In early October 1982, Janice's business partner, Marge, and my old college buddy, Hank, finally ended the fairy-tale romance that began for them in high school. They got married.

I was designated to be wedding usher number three, or maybe number four — I do not remember. On the night of the rehearsal, we had finished dinner and were edging toward the TV, when a buzzer in my head told me to call home. My sister, Virginia, answered and said that Dad was dead.

No surprise. It was one of those heavily telegraphed roundhouse punches, the kind you watch all the way to your jawbone. He'd been dying for weeks in super slow motion. It was like his comment about the cities that killed the Kennedys: you had to let it sink in and then decide what to do.

Everybody — Dad, most of all — had insisted that I attend the wedding. I'd phoned home that morning for an update, and either Dad was doing well or they simply lied and said he was; I never had the guts to ask. They had been debating whether to call me or leave me blissfully unaware until morning. But none of us had an option. They knew I would be calling.

I made it a point not to cry. I marched straight to Janice and delivered the news, like a TV anchor reporting a car accident: restrained emotion, deference to the victim, adherence to the facts. She burst into tears. I couldn't console her. I couldn't talk. I remember feeling ashamed that *she* was crying, not me, and that I needed to leave the restaurant before everyone saw just how cold and shallow I was. I don't think I said goodbye. I was afraid to look at people. They would see into me and know there was nothing.

A few minutes later, driving south on I-81, I turned on the radio. The Yankees were playing Boston. Ron Guidry was on the mound. *Good,* I thought. *A game will clear my mind, pass some time.*

Guidry threw a pitch, and I realized that my dad was dead.

At that point, I lost my bearings in a way that I had never done before (nor have since). I pressed the gas pedal as hard as I could and rammed down the highway, screaming over the Yankee game, as fast as my car could go and as loudly as my throat would allow. I must have gone thirty miles that way, drowning out the game. I yelled to God that I was sorry. I yelled to my dad that I loved him. And I yelled to anybody else who was listening that I was a damned fool, the damnedest fool of all.

I had seen him a week earlier. He knew the deal. They'd moved him into a special section of the Robert Packer Hospital, where it seemed every member of my high school graduating class now worked. In a matter of days, he went from sick to dying. The lungs, the liver, the heart—you could take your pick. For months, my mom and sister had tended to him, letting me pretend to be the crusading reporter up in the big city. Their updates worsened, but I always had a big story cooking or some big event on the calendar. Finally, they said Dad was asking for me, and only then did the light come on in my head. He had never done that before.

I found him lying inside a tangle of tubes and wires that ran into a *Star Trek* console of electronics. His entire face had turned the color of a bruise. His hair was a thistle, he hadn't shaved, and his front teeth were missing. He resembled no one I knew. He opened his eyes and rolled them, as if to say, *Check this out.*

I asked how he was feeling, how they were treating him, how the food was — the questions a game show host would ask, which he waved away like houseflies.

"Missed that damned fool, didn't we?" he said.

"That damned fool," of course, was Reggie Jackson. My dad never called him by name, just "that damned fool." The previous winter, the Yankees had let Reggie go to California, and Dad had switched from hating his image to celebrating his every home run. Once upon a time, a fifth-place Yankee team would have meant Dad's sun was shining, his roses were blooming, and his God was smiling. Now he was missing that damned fool.

"Shouldn't have let him go," I said.

"Damned fool."

I hadn't come to talk about the Yankees. I had come to cheer him up, and damn it, I was going to deliver. So I piled lie upon lie — upbeat fabrications about my life, like a fraudulent fortuneteller working his mark. I told him my novel was rounding into shape. I said I was thinking of moving up to the *New York Times* or the *Washington Post*. I told him Janice and I would marry. I told him everything was great. He just rolled his eyes and waved away my words.

"Damned fool."

(I've often wondered what Reggie Jackson would have thought about this: a father who hated his guts in life, remembering him to a son on their final talk. Would it have made Reggie laugh? Drop to his knees? Do ballplayers realize the roles they play in the lives of the people who love them or hate them, the faceless voices up in the stands, those of us they will never know?)

"Damned fool," he kept repeating, and after a while, I wasn't sure if he was talking about Reggie.

It is my last memory of my father.

In his final months, Dad rented a small office in downtown Waverly, located over a business that sold grave markers. He filled the place with railroad memorabilia that he'd collected, and he went there every day just to be with it. From his window, he could watch the trains pass through Waverly Station and check his watch to see if they were on time. Once, long ago, those tracks were his ticket out of town. He was going to work on the railroad and see the world. No dice. He returned home to stay.

Every day, he recorded arrivals and departures in the same business ledgers he'd once used to score Yankee games. Every day, he walked to the nearby Terminal Barber Shop to argue with Stan the barber, a big Yankee fan. From there, he would wander down to the tracks, where the rail hands knew him by name. This was his favorite place in the world.

I hope he is there now.

There was a nice memorial service at the Grace Episcopal Church, across the park from our home, where he and I both grew up. People talked about the Kennedys and Dr. Joyce Brothers and his feud with *Hollywood Squares.* We remembered the sawhorse with the mystery piece and his silly headlines in the *Waverly Sun.* One old friend told me the Yankees would someday lose a big game on a crazy bad hop, and I should smile because that would be my dad.

That night, my mom sat in the kitchen, fidgeting with the radio. I realized after a while she was searching for the Yankee game. She didn't realize the season was over.

"Bad year," she said. "You know, we really missed that damned fool."

JUJU RULE 13

Curses

In 2004, Boston finally ended the alleged "curse" that had allegedly been placed by Babe Ruth as alleged punishment for his alleged betrayal. What a joke.

That left the Chicago Cubs, who hadn't won squat since 1945, in sole possession of the last great media-fueled whammy, the "Curse of the Billy Goat," which offered far less appeal. In fact, the billy goat hex was little more than a marketing scheme ginned up by FOX Sports during the 2003 National League Championship Series, when the Cubs and Braves sought to compete for viewers against the Yankee-Redsock brawls.

I don't bother with curses for one reason.

Rule 13: Curses don't work.

Seriously, if curses worked, nobody would ever win a game. The whole season would be obliterated by meteors.

We are a nation of cursers and counter-cursers. I curse you, so you immediately curse me back. Both actions go to the cosmic curse court, where everybody is throwing the evil eye, and after years of depositions, while the lawyers run their tabs, the sides finally settle for a lifelong feud and several grudges to be named later. Then, of course, they curse the juju gods for not accepting curses.

I've seen wren-faced grannies on scooters, angry because the traffic light changed, pump out hexes at passing motorists like cover fire from a Gatling gun. They shoot off a hundred in five seconds, like forwarding e-mails. (My sister sends me forty e-clunkers a day — half of which claim Barack Obama is an alien, and not in the border patrol sense.) They curse cities, nations, generations. In the time it took to read this paragraph, somebody probably cursed your smiling butt.

On that note, I would like to issue a clarification over an incident that has been eating at me since the previous chapter.

In dealing with the Ultimate Yankee Fan, I did not "curse" the Yankees in the FOX Sports/billy goat sense of the word. I merely announced that I would withhold future juju. I did not cause the thirteen-year drought of the 1980s and early 1990s.

Yes, I made a heartless decision at a time when the team desperately needed help. Yes, I was venting rage toward the Ultimate Yankee Fan, taking it out on players who had never harmed me. Obviously, if I had it to do over again, I would avoid the man. Maybe the Yankees could have won a pennant. Maybe Big John Mayberry would even have hit for us. Maybe he . . .

Wait a minute. Mayberry was *never* going to hit for us. Anybody with half a brain could see it. Anybody! *And the refusal of that empty-suited, moneytard Ken doll and his Jazzercise-chiseled Stepford honey bun wife to see the truth . . . And then* HE *had the audacity to say* I *don't know a goddamn thing about baseball?* HE *doesn't know a goddamn thing about baseball! Eight home runs! That's what we got from Mayberry!* EIGHT! STINKING! HOME! RUNS!

Hey . . . water under the bridge. As far as I'm concerned, it's forgotten.

15

★

Tar

By my second season in Syracuse, Janice had learned the cold truth about the guy she'd let into her life: *my act was no act.*

I was an up-close version of Reggie Jackson. On a hot streak, I could carry our relationship on my shoulders. In a slump, I threatened clubhouse chemistry.

This was the summer of 1983, when Don Mattingly arrived, Bobby Murcer departed, Dave Righetti tossed his no-hitter, and Reggie — at thirty-seven — floundered in California, his career in decline. After eighteen months with Janice, I had regressed into my Yankee lifestyle. Our running joke, laced with truth, was that she could tell instantly by my voice whether the team was ahead or behind. She claimed to be able to calculate the margin, but in truth, if we were down by a run, I made it sound as if we were down by ten. I still controlled her laugh button, but when the Yankees lost, I didn't want *anyone* to laugh.

Hank's family owned access to a thin, tree-covered sliver of waterfront on Otisco Lake, thirty minutes from Syracuse. There, on hot Sunday afternoons, we found refuge from the city. We'd bring chairs, a charcoal grill, burgers and dogs, and we would lounge on inflatable sea creatures, like Cleopatra floating down the Nile. Food, sun, beer, water, women, Yankees on the radio — what could be better in Syracuse, New York?

Let me tell you about my adopted hometown.

In the 1920s, Syracuse built Franklin cars.

In the 1940s, Syracuse built General Electric televisions.

In the 1960s, Syracuse built Carrier air conditioners.

Today, it processes health insurance claims.

Syracuse has the distinction of having built the giant machines that killed the economies of cities such as — well — Syracuse. Without air conditioning, the climates of South Carolina, Alabama, and Mexico were too unbearably hot for corporations to move factories there. Thanks to Carrier's giant systems, made in Syracuse, the companies could say, "Adios, suckahs!" Throughout the 1960s and 1970s, as Syracusans shipped out the big AC units, they were shipping out the industry of upstate New York. Basically, they were shipping out their kids.

As the Weather Channel often notes, Syracuse receives a shitload of snow between October and May. We annually win the Golden Snowball Award for most accumulation among upstate cities, and we usually rate as the snowiest city in America. We are the New York Yankees of snow.

I've ridden on the streets of Baghdad during a war and on the New York State Thruway during a blizzard. Given the choice, I'd prefer Iraq. But there is no happier place in creation than Syracuse on that first sunny spring day, when everybody emerges from hibernation, huddling in their front yards and shouting, "Holy shit, we made it!" And for me, no snapshot of nature has ever topped the glow of the moon on the Finger Lakes.

But hey, what do I know? I thought Steve Balboni would break Maris's home run record.

One hot Sunday afternoon that July, as we loaded the wagons for Otisco, Hank and I were reeling from criticism over a recent visit by his brother-in-law, Alphonso.

"Alphonso" is not his brother-in-law's real name. In the early

2000s, I cofounded an elite Secret Yankee Club, which required each member to choose a secret Yankee name. We had a "Rocket," a "Godzilla," a "Moose," and a "Lieber." Hank chose "Jeter," a pick that angered everybody. We felt the name should have been off-limits, like a retired uniform number. (*Note:* If anybody had tried to claim "Mariano," there would have been real trouble.) I chose "El Duque."

Alphonso was a bank executive who had attended an Ivy League school and lived most of his life in New York City. He could project the lobster-fork-wielding elegance of a Manhattan dandy — until somebody mentioned Steinbrenner. At that point, he'd turn into a Pabst-swilling guest on *Jerry Springer* (*Yankee fan, by the way*).

During the 1970s, Alphonso wrote regular dissertations to a New York Football Giants fan newsletter, advising the team on roster moves. His letters, sometimes published, often ran seven pages, single-spaced. During the 1980s, he found that whenever he videotaped Giants football games and watched them that night, the team won. He rearranged entire Sundays to aid the Giants. This required incredible discipline, because when the Giants started winning, he yearned to watch in real time. Trouble was, whenever he broke down and turned on the game, Phil Simms threw an interception or Joe Morris fumbled. Alphonso mastered his impulses, switched back to tape, and the Giants won two Super Bowls.

I immediately recognized him as a juju genius.

But on his most recent visit to Otisco, rather than frolic in the water, Alphonso, Hank, and I huddled around the radio for nine innings, discussing Yankee issues. We covered the entire forty-man roster, devoting at least ten minutes to each player. That we rendered hilarious, witty, and fact-filled Yankee commentary, which the civilian guests chose to ignore, was never taken into account. Amazingly, *we* were accused of being antisocial.

"He's come a long distance to see his in-laws," Janice said of Alphonso. "I certainly don't think he wants to spend all his time talking about the Yankees."

Of course, she knew nothing about Alphonso.

Nevertheless, the not-so-subtle warnings were received, with Hank, Alphonso's official host and in-law, absorbing the sharpest jabs. We promised to change our ways. A few Sundays later, Hank and I vowed to establish a Yankee-free afternoon: no radio, no sports page, no talking. We would force ourselves to mix with the civilians and discuss Literature, Capitals of the World, Actors and Their Roles, Potent Potables — whatever the dimwitted, non-Yankee population thought important in their *Daytime Jeopardy!* game show worlds. No baseball. No Yankees. No fun. We would sacrifice for the enjoyment of others.

But, *damn it,* we were in a pennant race: two games out and facing the Royals. We couldn't just pretend the game wasn't happening. So Hank and I devised a plan: Every few minutes, one of us would wander to the car and catch an update. The other would create a diversion. We'd work like a pro wrestling tag team. No one would suspect.

It worked flawlessly. In the sixth inning, Hank whispered that Dave Winfield had just driven in Don Baylor, giving us a 4–3 lead. We slapped fives, and I loped off to "check the car." I returned to report that our reliever, Dale Murray, had mowed down Kansas City one-two-three in the seventh. Hank returned to report a one-two-three eighth. In the top of the ninth, I caught Murray's first two batters — two up, two down — and motioned for Hank to come in and close.

As Hank slinked off to the car, I lobbied everyone for a dip in the lake.

As a rule, I didn't swim until a game was secure.

A few minutes later, Hank tugged at my elbow. A Royal had singled, prompting Billy Martin to bring in Goose Gossage for the final out.

"Nature calling," I said, heading toward the cars. "Don't want to pee in a clean lake."

At the car, I sensed something wrong. Phil Rizzuto was yelling about "a monumental decision" about to be made.

I ran to the clearing and waved to Hank. As I feared, he was being led to the water. He glanced my way helplessly but kept marching with the herd.

I ran to the car. The game had ended. George Brett was fighting with the umpires. He'd homered, but somehow we'd won. *"Three men are holding him!"* Phil shouted.

I ran to the clearing.

"Hannnnnnnnnnnnk!" I yelled.

He glanced at me, uncertainty in his eyes. He stood knee-deep, preparing to board an inflatable alligator. Once his testicles hit the cold water, it was over. He'd never get out. He struggled, but the group's social tentacles pulled him deeper. They were peppering him with questions about politics, food, celebrities — seeking to confuse him, to absorb him, to break him.

I ran to the car. The game was over. Brett was out. His home run had been nullified because his bat had been illegal. Billy Martin had challenged the bat and won. *"One of the most unbelievable endings I have ever seen!"* Phil shouted.

I ran to the clearing.

"Hannnnnnnnnnk!"

As I feared, he'd gone horizontal on the alligator, his belly submerged. He paddled toward me, but the group pulled him back.

"The water's great!" Janice said. "Come on in!"

"It's really nice!" someone added.

"Gotta go," I said. "Beer going right through me."

I ran to the car. The Royals were arguing. Phil was screaming. I fished a transistor radio from the trunk and returned to the picnic table.

"Hey, look what I found!" I said. "An old radio! Let's see if it works!"

I turned on the game. The weak batteries barely made enough sound for me to decipher what was going on. I pressed it to one ear and covered the other with my hand.

"Wow, check this out!" I said. "There's a fight going on!"

They studied me coldly from the water.

"Put down the radio and come in the water!" someone shouted authoritatively, like a cop.

"George Brett . . . Apparently he hit a . . . But they . . . So now he's . . . *Hannnnnnk!*"

I could feel them glaring, shaking their heads.

"Come on in. It's so warm, it's practically bath water!" someone shouted.

"You can do it!"

I hunched over the radio. I could hear them splashing — frolicking extra loudly, trying to destroy my resolve.

"Seriously . . . It's a fight . . . This is history . . . It . . . *Hannnk!*"

He could not move. Someone on a sea turtle was attacking his alligator. On the radio, the authorities had hauled away Brett, maybe in a straitjacket. Phil was waiting to interview Billy. I maneuvered the radio over my head to improve the reception. I felt the heat of their eyes on my back.

Something touched my neck.

"Okay, what is it?" Janice said. "Do you know you are hopeless?"

Together, we listened to the aftermath of the famous Pine Tar Game. Hours later, it would appear prominently on every network newscast and in every newspaper. For months, the nation would debate the legality of Brett's home run, which had been negated because of excessive tar on the handle. The commissioner would overturn the umpires' ruling, and Kansas City would win. The bat, like Brett and Gossage, would wind up in Cooperstown.

"Hey, Hank," Janice yelled. "You gotta hear this."

Soon everyone was huddled around the radio, arguing about the legality of pine tar. Janice and I went swimming.

A few days later, I asked her to marry me.

She said no.

No? I shifted into joke mode. I said that I'd meant she could serve as my second wife — after Yogi.

She laughed.

I could still make her laugh.

But I think she foresaw the day when I would make her cry.

JUJU RULE 14

Screenplays

The Arizona Diamondbacks won the 2001 World Series on a fly ball that floated into left-center field like a flaming paper bag filled with dog poo.

I stood in my living room, shoulders square to the TV — stunned, drained, frozen in my lotus position. It was a few minutes shy of a Monday morning, and my family had gone to bed. I was alone with the TV, which looked ready to cry. In another era, I might have gone Mike Tyson on the first lamp that winked. Now I had nothing. I just stood there, refusing to believe that what had happened had *really* happened.

It didn't seem possible, the Yankees losing that series. It was more like a practical joke that had backfired, embarrassing everyone in-volved. Over the last seven games, the Yankees — with heroic juju from Alphonso — had achieved miracles worthy of my dice-rolling days of the APBA. Twice, Alphonso had called to say the game was over, that he had turned off the TV and was going to bed. And twice, minutes later, on successive nights, Tino Martinez and Scott Brosius had hit two-out, bottom-of-the-ninth home runs off an Arizona closer who'd been touted as unhittable — tying games that we won in extra innings.

"Groundhog Day," Yankee manager Joe Torre called it.

"It borders on the surreal," FOX Sports play-by-play announcer Joe Buck said.

"Adam raised a Cain!" the Dog Man said, calling from somewhere in Jersey.

These were not wins you experience in real life. These were car-toon victories, the endings to Jimmy Stewart movies. The cavalry came; the potion worked; the alien saucers fell from the sky. These were the types of victories that launched religions, the kind that suspended one's faith in pessimism. I had never been prouder of my team. The Yankees — playing for a city and nation hit by terrorism, and wearing caps to honor the New York City firefighters who had been lost in the 9/11 attacks — had done the unimaginable. It was as if America's entire emergency juju reserves had been channeled into the team. It was as if an Uppercase God had said, "Screw this! I'm personally taking over the operation!"

Everybody knew it: We were *not* supposed to lose that World Series.

Then the flaming bag fluttered down into left field, and it was over.

Listen: Baseball is not a movie. No matter how much we want the Bad News Bears to win the pennant or Rocky to take the heavyweight crown, the plot lines of Hollywood movies must never be confused with the stark reality of what one can reasonably achieve through juju.

Rule 14: Never pitch a movie script to the juju gods.

It seems obvious. Nevertheless, fans do this all the time. We stand before the TV and recite Gene Hackman's speech from *Hoosiers*. We lie in bed and create mash-ups between George Gipp and Brian Piccolo, then throw in some Gary Cooper and Sylvester Stallone. We compress a lifetime of Hollywood threads into a two-minute verbal trailer, which we fling at the television, or the stars, or whatever juju god we have on the line, and we plead for outcomes that even an Uppercase Deity could not reasonably supply, no questions asked.

We do this all the time. We want reality to be like the movies. And it always comes up short.

Good grief. When you pitch such formulaic ideas, do you honestly believe the juju gods have not seen the movie, read the book, and watched the TV adaptation ten times?

Listen: They were there for the early outtakes of *The Natural*, when Robert Redford was swinging the bat like Ethel Merman. They've sat through a million showings of *Radio*, where Cuba Gooding Jr. plays the mentally challenged fellow who becomes a football coach and teaches everyone the importance of love. Do not try to convince them that your Yankee plot will be a box-office hit on a B-movie budget. They don't want to hear it. If they want crapola, they can access my sister's forty forwarded e-mails and follow her links to the latest kitten videos on YouTube.

You can dream about that last-place team suddenly catching fire based on the prayer visions of a little girl, but when you get that juju god on the line, don't embarrass the rest of us. Don't make him put you on hold and grouse to his colleagues, "Damn, it's another dolt who wants us to do a Mariners' version of *Angels in the Outfield.*"

I suspect the juju gods hate Hollywood. No Oscar recipient ever thanks them from the podium. They'll never be portrayed by Charlton Heston or Morgan Freeman. They'll be played by Danny DeVito or Harvey Keitel, and instead of computer-generated graphics, they'll be lucky to get the Muppets. Worst of all, the studios once again will rewrite their original scripts.

Consider the 1948 film *The Babe Ruth Story,* the so-called *Plan 9 from Outer Space* of sports flicks. The plot merges two home run miracles into one. The Babe, played by William Bendix (*Yankee fan, by the way*), visits a dying kid and promises to hit a homer. Later that day, he calls his famous shot. If either event happened, they occurred at least five years apart. Most maddening is that the coscriptwriter, Grantland Rice, spent his sportswriting career ignoring the Bambino's life as a wild party animal. Now *that* was the stuff of legend.

Remember, movies are supposed to be an escape. They're supposed to let us briefly forget the suffering, the pain, the losses that life and baseball bring.

Never confuse Hollywood and baseball.

Besides, if Jimmy Stewart had been a Yankee, Billy Martin probably would have punched him.

16

★

New Hampshire

I moved to Syracuse for love.

Nevertheless, "the Salt City" also offered a compelling secondary attraction, which I saw no reason to ignore. Twice each summer, the Yankees' International League farm club from Columbus, Ohio, came to town, showcasing our young talent for the future, and I tried never to miss a visit.

Janice accompanied me on a few frosty outings but then declared that she didn't want to "get in the way" of my fun. Also, she wanted to keep her toes from falling off.

In Syracuse, to watch a night game in April generally requires a down-filled parka, insulated boots, long underwear, earmuffs, and, if you can sneak it in, a can of Sterno. I once watched a Yankee prospect named Jim Deshaies twirl a complete-game shutout while snow devils swirled around his head. It was so cold that the wind froze the mustard on my hot dog. I stayed to the end using the survival techniques of a Jack London story. I stuffed my pants with game programs and concessionary napkins. I stood in the men's room, with a wall-mounted hand dryer blowing directly into my shirt. By the ninth inning, I was one of maybe a dozen fans in MacArthur Stadium. We could practically hear the players' teeth chattering.

Feeling a survivalist bond with Deshaies, an upstate New York native, I ran around predicting to everybody that I had seen the next great Yankee pitcher. As a result, Steinbrenner dealt him to Houston, where Deshaies enjoyed a fine career.

"You hexed him!" Alphonso raged. "What the hell were you thinking? You might as well have packed his bags and bought his airline ticket!"

This was 1984, the year we had grown up learning to fear, thanks to George Orwell. We anxiously noted the presence of Big Brother and Newspeak, but Orwell never foresaw a Yankee team as horrible as this.

Steinbrenner had traded Graig Nettles and signed Omar "the Out Maker" Moreno, who quickly became my second coming of Big John Mayberry. By April 30, we were ten games out. We finished third, 100 million light-years behind Detroit. The season highlight came in August, when two Yankees, Bobby Meacham and Dale Berra, were tagged out at home plate on the same play.

"I can't take it anymore!" Alphonso shouted. "Every time I say that it can't get worse, they hear it and hold it against me!"

I had quit my job at the paper to devote time to the novel. I had one character called "Eddie from Syracuse," a mental patient who roamed the country ranting about the Yankees. That spring, I sold ice cream from the back of a freezer truck, which meant roaming the city from dawn to dusk, ranting about the Yankees. By August, I was back in the newsroom, beaten and depressed, much like the team.

I returned to find the usual changeover of colleagues who had jumped to bigger papers in warmer cities. For young reporters, the *Post-Standard* represented a steppingstone, a résumé builder. Friends were always leaving, and I was always coming back. For the first time, I began to see Syracuse as my final stop, the Triple-A city where I would play out my career. Of course, I would always have Eddie from Syracuse to keep me company.

Janice and Marge had grown their jewelry business into a company with twelve employees, each one a walking life crisis. They bought a building with fire code violations, a thriving rodent population, and a roof made of Swiss cheese. Once, they had worked sixty hours a week designing earrings. Now they worked eighty designing schedules.

We were caught in the steady working grind, the seasons seeming to change ever faster.

That fall, Janice announced that we needed a whimsical weekend getaway: just gas up the wagon and drive. We'd eyeball Vermont, hike New Hampshire, and land on some Massachusetts shore, eating lobsters that sold for the price of a Big Mac. I jumped onboard. To me, "weekend getaway" was code for "sex in motel." I made a music cassette for the trip — some Peter Gabriel and a few rare Springsteen bootleg cuts — collector's grade — with a B-side of Paul McCartney and Billy Joel lovey-dovey. We packed as if anticipating a month at sea: winter coats, swimsuits, boots, sneakers, a boom box, bug spray, visor caps, chips, dips, everything but the Kama Sutra and beer — which we'd buy cold when we arrived.

Friday, we set out on the least whimsical stretch of pavement known to humanity: the New York State Thruway. From there, we'd let the Fates lead us wherever they desired.

Some folks drive remote dirt roads just for the excitement of learning what vagaries of life might lurk at their darkened dead ends. Those people never watched *The Last House on the Left*. The truth is, I've never been a Fates kind of guy. I am a "let's get there" guy. Even without an estimated time of arrival, I vowed to cut the drive by thirty minutes. We could use that half-hour to floss, read the paper, or just sit in the idle car. (To me, sitting in an idle car is preferable to riding in a moving car.)

We barreled through Albany, never even cracked the windows on Vermont, and reached New Hampshire by twilight. There we wheeled onto a secondary route to let the travel faeries guide us to our romantic pleasure-rama, wherever it might be.

Around sunset, I tuned in to the Yankee game, not because I cared who won — I explained this at length — but out of respect for Don Mattingly and Dave Winfield, who were challenging for the batting crown. Soon we decided to start looking for a romantic setting to spend the night.

"That one looked nice," Janice said as I sped past a motel.

"Let's push on a little farther," I said. "Less driving tomorrow."

A few minutes later, I slowed for a motor lodge.

"Keep going," she said.

The next few miles offered options we separated into two categories: "Not Paying a Hundred Bucks for *That*" and "Owner Makes Sausage from People." Next came a train of No Vacancy signs, which spooked us into questioning what was wrong with the places that *did* have rooms.

"This one has vacancies," I said.

"Let's not find out why," Janice muttered.

We slowed for the next sign.

"Stop here," Janice said.

"It says 'No Vacancy.'"

"Sometimes they actually do have rooms."

We pulled into the lot. I refused to go inside and ask if the No Vacancy sign was a carefully calculated attempt to weed out travelers who can read. Janice glared at me.

A few miles down the road, a place looked promising to me.

"No," Janice said.

Around nine o'clock, we were hungry, tired, and lost, having left the reach of Yankee radio — which was like leaving the Milky Way. The car's tape player had eaten my cassette halfway through Billy Joel's "Just the Way You Are" (which I had immediately regretted adding to the mix). Janice was still praising a place I'd vetoed fifteen miles back. I explained that I would rather drive up the side of an active volcano than turn around.

"Next place," she said. "No matter what."

We pulled into a pine-shaded stretch of log cabins with a sign that said "Vacancy." As we sat in the car, a curtain moved in the office window, and two large eyes peered out at us.

"What the . . . ?"

"Go! Go! Go!" Janice shouted.

I stomped on the pedal, screeching the tires until we were a mile down the road.

We eventually reached a highway interchange, where prison-grade light towers illuminated a Burger King, a gas station/mini-mart, and a chain motel. We hit the fast-food drive-through and devoured in our seats two bacon-cheeseburgers that were the size and chewiness of footballs. As we fished for the last fries in the bottom of our bags, we watched the beer lights snap off at the mini-mart. Our hearts sank. We checked into the motel and asked where we could find the nearest six-pack. The guy directed us twenty miles back — about fifty yards from the motel I had vetoed. There we bought quart bottles of Miller High Life and a pair of needle-nosed pliers. (I was determined to fix that tape deck.)

We settled in around midnight and stayed up late, swigging beer in our winter coats, sitting in plastic chairs beside a dead swimming pool, listening to the crickets and the distant whine of the prison-grade towers.

There I gave Janice my best smile, my best kiss, and my best embrace.

"Hey," I said, "you want to get married?"

She winced, kissed me, and shook her head. "Let me think about it."

That weekend, we ate lobsters on a rocky pier in Massachusetts and watched the sunset on a mountain in Vermont. I fixed the tape player and fast-forwarded through every Billy Joel mistake. It was a wonderful trip.

But we were both still looking down the road, figuring the next stop just might be better.

JUJU RULE 15

Condemnations

With the exception of the Uppercase Deities — who, as we are constantly reminded, are 100 percent perfect — everybody makes mistakes.

Even the juju gods. Immortality does not imply immunity to imbecility.

I don't believe the juju gods will deny this. In fact, I considered devoting this entire book to exposing their blunders and mismanagement: the Pine Tar Game of 1983, the Mark McGwire/Sammy Sosa home run chase of 1998, the Yankee franchise between 1983 and 1994, and various scandals involving the Mets. Such a book would turn heads, down here and up there. Did you know the Cubs once traded Lou Brock for Ernie Broglio? I'd love to read the juju god e-mails surrounding that deal. *Somebody* would go to jail.

So when the juju gods blow a game, the thinking fan here on earth should be ready to tear them a new astral plane.

Okay, I know what you're thinking: *Only a fool would tell off the Fates who control the universe. Anger them, and — bam! — you're a pillar of salt. Piss off the gods? The last "thinking fans" to do that were probably rooting for Atlantis.*

I do not advise anyone to say things about supernatural entities that could get posted in a locker room. Surely, one reason the Phillies have lost more games than any other baseball team is the collective potty mouth of their fan base.

But when you have a case, prosecute it.

Rule 15: The juju gods accept honest criticism.

Once again, keep in mind that we're not second-guessing Jesus, Allah, Yahweh, Joseph Smith, or even Yoda (if you're into the *Star Wars* trilogy). We're not nitpicking or yelling at the Uppercase Deities who own churches and TV networks. We're talking about the *juju gods,* the grunts who fix ballgames. They do *not* hold the whole world in their hands. They do *not* carve whole mountain ranges with their fingers. They do *not* drive fancy red chariots across the sky. They work desk jobs. They drink coffee from the vending machine. Some probably wear Velcro wrist supports. Certainly, these underappreciated deities don't need to pick up the phone and hear you call them snake-faced cockroaches just because Javier Vazquez ruined eighty-six years of happiness with one pitch. But they are not so uppity, so godlike, that you can't call them and demand a retraction.

For example, one night long ago, a certain humpbacked line drive fell into left-center field, ceding the 2001 World Series to the Arizona Diamondbacks. As I stood there, watching it on TV, I delivered this message to the juju god hotline:

> All right, let me get this straight.
>
> For the last month, our team, the New York Yankees, has been carrying the heart and soul of a city and a country that was attacked by terrorists.
>
> This week, we twice hit home runs in our last at bat, leading to arguably the two greatest comebacks in World Series history.
>
> We had the great Mariano Rivera on the mound, the great Derek Jeter at shortstop, and the great Joe Torre in the dugout. And . . . now . . . this . . . ?
>
> We lose in the bottom of the ninth on a blooper? *Are you serious?* Is this an attempt at literary irony? Is this supposed to be satirical? Who wrote this? Who edited this? Who the hell proofed it? *Does anybody even read this crap before it gets put on TV?*
>
> Just tell me, so I can understand. Is there a rhyme or reason to this? *Is this what's supposed to pass for reality these days?*

Yes, I let them have it. And you know what they did? They just sat there, listening, taking it, nodding — knowing I was right. It was all I could do to hold off thinking words that I would later regret.

Then the Diamondback franchise did something incredible. Its public-address system played Frank Sinatra's "New York, New York," *the Yankee victory song.*

Arizona had won its first-ever World Series. Now, to christen the magic moment in their home park, they were rolling out the musical version of "Yan-kees suck!" They were ridiculing not only New York City but all of America, heroes, the juju gods themselves. It was the worst example of bad sportsmanship since the Moors were driven from Spain.

As I watched in astonishment, I composed an addendum to my earlier message:

> Hey, are you listening to this? Turn up the volume. What do you think of *that*? That's on your hands. Hey, are you watching? *Don't turn it off!*
> *Five years!* That's at least a five-year violation! I'd say ten! I say, put them on permanent suspension! Are you gonna let those guys get away with it? Look what you've done! *You guys have screwed up everything!* I want this corrected!

I had begun working for the next call.

Within a year, the Diamondbacks faced bankruptcy. Within two, they started selling off star players. Through 2011, they had yet to win another championship series game. They had finished last three times.

I didn't curse Arizona. If anything, they cursed themselves. Or maybe the juju gods were hoping to avoid a criminal probe.

Call them on mistakes. Press them to achieve excellence. Never assume they're perfect.

Remember, ascendance does not ensure transcendence above incompetence.

Lou Brock for Ernie Broglio? If I ever get the WikiLeaks on that one, somebody up there will fry.

17

★

Touching the Stone

For my eleventh birthday, my dad took me to the Hall of Fame Game in Cooperstown, New York, a pageant of religion and hokum that annually reaffirmed baseball's pastoral roots in American society. (*Note:* Major League Baseball killed the tradition after the 2008 game because its pastoral roots weren't generating a sufficient revenue stream.) We watched the Boston Redsocks beat the Milwaukee Braves, the highlight being a Hank Aaron home run that left the park in a banjo twang, landing beyond the clapboard houses that overlooked Doubleday Field. We sat close enough to hear the players fart, although at Cooperstown, so did everybody else. Dad wore a suit and tie. He bought me a program, a pennant, and all the candy I could eat. Unlike most events, we stayed to the end. But my most vivid memory came before the game.

Down the left-field line, Dad confronted a Braves pitcher named Claude Raymond. I vaguely remembered Raymond's APBA card. He was a Class B reliever — a middling star, with no known history of hurting the Yankees. He was standing in the bullpen, minding his own business, when my dad started in.

"Raymond! Hey! Raymond!" The pitcher didn't move. "You! *Raymond!* Get over here!"

I couldn't believe my ears. My father was addressing Raymond like an errant dog. The pitcher had to hear it, but he wasn't responding. I wanted to cry. I tugged at Dad's jacket, but he persisted.

"Raymond! Yeah, you! *Get over here!"* The louder Dad yelled, the more Raymond ignored him. *"Right here! Now!"*

I ran to my seat, mortified. Mortals weren't supposed to yell at gods. This was a baseball player, and a big one at that. Dad would be kicked out of the game or punched in the nose. I curled over and looked down at my sneakers. I wished we hadn't come. I wished we were home, watching on TV, where we would be safe. Anywhere but here.

Then I felt a touch on my neck.

Dad pressed out a scorecard with a purple squiggle in the margin. A signature.

"Happy birthday, Harty!" he said, beaming. "Look, Claude Raymond! He's pretty good!"

I never saw my father happier to be alive.

I believe such moments affect us in ways beyond our capacity to understand. It would be twenty-three years before I would ever dare watch a major league baseball game that couldn't be turned off with a knob or channel changer. And throughout that period, most folks figured me as one who routinely visited the Bronx.

Naturally, I gave them that impression.

In the early winter of 1986, a friend I will call "Lieber" — his Secret Yankee Club name — came to me with a proposal: we should recruit a group and attend Opening Day at Yankee Stadium. He volunteered to drive, which eliminated 98 percent of my hassles. Lieber saw me as the natural starting point, considering my vast experience in attending Yankee games.

(*Note:* Lieber had achieved blue belt status in my Yankee Fan Martial Arts rating system. Generally, a white belt, or beginner, is aware that there is a player named A-Rod. Then come yellow, pink, orange, and blue — two notches below the exalted black belt status. A blue can recite the Yankees' twenty-five-man roster, speak for thirty minutes on why Thurman Munson belongs in the Hall of Fame, and name at least ten washout former Triple-A prospects, such as Tucker Ashford and Hensley "Bam Bam" Meulens.)

To me, the gap between upstate and downstate far exceeded the drive. It was the difference between earth and Mars. Besides, I viewed Yankee Stadium as a place that existed in my imagination. I'd played in its outfield. I'd pitched on its mound. In my mind, every blade of grass stood perfect and proper, like Colonial Williamsburg. But I had no desire to go there. It could only be a letdown.

All my life, I'd watched Yankee games from my personal TV luxury suite. I never waited in traffic. I never spent five bucks on a warm beer or stood in a winding line of doubled-over men desperate to pee. In my private skybox, I worked my juju and helped my team. And if we lost, I just snapped it off before the beer commercial even began.

Why would I give this up? In fact, the idea of going to Yankee Stadium filled me with dread. It would ruin my own Opening Day tradition: chips, couch, channel changer. I had no interest in such a trip. None.

"Sure," I told Lieber, showing my smile teeth. "It'll be fun! Count me in!"

Why did I agree?

1. **Image.** Juju required showing faith in your team. Opening Day was no time for pessimism.
2. **Appearance.** Not to attend would be like a four-star general calling in sick for the Army-Navy game. A leader cannot decline such an invitation.
3. **Strategy.** I would scuttle the trip. By working on the inside, I would make sure it never came to pass.

Lieber launched a recruiting program worthy of the Notre Dame Alumni Association. He envisioned a rented van full of jubilant Syracusans arriving the night before the game, painting Manhattan the color orange, and returning home flushed with joy from a Yankee victory. It would evolve into an annual event, a Yankee rallying point, a morale booster.

In my recruitment speeches, however, a slightly different picture emerged. I noted that we'd sit in the upper deck, we would need to take two days off from work, and it would cost $400 — *if* we wanted to avoid bedbugs. I said we should not worry about rain, bad food, or being overcharged for basic services. We'd probably be hacked to death for our sneakers. Other than that, it would be fun.

Nobody signed on. Trip quashed, I thought. But Lieber had already purchased tickets. So Monday afternoon, he and I headed to Gotham.

We found our hotel, sampled the minibar, and took a cab to a place that held an exalted position in our minds: Mickey Mantle's Restaurant. We stood outside, nervous about entering, watching for Yankees to emerge from their cabs and march in with their entourages. After a while, a woman dressed like Minnie Mouse sidled up to me and asked if I wanted anything.

"A new life and a day without fear!" I replied wittily.

I'd forgotten to remove the sign on my forehead that said "Dork from Upstate."

She snarled something derogatory about my shoes and marched away. Despite our nerves, we decided it was safer inside. We entered Mickey's and headed straight for the bar, looking for Yogi and Whitey. The place was quiet.

"Where are all the Yankees?" I asked the bartender.

He said we had just missed them. A few minutes ago, Mickey, Yogi, Whitey — practically the whole 1961 team — had been there, signing autographs and cavorting with out-of-towners. He expected them back any time now. They were probably on the way!

I wondered if my "Dork from Upstate" sign was flashing.

We ate dinner, drank a beer, and eyeballed every guy who walked through the door, convinced that it would be Ross Moschitto or Roger Repoz. No recognizable Yankees showed.

From Mickey's, we walked the streets until we found an old man's bar, where the cultural gap between NYC and CNY (central New York) shrank, along with the hairlines. There we might as well have been drinking in Syracuse.

The next morning, we rose early, took the subway to the stadium, and, moments after the gates opened, marched triumphantly into the House That Ruth Built.

I remember my first impressions, the same thoughts I'd had during my first sexual experience: *"Holy cow! I'm in!"* I had finally made it! The place wasn't so scary after all, though it seemed smaller than I'd expected. I felt as if I could stand behind home plate and touch the outfield walls. In my backyard in Waverly, I'd made longer pegs to the garage wall than this place seemed to offer. Also, everything seemed to glow, as if charged by its own energy. I felt like an astronaut.

While the players took batting practice, we roamed the park. We climbed to the right-field upper deck and sat in the front row. We imagined George Brett's pine tar home run coming at us. We moved to center field, to relive Reggie's third blast in the 1977 World Series. We remembered the time Bobby Murcer had chased a ball around the center-field monuments on an inside-the-park home run. Then we worked our way toward left.

"That's where Thurman's home run landed against Kansas City," I said, pointing to the bullpen in deep left-center. "I was here."

I had touched the stone. Of course, it's gone now.

I believe future generations will wonder what the Yankees, New York City, and America were thinking in 2010 when we razed the House That Ruth Built. During the steamroller campaign to fund a replacement, politicians often called the old park a "cathedral." *Sports Illustrated* described it as the holiest venue in American sports. ABC News named it "Person of the Week." It arguably hosted pro football's greatest game (Colts vs. Giants, 1958), college football's greatest game (Army vs. Notre Dame, 1946), boxing's greatest bout (Louis vs. Schmeling, 1938), and baseball's greatest game (Aaron Boone home run, 2003). (*Note:* Apologies to Bill Mazeroski, Carlton Fisk, Ray Knight, and Bobby Thompson.) It hosted the two greatest speeches in American sports history: Lou Gehrig's farewell and Knute Rockne's "Gipper." It welcomed three popes, Nelson Mandela, Muhammad Ali, Billy Graham, Billy Joel, Pink Floyd, Walt "No Neck" Williams, and a grounds crew that formed human letters while the Village People sang "Y.M.C.A." Meat Loaf wanted his ashes spread there.

In its last four seasons, the old stadium drew more than four million people. *Four million people.* How bad could the experience have been?

We tore it down.

Did China raze its Great Wall to build one with energy-efficient windows? Did England replace Windsor Castle to provide broadband Internet? Did the Egyptians rebuild the Great Pyramid to install a JumboTron?

They claimed we had no choice. The old park—the one with all that pesky history—had lousy plumbing. The old park—where Jeffrey Maier snagged Jeter's home run, and where Don Larsen, David Wells, and David Cone pitched perfect games—did not possess adequate kitchen facilities to serve quality shrimp scampi.

At the end of the day, baseball is nothing more than a sandlot game played by kids who were once sent to the school nurse's office with foreign objects in their noses. But a baseball field is the most beautiful sandlot in sports.

They say it takes a lifetime to grow a tree. Same with a ballpark. The colors must fade, the seats must squeak, and the outfield walls must be climbed for a season-saving catch. A terrified rookie needs to walk out one day and then, twenty years later—the blink of an eye to a ballpark—wave farewell. A home run hero from long ago needs to stand at home plate and weep. Romances need to spark, and fathers need to see their kids go wide-eyed, and then remember how they felt when their own dads watched them in those very seats.

At one point, near the Yankee bullpen, I saw a journeyman reliever named Rod Scurry hanging out and minding his own business.

"Hey! Scurry!" I yelled. "Yeah, you! *Scurry!* Get over here!"

I got there late. But holy cow, I made it!

JUJU RULE 16

The Snap-off

Few rookies break into the majors as stars. In his first go-round with Seattle, Alex Rodriguez batted .204. In his Yankee debut, Mariano Rivera surrendered five runs in three innings. Lou Gehrig, at age twenty-five, grew so dispirited by his play that he asked the Yankees to demote him to St. Paul.

So it is with juju. For youngsters, the greatest challenge is playing through the humiliations that come with bringing your stuff to the Show.

Many newcomers, having mastered the Lookaway, start thinking they'll never lose another game. They hit their first slump and start questioning juju — or, worse, their worthiness to command it. Soon they see themselves as empty vessels in the paranormal powers sweepstakes.

What a terrible self-image to bear: the universe bestowed magic on others but left them with nothing. And it's all because they have forgotten:

Rule 16: Nobody wins them all.

Think about it. The Yankees, in their greatest seasons, *must* lose at least fifty games. So rather than blast the juju gods on call-in radio shows, let's be thankful they know what they are doing.

Listen: If the Yankees went 162–0, people would get suspicious.

In fact, if we won a mere 150 games, Major League Baseball would want to break up the franchise. Commissioner Bud Selig would order a probe (headed by some Redsock official), and soon media witch-hunters would be scouring A-Rod's locker for rosary beads and chicken blood.

(*Note:* In 2006, that's practically what happened. Selig appointed former U.S. senator George Mitchell, a member of the Redsocks' board of directors, to investigate the use of steroids in baseball. Over the next twenty-one months, Mitchell's panel met publicly with *one* player: Jason Giambi of the Yankees. Giambi spilled his guts, shriveled to the size of Betty White, and began hitting like her as well. Later, twenty of eighty-nine players named in the report were Yankees. No key Redsocks were mentioned.)

If the Yankees were to win all their games, the state of Massachusetts would criminalize the sport. And what about the Bible belt? Does the word "antichrist" come to mind? We only won four world championships under Joe Torre, but to hear our enemies wail, you'd think we were Sherman's army marching to the sea.

By throwing at least fifty games a year, the juju gods keep the hounds off our trail.

Nevertheless, it's not clear how the thinking fan should react after Boston wins four straight to take a championship series that we led three games to none. How should we handle such an open display of contempt?

Consider "the Snap-off," a quick and easy way to shame the juju gods after they just wrecked pitcher Chien-Ming Wang's career while he was running the bases. You neither fume nor grovel, and the bastards don't get to see you cry.

For me, the final moment of a Yankee loss would sound like this:

"Ground ball to second. Pedroia up with it —"

SNAP.

"Fly ball to center field, this should —"

SNAP.

"Called strike thr —"

SNAP.

The Snap-off is simple: don't let the ump raise his thumb. Hone your reaction time to a millisecond and — *bam!* — you're gone before the juju gods know the game has ended. They wanted you to weep? Well, boo-hoo. You're already in bed.

I view the Snap-off as a tersely worded letter of complaint, designed to work on the next game. But some fans swear it can become a fail-safe weapon in the event of another catastrophic attack of locusts. We're still studying the bizarre juju occurrence of June 12, 2009, when a tsunami of Snap-offs may have crashed the global grid.

It was the opening game of a midseason subway series, and the Yankees were losing to the Mets 8–7 in the ninth inning. Basically, we had lost. With two outs and two runners on base, Alex Rodriguez hit a pop fly to right field. Met second baseman Luis Castillo, a defensive specialist, settled under it, and then —

SNAP.

Apparently, twenty million Yankee fans' TVs simultaneously clicked off, awakening the juju god on duty, who instinctively beamed down a pulse to Castillo, like a satellite phone call, causing his mitt to close prematurely. The ball popped out, the runners scored, the Yankees won 9–8, and the Mets' season was history.

Never let an umpire throw the final thumb on a Yankee loss.

Never ask to be demoted to St. Paul.

And never doubt your juju. It's in you somewhere. Snap it out.

18

★

Jay-bird

The phone would ring, and Janice would answer. She'd talk for ten minutes, laughing, lost in conversation. I'd conclude it was one of her friends. Then she'd wave for my attention and hand over the receiver.

"CONGRATULATIONS! YOU AND GEORGE JUST MADE RON KITTLE THE NEWEST YANKEE!"

Glavin.

The darkest omen for a Yankee fan to receive.

Glavin was a thin, bearded Redsock fan with wire-rimmed glasses and a forehead the size of a supermodel's back. A journalism professor at Syracuse University, he didn't look imposing, but he possessed a booming, otherworldly voice, which served as a battering ram. Although Glavin loved Boston, he followed the Yankees more closely than most New York fans, and he quickly lit upon any incident or clubhouse dispute, looking to coax a Yankee fan into saying something that would hurt his team. When we lost a tough game or a key Yankee fell to injury, the phone would ring, and after Janice was talked out and my defenses were low, the full magnetic force of his voice would crash upon my ear.

"WHAT IS WRONG WITH MATTINGLY? YOU AND GEORGE

ARE PAYING A TON OF MONEY FOR SOMEBODY TO LEAVE THE TYING RUN ON THIRD!"

"You and George . . ." It was always *"You and George . . ."*

In Glavin's fevered mind, every Yankee fan existed as a personal lackey of the Yankee owner, if not a second head sprouting from a cleft in Steinbrenner's shoulders. He phoned after any Yankee setback, sometimes even before the news hit the wires.

"WHAT IN THE WORLD DO YOU AND GEORGE HAVE AGAINST BOBBY MEACHAM?"

"YOU AND GEORGE MUST BE SINGING TONIGHT. YOU'VE GOT CLAUDELL WASHINGTON!"

Over the years, I would come to rate the severity of a Yankee setback by the amount of time it took for Glavin to grab the phone. He acted as the Yankee equivalent of a tsunami warning system. If we lost a backbreaker, he'd phone during the postgame interview. After a routine Yankee defeat, he might wait a day. But in a tight race, Glavin played his hand carefully. He knew that a premature celebration could backfire, juju-wise. When rubbing salt into a wound, you didn't want to cut your own fingers.

Later, same night, the phone would ring again. Janice would answer, nod into the receiver, and then point it toward me.

"Someday we'll look back on this, and it will all seem funny," the Dog Man would say.

No, we wouldn't. Ever.

The 1986 season would never be funny. It was the year that culled our Yankee fan herd. I watched longtime comrades suddenly cross-dressing in orange Met gear, calling themselves "New York sports fans." These traitors had no shame. It was like a Catholic bishop converting to Islam and saying, "What? This? I've always been a big Allah fan!"

I felt alone, defeated, under siege. Every day, in the corridors of the Syracuse newspaper offices, some newly transformed, smirking Met fan would bait me into a conversation that I could not win.

At the time, the papers consisted of the *Post-Standard* (morning) and the *Herald-Journal* (evening), with the two editorial staffs arranged to compete in a journalistic civil war. In actuality, it was like a boxing match between Siamese twins: if one punched the other, both sides yelped. The ownership, Newhouse News Corporation, had arranged the staffs like armies of toy soldiers on a kitchen floor. The guns were always aimed, but nobody fired. By day, the two sides waged combat for scraps of news. By night, they drank together and, in more than a few cases, shared a mattress. On the rare occasion when some editorial hotheads revved the rivalry to the point of undermining corporate revenues, the publisher quickly reminded everyone that they parked in the same lot.

Both papers traditionally tilted pro-Yankee, in part because Syracuse had been home to a Yankee farm team for decades. But this new Met insurgency threatened everything we had built. In retreat, Yankee fans even began to ponder what once had been unthinkable: The need to make peace with the growing Boston menace.

At the papers, the Redsock contingent was led by John Bonfatti — alias Jo-bo, Jay-bird, Jay-bo, John, Jay, John-Jay, or, as I called him, Bon-*fahhhh*-ti — a writer of concert reviews and entertainment features, who had a gift for crudity that could shock a monkey house. Bonfatti served as the newspapers' de facto social director, if one imagined the role played by Artie Lange (*Yankee fan, by the way*). Monday meant football night at Jay's. Tuesday meant recovering from Monday night at Jay's. Wednesday meant planning Jay's weekend. Thursday, Jay's weekend began. From there, nights melted into a blitz of bottle openers, Bic lighters, and scratched vinyl renditions of "Thunder Road."

Bonfatti loathed the Yankees. If you mentioned Don Mattingly, he'd throw an object just to spook you. A loss to New York sparked malevolent tantrums, and to mock Bonfatti afterward was a dangerous card to play. The sight of him — 260 pounds, "Weird Al" Yankovic hair, glasses the size of satellite dishes, in his XXL Bruins jersey, stomping through the newsroom after a Redsock loss — sent good Yankee fans cowering in bathroom stalls, feet hovering over the tiles.

In our Yankee support groups, after badmouthing the Mets, we would look at Bonfatti and ponder a troubling scenario: *what if the Redsocks won a World Series?*

Until Bonfatti, I never feared such an event.

A year earlier, I'd helped plan Jay's farewell party. He was moving up to the *Buffalo News,* yet another friend heading off to a major league journalism career. As much as I'd miss him, at least we were off the hook in 1986, when the end-times appeared on the horizon: the World Series between the Redsocks and Mets.

Which did we prefer: Scylla or Charybdis? Arsenic or cyanide? The firing squad or the electric chair?

After some contemplation, I reached a decision: I would root for a Category 5 hurricane to come ashore between Cambridge and Queens. I wanted floods, tornadoes, and a windchill approaching instant death. I wanted Tim McCarver, frozen in sleet, chattering "mockery of the g-g-game." To me, this was Wolfman vs. Frankenstein, Hitler vs. Stalin, herpes vs. clap. I wanted mutual destruction. I wanted it to stop hurting.

I hated — *hated* — the Mets for all the reasons Yankee haters hated the Yankees: they swaggered; they spent money; *they won.* Worst of all, they had hypnotized New York City and stolen its fans, like pod people in a body snatchers movie. I wanted those Yankee turncoats, now clad in Met colors, to burn.

But root for Boston? Nope. No way.

I would boycott the World Series, sequester myself, enforce a personal gag order: no TV, no radio, no print, no discussion, nothing. To me, baseball no longer existed.

Late that October, Hank and I had to drive twenty hours to a wedding in Chicago. Jay suggested we stay overnight in Buffalo. The only problem: it coincided with World Series game six, the likely clincher for Boston. We would be in Bonfatti's presence at the moment of a Redsock world championship. It would be like standing beside a nuclear bomb.

Then Bonfatti made a critical mistake: He decided to throw a party.

Listen: Never hold a victory party *before* the victory. For starters, if your team loses, your party sucks. Second, the loss will be your fault. Enemy juju throwers will have used you. They'll say, "Hey, juju gods, you going to Bonfatti's victory party? No? *You weren't invited?* Oh, sorry to mention it . . ."

With Boston leading the series three games to two, Bonfatti figured he had wiggle room. If they lost, it just meant a game seven. Besides, they couldn't lose. The Redsocks had Roger Clemens on the mound and two future Hall of Fame bats, Wade Boggs and Jim Rice. Plus, there was a championship feel to this spunky Redsock team. They had made heroic comebacks all season. This was a *special* group, a team of *destiny* . . .

As Bonfatti droned on about his team, I silently vowed to root for the Mets.

By game time, the house had filled with Jay's newspaper colleagues and network of Redsock comrades. His stereo, its speakers the size of Tom Cruise (*Yankee fan, by the way*), blasted Springsteen, and six-packs piled up in the kitchen beneath a smoky haze.

Jay sat next to the TV, pumping his knees, his face shining white from the screen. He baby-talked to some players, chanted cryptic intonations to others. In key situations, he stood and punched the chair, as if pounding stray Rizzutons from the cushions. He never strayed from his post. He had won the pennant in that chair, and he was sticking with it. (That's smart juju, by the way. I've seen people cut and run just because of a called strike.)

In the kitchen, Hank and I tried fruitlessly to ignore the game. Now and then, shouts would erupt over the wall of music, turning heads toward the tube. We'd see Jay hugging the cushion of his chair, exhorting his players like a sea captain lashed to the mast in a howling storm.

After nine innings, the game was tied, 3–3.

In the top of the tenth, Dave Henderson homered to give the Redsocks a one-run lead. Then Marty Barrett singled home Wade Boggs, making it 5–3. Three outs separated Boston from its first world championship since 1918. As the beer commercials rolled, Jay pressed the cushion to his cheek and began slow dancing.

"Three, three, three!" he shouted. "Three more outs!"

He set down the cushion and reared back to empty his lungs of air, without creating discernible words. He sounded like Yoko Ono. His shirt was soaked with sweat, his glasses were fogged, and his hair flew in every direction at once.

The first Met batter, Wally Backman, flied out. One down.

"Two, two, two!" he shouted. And the crowd roared: "*Two more outs!*"

Now Jay began to jump up and down, shaking the house with each landing. Friends removed picture frames from the walls. Someone killed the stereo and turned up the TV, until the stadium noise roared like the ocean. Partygoers surged forward, seventy people belly to belly in a room roughly the size of a one-car garage.

Keith Hernandez flied out. One out left.

"Get up, everybody!" Bonfatti shouted, climbing onto his lucky chair. "*Get up, get up, get up!*"

Then Jay made his mistake.

"*We did it!*" he yelled. "*We won the World Series!*"

Jay's mouth formed a Fruit Loop and started emitting a long, formless groan: "*AHHHMMM . . .*" It was the sound windshield washers make when they're out of fluid, but a thousand times louder. Soon everyone in the room was *AHHHMMM-ing*, the Redsock faithful moshing and tumbling like socks in a dryer. Above the crowd, Bonfatti windmilled his arms while doing the twist, his weight turning the chair beneath him. Lamps flickered, and he kept groaning: "*AHHHMMM . . .*"

In that moment, seeing Bonfatti's joy, I came to a psychic crossroads. *Juju gods*, I thought, *I have changed my mind. Let Boston win!*

Gary Carter singled. Man on first.

Nobody noticed. Carter's hit didn't even register with the revelers. If anything, the *AHHHMMM-ing* intensified. The windows had been opened to cool the place down, and the TV noise was peeling over the neighborhood.

Juju gods, I thought, *let Boston win.*

I joined in, humming *"AHHHMMM . . ."*

Kevin Mitchell singled. Tying runs on base.

This made the *AHHHMMM-ing* louder, madder, harsher, more crazed, as if to shout down the events on TV. The entire crowd was jumping up and down, leaping onto each other. The house was bouncing; the lights were out; drinks were sloshing in raised salutes.

"Go, Redsocks!" I shouted. *"One more out!"*

Ray Knight singled.

The jumping stopped.

I won't go into bloody detail. We all know what happened. Minutes later, Mookie Wilson's famous ground ball bisected Bill Buckner's infamous knees. As the Mets celebrated on TV, Bonfatti's house moved from prison riot chaos to the solitary voice of Sparky Anderson, saying that Boston was in serious trou —

SNAP.

Silence. Now you could hear beer being poured into a glass, loudly, as in a radio commercial. Jay sat in his chair, not moving, staring at his feet. A Redsock fan was writhing on the floor like a wounded deer. Another ran outside and vomited. The phone was ringing. Down the street, car alarms sounded. Hank looked stunned, as if he'd just witnessed a murder. He drained his bottle.

Bonfatti took off his glasses and rubbed the red spot over his nose where the rims had left a dent in the cartilage. A line of mourners formed. People patted his shoulder, whispered a few words, and moved on. Jay acknowledged no one. He didn't lift his head. He wasn't crying. He just stared at the floor.

I tried to process what had just happened. *The exact moment* that I began to root for Boston, the Redsocks collapsed. By switching the polarity of my juju output, I had inadvertently unleashed on Boston an unprecedented demise. It was like the moment when the three energy ray streams in *Ghostbusters* merge to blow up the giant Marshmallow Man. I felt like Edward Teller. I had stumbled onto a juju force I had never before considered: *Reverse Rizzutonic Juju Emissions.*

When my turn came with Jay, I could see he was critically wounded. I touched his wet shoulder and felt truly sad about what had just happened.

"Jay-bird," I said, "I'm sorry."

"That's okay," he said. "Hey, it's not your fault."

JUJU RULE 17

Cheese

In *Ball Four,* Jim Bouton's 1970s best-selling memoir of life in the major leagues, the former Yankee pitcher recalled watching a journeyman infielder named Julio Gotay slide into second base, causing a cheese sandwich to pop out of his back pocket. Nobody flinched. For luck, Gotay always played with a cheese sandwich in his pants.

"He also used to carry a fish on the plane, to make sure it didn't crash," Bouton later told an interviewer. "We never crashed. So I guess it worked."

Hence the essence and proof of juju: *they never crashed . . . so it worked.*

Listen: These days, it's not just folks with bad teeth and botched tattoos who still accept collect calls from Elvis. In 2011, the roster of guests on the noteworthy cable TV show *Celebrity Ghost Stories* included Ernie "Ghostbusters" Hudson, Gina "Showgirls" Gershon, Shelley "Cheers" Long, and Corey "Goonies" Feldman. Every fading star in Hollywood is dipping at least one ringed toe into the next realm. But it doesn't end with actors. The ranks of true believers have included inventors (Henry Ford), generals (George Patton), first ladies (Nancy Reagan), and first ladies who became secretary of state (Hillary Clinton, who reportedly once channeled Eleanor Roosevelt in a séance). Even Dick "Eight Is Enough" Van Patten conjured up a ghost story for the show.

But one earthly group long ago levitated above all others: pro athletes.

Since the days of Samson's untimely buzzcut, jocks have reigned as the world's most gullible dolts. As kids, they think sidewalk cracks will break their mothers' backs. As adults, they avoid the chalk lines jogging to the dugout. By the time every athlete turns pro, he or she knows exactly what it takes to win: a personal link to the juju gods.

Ever wonder about those black smudges under their eyes? The players claim it lessens glare. Yeah, right. They wear it at night. *Does the moon glare?*

Of course, some sports are ruled through sheer brute force. In his worst game, the 370-pound, all-muscle defensive end will still beat the lymph nodes out of the unlucky side of beef who must line up across from him. The guy spent puberty in a weight room, steroids long ago turned his testicles into Raisinets, and the team has a shrink on retainer just to keep him from throwing women off water towers. To play football, he doesn't need hoodoo. He needs a bail bondsman.

But that's football. No one masters baseball in the weight room.

Hitting a 90 mph curve may be the most daunting task in sports (after working as traveling secretary for Billy Martin). At least three times per game — *three, again* — the batter steps to home plate with the eyes of the universe on him. What comes next? Juju, of course. Just as every whale in the ocean has his own signature song and no two snowflakes are alike, every batter in the major leagues performs a unique sequence of juju moves.

Between pitches, Nomar Garciaparra unfurled a series of rituals worthy of a fifteenth-century exorcism. He would step from the box, kick the dirt with each toe, adjust both batting gloves, and then touch his helmet. *Every. Single. Pitch.* Then Nomar would swing and hurt himself — but, hey, that's another story.

The great hitter Larry Walker took *three* swings before every pitch. He wore number *33*. He batted *third*. He always showered from the *third* nozzle and set alarms for *three* minutes past the hour. Walker got married on November *3* at *3:33* P.M. In his career, Walker hit *383* home runs, with a batting average of — cue the theme from *The Twilight Zone* — *.313*.

Before every game, Wade Boggs ate chicken. Jim Palmer choked down pancakes. Denny Neagle went to the movies. After his pivotal home run in the 1996 World Series, Jim Leyritz decided to eat at the same restaurant every day until the series ended. The Yankees won. So it worked.

In 2008, Yankee slugger Jason Giambi revealed to the world his secret juju cure for a slump. Beneath his uniform, Giambi wore a gold lamé thong with a flame-line waistband. He had worn that type of thong for years, even shared the idea with teammates, including Johnny Damon and Derek Jeter. They both swore by it, although Jeter — in what may be the most interesting quote of his career — said the thong pinched while he ran the bases.

Giambi's juju thong inspired me to write this verse:

> *On days when drives are flying long,*
> *And pitchers wonder what's gone wrong,*
> *The Bronx winds sing this joyous song:*
> *"Giambi's in his golden thong!"*
>
> *Each swing reveals Giambi's might.*
> *Each wince inspires his mates to fight.*
> *They know too well his painful plight:*
> *One ball hangs left, one ball hangs right.*
>
> *He leads the veteran team attack.*
> *True courage, he shall never lack!*
> *He eyes the pitch, then takes his whack*
> *As golden threads ascend his crack.*

Then comes the time when life turns wrong,
When wins grow short, and losses long,
And Bronx winds sing their saddest song:
"Giambi's lost his golden thong!"

Giambi's thong upheld a grand juju tradition of Gotham sports: stupidity. In 1904, New York Giants players marveled whenever a team of white horses appeared at the Polo Grounds. They saw it as a good omen — except that it was no such thing. It was Giants manager John McGraw messing with their heads. Recognizing them to be dolts, McGraw paid a stable to send out the horses just as his players arrived for practice. Did it work? Of course it did. That year, McGraw's Giants became the best team in baseball.

To be sure, many ballplayers reject superstition. But by the time they reach the majors, every one of them comes to grips with one iron rule — whether they believe it or not:

Rule 17: *Never disrespect your teammate's juju.*

Did Julio Gotay's fish work? His team's plane never crashed.

Is the New York Yankees' juju working? They've won twenty-seven world championships, haven't they? What do you think — is it working?

19

★

The Knot

For six years, Janice and I lived happily in a gingerbread house on Thurber Street (that's not a literary metaphor) with a big, goofy German shorthaired pointer named Bullwinkle. On warm spring evenings, the kinds that seduce Syracusans into thinking that winter has packed its tongs and sailed to Australia, we would lounge in the yard on a box elder that had been toppled by a windstorm and now served as a unique piece of outdoor furniture. There, one evening, like Mariano outdueling Kevin Youkilis in a twelve-pitch at bat, I wore Janice down.

For two years, she had fouled off my proposals, fast and slow. Long ago, I'd exceeded my pitch count. Other suitors would have headed for the showers or demanded a trade, but I kept throwing. Maybe it was the hopefulness of April. Maybe it was my changeup delivery. I said it didn't matter if she never said yes; I would stay as long as she would have me. But if she ever *did* decide she wanted to marry somebody, well . . .

She nodded slightly.

I appealed to the third-base umpire, who said, *Yes, she went around!* That was a yes! *She said yes!*

That November, we rented an old Victorian manor where every

stick of furniture cost more than my car and the upstairs men's room held a regulation-size pool table. We decided on a mixed wedding — Yankee fans and Yankee haters.

Jim Wright came from Norwich, lugging a new generation of bad Reggie Jackson jokes. Bonfatti, still in mourning over the Redsock collapse, led a contingent from Buffalo. The Duke drove in from Massachusetts. Jocko brought a newly tortured cap from Rochester. Spry arrived with a fresh Steinbrenner rant. Hank, my best man, countered with his usual rant, which ended with, "Aww, screw it. We suck!" Alphonso brought news of new Yankee hope, a young pitcher named Doug Drabek. The phone rang, and from somewhere in Delaware, the Dog Man said, "Tonight we'll be free; all the promises will be broken."

The event produced two noteworthy moments.

1. We forgot to plan a musical processional. After sitting in silence for about ten minutes, a few guests began humming "Mellow Yellow," a 1960s Donovan hit that somehow captured the group mind. The whole crowd joined in. It sounded like a Stonehenge druid orgy, with everyone snapping their fingers on cue and whispering, "Quite rightly." People still ask how we arranged it.
2. Moments after the town justice pronounced us man and wife, my uncle Bert, a World War II veteran, shouted for all to hear, "Thank God!" Later, my aunt Connie, a librarian from New Jersey, called his comment "the lone element of religion injected into the ceremony."

She was wrong. By dinner, the ball caps and Buckner jokes emerged. I did not slink away from my own wedding to catch a Yankee game, but then again, it was late November.

If you expect salacious details regarding the superhuman sexual performances that marked each morning, noon, and night of our honeymoon, forget it. I will simply note that on our first night, we went to the same burrito joint twice. Decide for yourself if that's a literary metaphor.

The trip produced two noteworthy Yankee events.

One morning in the hotel room, an ESPN crawl reported the Yankees had traded three prospects, including Alphonso's hope, Doug Drabek, for the faded Pittsburgh Pirate washtub that was Rick Rhoden. I collapsed to my knees and began pounding the floor. Janice heard the thumps, rushed from the bathroom, and, seeing that it was just me digesting Yankee news, returned to her shower. Back home, I found a phone message in a helium-pitched delirium.

"Next five years, we're dead!" Alphonso screamed. "Five years! Maybe ten! *We're dead, DEAD!*"

The second incident involved the New York Football Giants, my second sports team. Back in 1961, I naturally assumed them to be the Yankees of the NFL and thought they would cruise to the title, like Mantle and Maris. The Green Bay Packers crushed them, 37–0, a beating so brutal that I hid behind the couch until my parents nearly reported me missing. The loss so traumatized me that I never took up juju for the Giants. I simply never believed in them.

Nevertheless, during our honeymoon, the Giants were clearly the NFL's best team (as long as Lawrence Taylor avoided jail). In a dark sports bar full of sunburned male walruses, I watched L.T. and company crush the Washington Redskins like an empty pack of cigarettes. New York owned the juju that day, thanks to one magnificent warrior voice who sat down front.

Whenever a Redskin fan shouted something derisive, the anonymous foghorn yelled, *"Wanna bet?"*

Nobody responded. It was as if he'd pressed the bar's mute button.

Minutes later, someone would shout a crudity about Phil Simms. *"Wanna bet?"*

Nobody wanted to bet. And since they didn't want to bet, they didn't want to open their mouths either. The guy might as well have shot off a gun. The place turned to stone.

That guy had Billy Martin–level juju.

We returned home from our honeymoon to find a new stereo system, courtesy of Bonfatti. He'd convinced some of our friends to contribute to a joint gift so that, instead of ice buckets and cupcake tins, we'd actually have something we'd enjoy. We still play that stereo.

Twenty-two years later, in late August 2008, Jay visited his brother in Massachusetts. From all accounts, they enjoyed a glorious day. I have to believe they watched the Yankee-Redsock game on TV that night. If so, Jay must have been giddy over the outcome: a Dustin Pedroia grand slam and an 11–3 rout, a loss that mathematically ended the Yankees' pennant hopes in a wretched, horrible year.

Jay went to bed that night and didn't wake up. He was fifty-two.

I still see him on that chair in Buffalo, twisting the night away, one out from paradise, daring the juju gods and shouting to heaven, *"AHHHMMM . . ."*

Listen: There is no rivalry between the Boston Redsocks and New York Yankees. It's a fraud. It's a marketing tool. There is no Youkilis vs. Mariano, no Fisk vs. Munson, no DiMaggio vs. Williams. Never was, never will be. They are just employees of the same company who wear different uniforms to work. They golf together. They exchange holiday gifts. Their children attend the same schools. There are no feuds, no wars, no curses, no hatred.

There is only a connection between their fans. And it is a *bond*, not a rivalry. Never forget that.

After Jay's death, it occurred to me that the miserable Yankee team of 2008 had finally done something right. It had given my friend a smile on the last day of his life.

The juju gods were thinking.

Sometimes it takes *us* a while to understand.

THE SOCIOLOGY OF JUJU

The New York baseball market comprises three tribes, which in modern history have been united only three times.

The first came around 1990, when George Steinbrenner's rampant mismanagement aroused a soul-on-fire rage in Yankee and Met fans alike.

The second was in 2007–2008, when Alex Rodriguez briefly opted out of his $252 million Yankee contract, the richest document in sports history. This occurred after A-Rod had dumped his wife to hike a nature trail of strippers, waitresses, and aerobics fiends, which would eventually lead to the Disney haunted castle known as Madonna. All of New York despised him so vigorously that A-Rod reconsidered and signed a *richer* deal — $275 million — to remain a Yankee. But he kept hitting, so the resentment disappeared.

The third time was on 9/11, after the World Trade Center attacks, when the Yankees gallantly carried the flag of New York City and America all the way to the desert of Arizona, where a few incompetent juju gods — who hopefully now work minor league games — allowed a humpbacked fly ball to flutter into left-center field.

The three New York tribes are the Yankgers, Dodgints, and Nyets.

Yankgers. The dominant tribe, as of this writing. Yankgers is an acronym of the Yankees, Giants, Knicks, and Rangers — YGKRs — the city's oldest teams, which inspire passionate, across-the-board followers. At any moment, the typical Yankger's joyful recollection of Roger Clemens beaning Mike Piazza in the 2000 World Series might segue into a weeping appreciation of Lawrence Taylor snapping Joe Theismann's leg like a frozen curly fry fifteen years earlier.

This fervor stems from bloodlines. In many cases, the Yankees represent the first adopted team of their ancestors, immigrants who celebrated their new life in America by watching Babe Ruth and Lou Gehrig kick the emerald-green snot out of teams from fancy-pants places such as Baltimore and Washington. Between 1927 and 1962, Yankee dynasties romanced New York's Italian and Irish populations like a millionaire industrialist sending pricey chocolates to a stripper.

The Yankees became the gateway drug to other New York franchises — starting with the football Giants.

In 1956, the Yankees and Giants both won world championships, inspiring New Yorkers to equate the two as looming dynasties. Both played in Yankee Stadium. Both retired uniform numbers by the bushel (Ray Flaherty, number 1; Tuffy Leemans, 4; Al Blozis, 32). The Giants — behind Frank Gifford, Andy Robustelli, and Sam Huff — seemed poised to become the Yankees of the NFL.

Then the dice turned cold. The guts of the Giants, Vince Lombardi, jumped to Green Bay, and the brains of the franchise, Tom Landry, skipped to Dallas. That left the clipboard of the team, Allie Sherman, to run the show. Between 1958 and 1963, the Giants played in five NFL championship games — *and lost every stinking one.*

In the 1980s, the Giants again flirted with greatness. Behind Phil Simms, Joe Morris, and L.T., they won the 1986 Super Bowl. Unfortunately, the players went on strike, and the owners broke the union like a certain Redskin quarterback's femur. The league imposed a revenue-sharing system designed to create what it called "parity."

Everyone knows the NFL loves America. It reminds us constantly in sugary halftime shows and United Way commercials. But the NFL's owners do have one problem with the United States: capitalism. They hate it.

The NFL is the world's leading communist organization. Each spring, its worst teams draft highest, receive the weakest schedule, and sign players shed by the winners due to a league-enforced salary cap. In a perfect NFL season, every team goes 8–8, all the players dress alike, and every TV announcer flutters his hands like Terry Bradshaw. Thus, the league's owners avoid their worst-case, nightmare scenario: an NFL version of the Yankees.

As for the other Yankger teams? When critics condemn New York fans for backing the rich and powerful Yankees, they manage to ignore the tortured histories of the Rangers and Knicks. Sadly, Yankgers cannot.

Dodgints. In the early 1900s, the New York Giants won three world championships under John McGraw, arguably the first coming of Billy Martin. They won again in 1933 and then in 1954, under Leo "the Lip" Durocher, the second coming of Billy. Their mortal enemy, the Brooklyn Dodgers, won just once — in 1955 — while losing eight World Series, making them the first coming of the Redsocks. (In fact, the *B* on their caps bore a striking resemblance to the Boston *B*.)

Both teams succeeded by signing African American players, such as Willie Mays and Jackie Robinson, long before the redneck Yankees woke up and acquired the majestic oak tree that was Elston Howard. (By the way, that disgraceful lag in morality cost us at least three world championships. Imagine Larry Doby in the Yankee lineup of 1954. Also, Boston could have ended its "curse" fifty years earlier if not for racist foot-dragging.)

In the winter of 1957, the Dodgers and Giants abruptly skipped to California. If that happened today, the National Guard would be deployed. Effigies would be burned, lawyers would sue, and elderly white mobs in Tea Party costumes would march on Washington. The anger would have a name: *coast traumatic stress disorder.* But in the post–World War II era of Dwight D. Eisenhower and Sandra Dee, the masses were too newly mesmerized by TV to mount an insurgency. They didn't have a team, but they could watch Milton Berle dressed in drag.

Fans of the Giants and Dodgers faced a hellish choice: keep rooting for the teams that had betrayed them, whose games now started after ten o'clock each night, or support the franchise they hated more than they hated life itself — the Yankees.

So were spawned Dodgints, Yankee fans created by the Great Dodgers/Giants Treachery of 1957.

Inside every Dodgint lurks a cork-popping rage that must be directed at somebody — anybody — but preferably a Met or Redsock. They cannot explain this anger any more than an emperor penguin can describe life outside Antarctica. They're always ready to detonate.

They always want to fight. The craziest Dodgints are the children of those who kept rooting for the Dodgers or Giants, like googly-eyed zombies milling around a shopping mall. They refuse to sign up for baseball's version of a methadone clinic, the Mets. In fact, Dodgints view Met fans the way brown ants view red ants: browns want to squeeze reds with their pincers until the reds' tiny heads explode.

Dodgints constantly fume. They want every Yankee manager fired, every Yankee pitcher pulled. They want the cleanup hitter to bat third, but they also want him traded. The Yankees can be leading 13–0, but if a star hitter strikes out with runners on base, their whole night is ruined. They love the Yankees. They hate the Yankees. They'd rather finish twenty games out than lose the World Series in seven games on a humpbacked blooper. They fear every Redsock acquisition, even players the Yankees wouldn't touch with a laser pointer. They want every free agent. They want every game, every at bat, every pitch. They want the season over, as soon as possible.

Publicly, they scorn juju. Privately, they are the most obsessive practitioners ever known. They weigh every subconscious movement for its impact on the team. Some may even dream juju in their sleep.

They never find peace. They never experience joy, except for the moments immediately following a Yankee win. It lasts until Frank Sinatra finishes "New York, New York." Then the shakes return.

I am a Dodgint.

Nyets. The polar opposites of Yankgers, Nyets take their name from the New York Mets, Jets, and Nets. They flourish mostly in areas of weed-whacked suburbia and its ancient holy land, Long Island.

Why there? The Mets, and originally the Jets, played at Shea Stadium in Flushing, and the Jets for years practiced at Hofstra University, in Hempstead. The New Jersey Nets' glory years occurred as the New York Nets, playing in Nassau Coliseum. In hockey, the Islanders are, well, *islanders*.

Nyets believe in the power of love, the magic of nature, and the greatness of God. They generally abstain from juju. As a result, their teams have suffered.

Met fans watched as the great Tom Seaver was run out of town by the blowhard tabloid sportswriter Dick Young. They watched little Lenny Dykstra go to Philadelphia and plump up into a steroidal behemoth. They saw Doc Gooden and Darryl Strawberry resurrected as Yankees. In 2007, they watched their team blow a seven-game lead with seventeen games left, the kind of meltdown that ended nuclear power in the Ukraine. In recent years, they've watched one of their last icons, Keith Hernandez, hawk hair coloring. (He couldn't snag a Viagra contract.)

Jet fans had to witness the transformation of Joe Namath from world's coolest bachelor to shaky groper of waitresses. They suffered the indignity of playing home games in *Giants* Stadium. In 2000, after head coach Bill Parcells resigned, they watched his handpicked successor — future Patriot legend Bill Belichick — quit after *one day.* He scribbled his resignation on a napkin: "I resign as HC of the NYJ."

Nets fans? Let's just say that, through their first thirty years, they never watched an NBA championship game that the Nets were playing in.

Even when touting his team, a Nyet's head will shake, as if to say, *Yeah, I don't believe me either.* They claim to disdain violence, but beneath every dinner table, a Nyet is choking a napkin with his or her bare hands. In dreams, they are dousing Mr. Met with gasoline and striking a match on Bernie Madoff's stubbled chin.

Many Nyets yearn to flee Long Island. But to the west, they face a city swarming with Yankgers and Dodgints, hungry for the chance to shred a David Wright jersey into animal bedding. New Jersey won't accept them; it's still pissed about the Nets. If they go north, they will find Redsock fans still seething over the 1986 World Series. (If the Yankees ever fall, "Mets suck!" will quickly become Fenway's favorite chant.)

Nyets who move to, say, Ohio face the obvious question: *Why aren't you a Yankee fan?* These days, a Met fan turning up in Toledo will trigger calls to the U.S. Department of Homeland Security.

Archie Bunker was a Met fan.

Tony Soprano rooted for the Yankees.

When Nyets inbreed, a mutation often results. See that bearded guy standing on Broadway, the one wearing a Met cap and a Minnesota Viking jersey? What caused him to support a team from a city he knows only from reruns of *The Mary Tyler Moore Show*? What happened to him? And do you really want to know?

The Russians have a one-word answer: Nyet.

20

★

"George Steinbrenner Must Die"

To this day, when people ask about the kitchen bomb of 1988, I blame George Steinbrenner and try to redirect the conversation. In truth, the bloody explosion that changed my life with Janice was not Steinbrenner's fault.

The story began two years earlier, when Hank and I attended a wedding in Rochester and crashed at a friend's house. The next morning, as we iced our lobotomies, our host unveiled a wooden crate containing twenty-four frosty brown bottles. He lifted one, uncapped it, toweled the foam from its pouty lips, and filled two pilsner glasses with a magical golden liquid. He called it homebrew.

Greatest. Guy-move. Ever.

Weeks later, Hank and I took over Janice's kitchen and lay boil to a gallon of mystical ingredients, until the impetuous froth leaped from the kettle and onto the floor, a sign of what was to come. A week later, we bottled three cases of a chocolate stout. A month later, we drank them like kings of the beer world.

To the uninitiated, I should note five critical elements of home brewing.

Safety. To avoid injury and lawsuits, never point a bottle at anyone. Treat it as a loaded weapon. Uncap it outside or in a secure shower stall. Wear safety goggles or a Kevlar vest.

Presentation. After the gusher subsides, *gingerly* pour beer down the side of a tall glass, trying to limit the foam. Leave the putrid final two inches of yeast residue in the bottle. *Do not drink that crap.* For proper disposal, contact your Department of Environmental Conservation.

Admiration. Sniff the glass, appear to be thoughtful, and then say something like "Hmmm . . . a bit throaty, woody . . . You can definitely taste the feminine hops."

Taste. Nobody cares. It will probably remind them of old sneakers. Nobody cares. They'll set it down after two sips. Repeating for emphasis: *No. Body. Cares.*

Bottle. *Important:* Each batch needs a cool label. *This is critical!* Decorate the bottles and give them as keepsakes. They are the only part that matters. (*See* Taste.)

We brewed a "Merry Christmas Stout," a "SeelCraft" lager, and a "Bullwinkle Beer," named for our beloved German shorthair. To celebrate our wedding, we made "I Do I Do Brew." The label showed Janice and me conversing. I say, "Get me a beer." She says, "Get it yourself."

But in the winter of 1988, Hank and I brewed our masterwork: "George Steinbrenner Must Die Beer."

It summed up my worldview. I had gone from a kid who saved the Yankees to a cynical adult who withheld a juju life raft from a struggling team. Moreover, for fifteen years, I had been rewriting a novel about a crazed Yankee fan who battles an egomaniacal baseball owner. I couldn't escape George, even in my literary solitude. He needed to go away.

We decided to unveil our achievement with a "George Steinbrenner Must Die Gala Beer-Tasting Soiree." The concept excited the Yankee intelligentsia in the way that comic book conventions lure chubby, bald men. Normally, we would expect one in three invitees to attend. This time, not only was everybody coming, but they wanted to bring friends. The notion of bashing Steinbrenner presented to Yankee fans and haters a grand unifying cause. Someone suggested we burn him in effigy or smash a George piñata. Rumors spread virally. On the day of the event, a local TV news anchor called to ask if she could come; she'd heard this was the party of the year.

Listen: In Syracuse, New York, when a local TV news anchor invites herself to your beer party, this *is* the party of the year. We practically needed a red carpet.

Unfortunately, the louder the buzz, the more Janice fretted. I assured her that all would be fine. Yankee fans were duty bound to be courteous and respectful.

"Have you ever even seen those guys sober?" she asked. "They'll stay for a week."

Nonsense, I said. Sure, the boys would let off some steam. It had been a tough Yankee decade. But the whimsical anti-Steinbrenner theme would bring a calming tone to the evening.

"How did we get roped into this? If those Bowery drunks want to party, let someone else host it."

Again I explained that this was not a party but a soiree, a beer tasting. We would unveil each bottle, so that people could sip and discuss. There would be conversation, reflection, mirth — no cause for alarm.

"And what's this about a bonfire?"

I explained that somebody probably misheard Bonfatti's name.

"Jay's coming? With his buddies from Buffalo?"

I explained that we shouldn't waste time talking. We had maybe five hours to move everything of value to an upstairs bedroom and find a reinforced-steel padlock to keep the door secure.

Actually, we had three. Folks came early. By seven o'clock, the living room was clogged with bodies. It didn't ease Janice's fears that the first to arrive were newspaper photographers, legendary late-raging killers of kegs. By eight, the crowd stood shoulder to shoulder throughout the house, with people chugging homebrew straight from the bottles, yeast deposits and all.

Around then, a delivery truck pulled up and dropped off a crate of Chesapeake Bay oysters, which a friend — a newsroom escapee — had sent from Baltimore. We hadn't planned on raw oysters. The excited crowd swarmed over the ice-packed box, tearing apart the insulation, and people began trying to shuck the oysters with bottle openers, car keys, and steak knives. After a few disturbing flesh wounds — one could do an interesting psychological study on how quickly a crowd will part in the presence of spurting arteries — folks dragged the dazed shellfish to the back porch, where guests began smashing their exteriors with hammers, snow shovels, and steel-toed boots. Shards flew everywhere, diffusing a seaside aroma that — we concluded later — would be likely to attract wildlife.

By ten, guests jammed the front and back porches, unable to enter the house, while cars circled the neighborhood for a place to park. Many gave up and went home. They'd be considered the lucky ones.

Around midnight, people on the back porch reported hearing a horrifying yelp off in the darkness. Moments later, they saw a black object hurtling fast and low across the hard-packed snow, advancing on the house like a live torpedo. It was Bullwinkle.

As the dog neared, porch sitters recognized the overwhelming, pungent odor of a skunk. Bullwinkle had been sprayed. The German shorthair, a veritable stink bomb, rushed toward the open kitchen door, and the crowd parted to avoid him.

Bullwinkle's knee-buckling stench hit the interior party like a flaming bottle of gasoline. Human waves spread in every direction as the animal searched for his doggy bed. The crowd surged out the front door and spilled onto the snow, where people stood coatless and shivering.

Janice and I coaxed Bullwinkle back outside. We calmed him, petted him, and hooked a leash onto his collar. We opened every remaining window, and Bonfatti handed out record album jackets, organizing volunteers to fan the stench toward the doors, like a bucket brigade for air. The indoor temperature fell to 30 degrees, but the rank smell soon subsided, and the tide of partygoers began to return.

Janice found a bucket and some jars of spaghetti sauce. On the back porch, Hank and I gave Bullwinkle a tomato shampoo. Now the kitchen was refilling, the downsized crowd more manageable and at peace. Hank rubbed red sauce into the dog's short hair, while I poured warm water over his back and talked softly to him. I loved that dog, and I stroked his forehead, making sure he knew I wasn't angry.

We had triumphed over adversity. We had saved the night. Bonfatti, in charge of the stereo, switched from the Cars to the Clash. Hank and I intended to break out our last case of homebrew. Already, people were calling this, the party of the year, "the night of the skunk." George Steinbrenner was dead, and he had not died in vain.

I cannot recall the precise sequence of events that followed. Apparently, Hank and I each thought the other was holding Bullwinkle's leash. Neither of us was. The dog lurched forward. Somehow, beneath the thick slather of tomato sauce, he slipped away.

There are moments in TV shows, usually violent ones, when time is suspended and the action grinds into a slow-motion dance, often accompanied by a wailing guitar and the hero shouting an elongated "No-o-o-o!"

For me, as Bullwinkle bolted into the kitchen, this was such a moment.

I still see Hank stretched forward, a towel in one hand, reaching for the frightened dog. I still see Janice leaning against the stove, wearing her favorite sweater. I see Bonfatti holding court among people who are clutching drinks, mouths open like flytraps, tongues exposed, soon to receive a taste they will never forget. I see men in suits and women in dresses, having come straight from the Syracuse Symphony. They stand frozen in time, like paintings of long-dead people on a museum wall.

Most of all, I see Bullwinkle — a black lump beneath a coat of red slop — halt in the center of the room; coil his sixty-pound frame; and then, from head to tail, *shake.*

Neighbors heard the screams. The explosion slammed bodies into appliances and walls. Someone crashed into the sliding kitchen door, knocking it permanently off its track. From the epicenter of the dog, a shock wave of red splotches instantly covered every square foot of the impact zone, including everyone inside it. Bullwinkle coiled, then shook again, a moment before Hank's towel could absorb the aftershock.

Later, people said it looked as though *The Texas Chainsaw Massacre* had been filmed in our kitchen. Every wall, every hanging plant, every utensil, and every living person was coated with a microscopic spray of skunk, dog, and Ragú.

For months, people would ask to see "the house where the dog exploded." Strangers on the street would point to it. Thousands claimed to have attended, and no one could disprove them. Some returned to look for lost items, though we sensed they just wanted to see for themselves the detonation zone.

Years later, we sold the place. I'm sure splotches still lurk in the crevices.

That night, George Steinbrenner did not die. But a segment of our lives did. The next day, Janice and I agreed that we were getting too old for this. It was time to settle down, to take things more seriously. Time to raise a family.

On a hot summer day three years later, Janice heard mysterious noises above our bedroom. She climbed into the attic and found an unopened case of George Steinbrenner Must Die Beer. A few bottles had exploded in the extreme heat, embedding shards of glass in the walls. She carefully carried the case out to the backyard, where over the next few days, the Steinbrenners detonated, one by one, inside the box.

A few bottles survived. I have kept them cold for more than twenty-five years. In 2009, to celebrate the Yankees' twenty-seventh world championship, I opened one. It was a bit throaty, woody . . . You could definitely taste the feminine hops.

JUJU RULE 18

Thirteen

Following the 2011 season, the Yankees' all-time record stood at 8,915 wins and 6,514 losses. Crunch the numbers: that's an average of 94 victories per season.

Thus, every year Yankee fans enjoy thirteen more wins — and suffer thirteen fewer defeats — than the average .500 team. Think about it: if you root for the Yankees, you can expect to celebrate thirteen more victories and suffer thirteen fewer losses every season for the rest of your life.

Thirteen more victories and thirteen fewer losses. Every season. For the rest of your life.

I respect that some readers already have a favorite team and it is *not* the Yankees. Moreover, a few might consider it insulting — no, *infuriating* — to hear a Yankee fan boast about his thirteen extra wins and then attribute them to some personal New Age dorkcraft. You might even view me as a quintessential Yankee fan asshole, just another valueless jerk who thinks the universe revolves around his team.

Okay, fine, I get it. I understand your rage. If *I* suffered thirteen needless defeats every year, I'd be bitter, too.

But, reader, do you love your children? Do you want them to follow the great American pastime? Do you want them to be happy?

As Yankee fans, they will likely celebrate thirteen more victories . . . *and suffer thirteen fewer losses* . . . every season for the rest of their lives. If they live to age sixty-five, that's 845 victories — more than five undefeated seasons. Five years . . . *without a loss.*

Those creamy victories will replace 845 acid-tinged defeats, including a few walk-off heartbreakers that will haunt your children to their graves, if not send them there before their time. Imagine it: *five seasons without one victory.* Not even over the Marlins.

Would you knowingly subject your children to five years of unrelenting loss and humiliation? If your answer is yes — well, hey, Parent of the Century, here are a few more child-rearing tips: Buy them crack pipes. Teach them to bungee jump. Show them how to make Halloween masks from plastic bags.

Defeat is a terrible thing to inflict on a child. It destroys self-esteem. It breeds juvenile delinquency. Kids come to expect cleanup hitters who bat .230 and relievers who cannot throw strikes. They turn to fast food, video games, and phone sex. They quit school. Why learn to read when the sports pages tell only of losses?

Do you want your children striving for life's wild card?

Of course, if your children were to become Yankee fans, not only would their lives be brightened, but their juju would be added to the collective cause, resulting in an even higher annual winning percentage. If it grows by just 4 percent, compounded over ten years, they could expect up to *eighteen extra wins per season.*

With the lack of stress from losing, they could live to be 110. With conservative estimates of overage juju, they could squeeze out a few more victories, spending their retirement years never experiencing even one loss. That, in turn, would mean fewer strokes and heart attacks, prolonging their lives indefinitely. Think of it: No defeats! No death! Eternal life!

Okay, maybe that's overstating it a bit. But a tiny investment now, and everybody wins later.

Rule 18: *The more successful the team, the stronger the juju.*

I know what you might be thinking. *What is this fool saying? I don't have kids. I hate kids. Why would I care about kids? What's in this for me . . . me . . . ME?*

First off, you really should be a Yankee fan.

Second, if you're not rooting for the Yankees now, you may be suffering the consequences without even knowing it.

Reader, answer these questions:

1. Have you ever been shut out of an important meeting?
2. Did you ever learn, *after the fact,* of a party to which you weren't invited?
3. Have you ever walked down the hall at work to find colleagues whispering to each other and then, as you drew near, abruptly going silent?

They are Yankee fans, talking Yankee baseball.

Somewhere on Wall Street, Main Street, K Street, or Easy Street, a Yankee fan right now is turning the dials on your career. Almost all the big-money CEOs root for the Yankees. They can't help themselves; it's instinctive. How do you think they made it to the top? By turning their backs on *thirteen free wins per year*?

Right now, your boss, or your boss's boss — some pompous Ultimate Yankee Fan gasbag from the world of gated communities, gourmet marshmallows, and Tibetan nannies — hungers to discuss the clutch-hitting legacy of Yogi Berra with a lunch-bucket underling just like you. That is, *if you're of the pinstriped cloth.* The chance for some Yankee chitchat appeals to a VIP like a dangling yellow strip of sticky tape beckons to a housefly.

Ever hear the term "yes man"?

Ever wonder why it's called the "YES Network"?

I sense some readers bristling, perhaps violently, over my good-faith call to join the Yankee self-help movement. You vow to remain loyal to your favorite Marlin, the one everyone calls "Mr. Marlin," or the "Marlin Clipper," or "the Pride of the Marlins," and it infuriates you to think of "Donnie Marlin" or "Stan the Marlin" ever signing with the hated Yankees.

Listen: This isn't about hometown loyalty. It's about pro athletes with short careers. Any ballplayer seeking to turn his children into trust funds will flee to Los Angeles or New York before you can say "seven years, ninety mil, no-trade clause, and complimentary sky-box." Yes, your Labrador retriever loves you, but when the neighbor offers porterhouse, don't expect him home for kibble. And when he strays, don't blame the dog. Join him! The steaks are on the grill, and that's not Alpo, brother!

As a Yankee fan, you'll follow not only your lineup of millionaire stars but also the high-maintenance actresses and emaciated-yet-busty supermodels they date in public. You can read about their sexual exploits in the grocery store checkout line. You can regale small-market fans with your worldly insights and insider knowledge.

You'll project Yankee pride into every conversation. The phero-mone scent of juju will boil up from your swaggering Yankee-fan frame. You'll be Pamela Anderson in a room of Olive Oyls, Springsteen in a hall of Eddie Rabbitts. You will be Gotham. You will be Wall Street. You will be Trump, Murdoch, Soros — *Steinbrenner!*

And your juju will grow in size — *by thirteen extra wins per season!*

Unless, of course, you're a Phillies fan. In which case, *make it seventeen!*

21

★

Frank Crosetti

In my life, I have met Dan Quayle, Al Gore, Timothy Leary, Southside Johnny, Sam Huff, Mario Cuomo, Robbie Knievel, David Byrne, the bass player for the Tragically Hip, a saxophonist for Ray Charles, a guy who delivered pizzas to Shania Twain, Eddie Money, Daniel Patrick Moynihan, Kurt Vonnegut Jr., Colin Powell, Betty Friedan, Tom "SpongeBob" Kenny, Commander Cody, and Phil Rizzuto.

None of those meetings compares to meeting my children.

Our first son arrived on December 12, 1988. To be honest, I recall no Yankee events in the weeks leading up to it. George could have signed Sarah Michelle Gellar (*Yankee fan, by the way*), and I would have missed it. During that period, my beautiful, loving Janice had turned into a malevolent, watermelon-lugging denouncer of God. For me to harp on a Yankee defeat would be cruel, if not dangerous. I once briefly floated the idea of naming our child "Mattingly." I nearly lost a limb.

We took the obligatory Lamaze classes, which are designed to terrify prospective parents. Janice enrolled with the hope of learning to "breathe away" the pain. After two sessions, her plan changed to arriving early and demanding hard-core drugs. I was assigned to drive the birthmobile and serve as coach, a designation I accepted proudly.

I viewed myself as Frank Crosetti, "the Old Crow," the legendary Yankee third-base coach — flashing signs, slapping butts, and keeping Janice loose with my lively banter and contagious smile. As she rounded third, I would windmill my arms and wave her home. Plus, I'd be prepared. I assembled an emergency "Break Glass in Case of Baby" kit: towel, bottled water, Chiclets, Kleenex, blow-up pillow, change of clothes — plus whatever Janice might need. I recorded a "delivery mix" tape for our ride to the hospital. It included some Peter Gabriel and a few rare Springsteen bootleg cuts — collector's grade — with a B-side of inspirational birth anthems, such as "We Are the Champions" by Queen and "Jump" by Van Halen. Unfortunately, when the big moment arrived, I couldn't find the tape. Janice grew testy while I searched the house and then crabbed nonstop during the ride, not even listening to the songs.

I held my tongue, though. No complaints. *Frank Crosetti . . .*

At the hospital, Janice flagged down the first nurse and said the magic word she had learned from eight weeks of Lamaze: *"Epidural!"* They assigned us a room with stirrups and cable TV, and we waited for the baby shoe to drop.

And we waited . . .

About three hours later, a condescending doctor said that Janice wasn't dilated enough, hadn't suffered enough, wasn't apparently *tough* enough, and that she should go home and not come back "until it really hurts."

Those words hit her like a frying pan. Humiliated, Janice went home, bucked up, hissed like a runaway steam engine, and, twenty-four hours later, nearly hiccupped our baby onto the kitchen floor. I'd gone in to work and was sitting at my desk when Marge phoned from the emergency room, yowling like Mariah Carey (*Yankee fan, by the way*). She had rushed Janice to the hospital. Our baby was due any minute.

I arrived just in time for Janice's final "You bastard, you did this to me" glare.

"Breathe," I said.

Frank Crosetti . . .

Soon Janice started yelling, the nurses started scrambling, the doctor shouted *PUSH,* and we had a son — Hart Emerson — who was looking around and screaming: *Holy cow! I'm out!*

Three years later, Janice found herself back in the saddle. It was mid-August, the Yankees were mired in fifth place, and I assured the maternity ward staff that everything was "most excellent," as I had done this before. I was detailing, in my own delightful way, Janice's penchant for false alarms, when she started yelling, the nurses started scrambling, the doctor shouted *PUSH,* I waved her home from third — *Frank Crosetti* — and our second son, Kyle Everett, emerged from the clubhouse to join the team.

In May 1994, our third baby loomed. By now, I viewed myself as a seasoned sea captain, the serene and steady hand at the tiller. I knew my job: Say "Breathe" and let the pregnant lady run the bases.

But this time, the stakes were higher. This time, we were riding a ten-game winning streak and leading the American League East.

To repeat: *After fifteen years as also-rans, not only were the Yankees the hottest team in baseball, but they also held first place in the American League East.*

We arrived at the hospital around 9:00 P.M. and were given a room. Knowing we might be there for many hours, I quickly ordered the premium channel TV package. After tending to Janice's needs, I scrolled through the listings and found that the game happened to be on.

Some have asked — rather accusingly, I might note — what manner of man sits and watches a regular-season Yankee game while his wife is giving birth. Let me address this on four fronts:

1. *I did not "sit and watch" the game.* I "kept tabs" on it. There is a huge difference, so vast that I could write a whole book

about it (but I won't). While keeping tabs, I monitored Janice and periodically asked if she needed anything, such as a glass of water or a towel to bite down on.

2. *This was no ordinary regular-season game.* As stated earlier, we had won ten straight. We were more than halfway to the all-time team record for consecutive wins — nineteen games (which, for history buffs, was set in 1947).

3. *Janice never requested another show.* Had she asked to watch something else, I would have switched channels without hesitation. It was her call. She made no request. Keep in mind, she was in excruciating pain. Giving birth is no picnic. What was she going to do, lie there and watch *The Nanny*? (Fran Drescher is, by the way, a Yankee fan.)

4. *It was a good game.* It was not a blowout. It was a close contest, just the kind of real-life drama that could provide a well-deserved diversion from Janice's ongoing agony.

In the top of the seventh, the plucky Yankee shortstop Mike Gallego homered to give us a two-run lead. In the bottom of the inning, our starter, Jimmy Key, faced the heart of the Twins order.

"First-pitch strike," I whispered, and Key obliged.

"What did you say?" Janice asked.

"Nothing."

"You're doing your eyeball stuff?"

"Breathe."

In the eighth, manager Buck Showalter brought in Bob Wickman, a promising young pitcher with a great background story. As a child, Wickman lost part of his finger in a freak accident. For most kids, that would make pitching impossible. But "Wicky" had fought his way to the majors, a truly inspirational tale. In fact, I told Janice about Wickman's journey. I figured this a great omen — that such a fine, strapping young man would be pitching while our child was being born.

"No," she said.

"No?"

"We're not naming the baby Wickman."

"First-pitch strike," I whispered, eyeing the TV.

"Wait a minute," a nurse butted in. "Do I see Dad here actually watching the game?"

"No, I'm not."

"Inspirational story on the mound," Janice said.

"Breathe," I said.

Wickman (the bastard) gave up a leadoff double.

Showalter brought in a young lefty, Sterling Hitchcock ("Sterling Seely"?), who promptly yielded a single. I was fuming. But it didn't matter. To my absolute horror, Showalter turned to Xavier Hernandez, a bullpen disaster who lately had been a human gasoline can for fueling opposition rallies.

"Game's over," I said. "Might as well turn off the TV. We lost."

Janice let out a moan, which I accepted as agreement.

"Thank you, Lord Buckington!" I told Showalter, through the TV, using my most derisive nickname for him. "Thank you, thank you, *thank you*, for totally wrecking this moment! Thank you sooooo much."

Kirby Puckett singled, tying the game. Soon Minnesota led.

"Thank you *sooooo* much, Bucky!" I said. "Thank you, thank you, *thank you*, for driving a stake directly into my — "

"*EEEEEEEAEAHHH!*"

"Breathe."

In the ninth, we went down like lambs.

"Hey!" I yelled to the nurse, motioning with the remote. "You want the TV off? Well, here! *Let's turn it off!* There's nothing worth watching, right?"

"*EEEEEEEAEAH!*" Janice said, which I interpreted as agreement.

After midnight, Janice started yelling, the nurses started scrambling, the doctor shouted *PUSH,* I waved her home from third, and — oh, God — suddenly we had a beautiful baby girl.

We named her Madeline. It was as close to Mattingly as I could get.

JUJU RULE 19

Discipline

We have studied the Lookaway as a first-stage defense, perhaps to be used by an international Yankee juju militia in case of an attack. This might work against a collection of bored Long Island housewives trying to revive the Mets with inside-out bras and Shake Weight exercisers, but it won't stand up to the likes of Gino Castignoli and Vladimir Shpunt.

The Lookaway can work only if it is focused like a laser, on a wide scale.

Here's the scenario:

We lead by one in the bottom of the ninth. One out, bases loaded, their best hitter striding to the plate.

In the first inning, you struck him out with an evil eye. In the third, he homered while you rubbed the now shattered ashtray. In the seventh, you induced a pop-up by jogging in place. He's expecting the evil eye. On TV, he's giving you his own version of it.

But he's not going to get the evil eye. We're going to pull the string and throw the changeup, the Lookaway, which he hasn't seen all night.

Before you whip your head from its moorings, yanking the ball with it, think: *Toward what outcome should Yankee fans across the world be applying our collective juju?*

1. Double-play grounder, ending the game
2. Infield pop-up, putting us one out closer to winning the game
3. Fly ball, which could mean a play at the plate
4. Home run, costing us the game
5. None of the above

The answer, of course, is 5, none of the above.

If we always seek big plays and knockout punches, we will lose. And unless everyone pulls in the same direction, our juju will be worthless. We must aim our juju toward a single, direct, and *attainable* outcome — always seeking the smallest increment on every scale.

A first-pitch strike.

Rule 19: *Ninety percent of juju is pitching, pitching, pitching.*

Think: *First-pitch strike.*

Now concentrate on the little white dot and quickly twist your neck like a broken marionette. Paint the corner with your skull, freezing the batter at the knees. *Steeeeee-rike!*

Think: *Second-pitch strike.*

And so on. Small steps. Increments. Every Yankee citizen on the same page. That's all it takes.

That's how we keep our world safe.

22

Peyer

In 1989, seven years into the Great Drought, Yankee fans found themselves rooting for lineups that greased the monologues of late-night comics and fashioned George Steinbrenner into the human face of American incompetence. By September, we would view our starting rotation — Andy Hawkins, Clay Parker, Dave LaPoint, Greg Cadaret, and Walt Terrell — like a list of common criminals.

Adding to my woes was the growing fury of Tom Peyer, my friend and writing partner, who had recently chosen to board the Yankee bandwagon.

Peyer drew political cartoons for the *Syracuse New Times,* a weekly paper that sought to ridicule the second-generation country-clubbers who ran the city. He had amassed fans and critics, maintaining a persona as an aboriginal Syracusan. Peyer rolled his own cigarettes, which most people assumed were joints, and dressed in black long before it became fashionable. Physically, he looked like a pencil with an Afro. Politically, he espoused views that were half Eugene V. Debs, half Bart Simpson, and he drew Ronald Reagan with so many chins that senior citizen groups complained, saying he made dementia look bad.

Peyer had dropped out of high school and wandered the country as a teenager. He never went to college, never learned to drive a car, and never followed sports. Instead, he channeled everything into comic books. Peyer always knew who Superman was fighting and what babe Peter Parker was pining for. He could even outline the deep-seated traumas of J'onn J'onzz, the Martian Manhunter. He claimed that male superheroes were named for their penises: Iron Man, Hawkeye, Colossus, Black Bolt, the Punisher, the Thing, the Hulk, the Beast, Nightcrawler, Mr. Fantastic. (By the way, the Yankees also have their share: the Iron Horse, Stick, the Babe, the Boss, Moose, Superchief, Old Reliable, King Kong, Catfish, A-Rod, Godzilla.) We never did figure out Swamp Thing.

In the mid-1980s, Peyer approached me with a confession. He had grown up in a Yankee household, but during his rebellious teen years, he had rejected the great traditions and history of his subculture. Now pushing thirty, Peyer wanted to reconnect with his lost heritage and start enjoying his birthright: the Yankee championships that arrived every October like apples in the orchards. He asked me to tutor him as a Yankee fan.

Well, what could I say? What manner of friend would say no? Here was a fellow whose intellectual development had been limited to art, politics, culture, religion, science, music, literature, news, ex-wives, and family. I told him, *Yes, of course — I'll do my best.*

I assumed the role of a Yankee Professor Henry Higgins, with Peyer as my Eliza Doolittle. I assigned books and movies. I lectured on critical issues, such as how no Yankee dynasty has ever evolved without a homegrown catcher. I explained that Whitey, Mickey, and Billy were called "the Unholy Trio" due to their superhuman abilities to consume liquor, and that Babe Ruth's pumpkin-size cranium had won him the nickname "Two-Head." I taught basic home juju — where to sit, the Lookaway, furniture pressure points, and the like — kindergarten stuff, nothing that could get him booted from the diocese.

Had I known the Yankee teams that were coming — the Eric Plunks, Jim Walewanders, and Lee Guettermans — I would have told him to visit Alaska, write a screenplay, take up morris dancing . . . anything but become a Yankee fan.

The sad truth is, Peyer enlisted at the start of a six-year barf, from 1987 to 1992, perhaps the unkindest era in Yankee history. We would spend more money than any other sports team, yet we would finish dead last in 1990. Steinbrenner would rip through managers like my Maverick went through quarts of oil.

Worst of all, in Peyer's comic book mind, it was *my fault*. Soon he was running around Syracuse claiming that I'd recruited him, hypnotized him, and made promises that I did not keep.

I write here with a clear conscience:

I sold Tom Peyer NO bill of Yankee goods.

I led Tom Peyer down NO primrose pinstriped path.

By 1989, Peyer was openly defiling my ban on excessive swag. He bought a Yankee jersey, a Yankee warm-up jacket, several Yankee caps, and a Yankee wall clock the size of a capitol rotunda. He began parading around Syracuse like the illegitimate grandson of Lou Gehrig, dropping the names of obscure Yankee players into conversations. (Instead of "Oh, shit!" he'd exclaim, "Hensley Meulens!") Without me, the guy wouldn't have even known we had a farm club in Columbus. Now he was "Mr. Yankee," "the Man in the Cap," "the Back-Page Know-It-All" — and everything that ever went wrong with the Yankees, *everything*, was my fault.

"You said we always win," he'd grumble.

"Nobody can guarantee wins," I'd reply. "Life doesn't work that way."

"You said we always challenge for the pennant."

"I said we *try* to challenge for the pennant."

"Thirteen extra wins a year. That's what you said!"

"That's the average. You can't expect it every year."

"As opposed to *thirteen losses!*"

"Wait a minute. I didn't recruit *you*! You came to *me*!"

"Hey, everybody, look at me! I'm Bruce Springsteen in a hall of Eddie Rabbitts!"

The Yankiverse was wobbling on its axis. Alphonso had reached a perpetual state of rage over the trading of Doug Drabek, now the National League's best pitcher. He denounced every trade, convinced that Steinbrenner could do nothing right. He focused his hopes on a new Yankee farmhand, a pitcher named Al Leiter, whom Alphonso had scouted on a spring training trip to Florida.

"Write this down: Al Leiter, Hall of Fame, class of 2015," he proclaimed. "I think we're turning the corner."

I agreed. With this crop of future superstars, such as Marcus Lawton, Stan Jefferson, and Lance McCullers, how could you *not* burn with hope? On April 30, 1989, four weeks into the season, we beat the White Sox to move into a tie for first in the AL East. Late in the game, the Yankee announcers broke in with stunning news: The Yankees had obtained Blue Jay outfielder Jesse Barfield!

The broadcast team sounded jubilant. We'd found a slugger to anchor the order. That crackerjack Yankee front office had outwitted stupid, incompetent Toronto (baseball's best-run team throughout the 1980s, by the way). We'd stolen a former all-star who was merely slumping (batting .200) and given up only (*cough*) young (*cough*), little-known (*clear throat*) . . .

Al Leiter.

We traded Al Leiter.

I started screaming. I fell to the floor and lay on my back, kicking my feet like a dung beetle. Janice sauntered in from the kitchen, saw it was a Yankee game, and returned to what she was doing. I kept screaming. I wanted to hurt the TV. I wanted to burn down the city. The announcers kept celebrating. They gushed about Barfield's big bat. They marveled about Barfield's arm. They raved about how wily the Yankees were, cutting such a great deal. I just lay there, screaming. The phone rang.

"You lied to my face!" Peyer roared. "Hensley Meulens, I hate this team!"

"*Five years!* We're dead for five years!" Alphonso shouted. "Maybe ten!"

"Barroom eyes shine vacancy," the Dog Man said from somewhere in Jersey.

"YOU AND GEORGE MUST BE MIGHTY PROUD. I HEAR YOU OUTWITTED THOSE STUPID CANADIANS AGAIN."

A cackle call from Glavin, the ultimate bad omen.

Over the next few days, as the Yankee propaganda mills churned upbeat Barfield crapola, with many sportswriters in tow, we smoldered with indignation. These were Steinbrenner's "baseball men" — seasoned scouts, career general managers and appraisers of talent, some of the highest-paid, most experienced professionals in the field — and they were *idiots! Dolts! Fools!* They didn't know a goddamn thing about baseball!

But from the vast Yankee echo chamber, one voice of sanity emerged.

The Scooter. Phil Rizzuto.

Phil couldn't believe the Yankees traded Al Leiter. It made no sense. How could they give up a pitcher with such potential?

Phil was speaking truth to the Yankees. We had found the Prophet.

JUJU RULE 20

The Micrometer

In 1989, after the Yankees obtained Jesse Barfield, the WPIX broadcast team sought to inject hope into the game whenever our new slugger strode to the plate. Even Phil would brighten with the thought that, any minute now, six grinding years would vanish, Barfield would magically change back into the handsome Blue Jay prince he'd once been, and we would win happily ever after.

Then the pitcher would wind up, the ball would soar, and Barfield would take his mighty cut — *bam!* — rocketing the ball skyward. And while the infielders decided who should catch it, Phil would give viewers a lesson on the physics of life.

"Aw, Jesse jussssssst got under that one," the Scooter would say.

"One-tenth of an inch, and that ball is in the upper deck! He jusssssssst missed it."

And he did. He just missed it.

Jesse Barfield just missed them, as Big John Mayberry just missed them, as Ron Kittle just missed them, as Peter Best just missed being a rich Beatle, as Al Gore just missed becoming president, as tomato juice just missed tasting good, as Julius Caesar just missed listening to his suspicions and living to an advanced age, and as Hitler's mom and dad just missed having sex without conception. They all jusssssssst missed them, just as I just missed them back in Little League.

The difference between the grand slam and the infield fly rule.

A micrometer.

In juju, remember: You are not trying to move the outfield walls fifty feet closer. You are not trying to dislodge the 240-pound catcher blocking home plate or topple the six-foot-ten Randy Johnson with a gust of wind. You're not trying to tackle a sprinting fullback or block out a charging LeBron James (*Yankee fan, by the way*). You are seeking to affect the spin of a five-ounce, cork-filled ball as it hurtles through the air. You are seeking to reduce the ball's rotations per second from 50 to 49. That's all.

You are not trying to enter an opposing batter's mind and re-create the "elevator of blood" scene from *The Shining*. You are not trying to control the wind, the birds, the grass, or the locusts. You are not trying to rescind the laws of physics, or even those of the state of New York. You have one point on which to concentrate.

Rule 20: *Never take your eyes off the ball.*

Reduce the spin, or accelerate it. Paint the corners. Shave the plate. Don't try to move the planet. Just concentrate on your micrometer.

In life, it can be the difference in your foot on the brake pedal that stops your car ten feet shy of the oak tree. It might be the difference between life and death, happiness and despair, a world championship and third place. That's all it takes.

A micrometer.

23

★

The Trip

In 1991, Lieber and I returned to Yankee Stadium for another Opening Day, this time backed by an all-star lineup. We had recruited Pudge, a pharmacist from Oswego; Fronz, a former Penn State linebacker; Steve, a token Twins fan; Moose, a cartoonist and travel authority; and Peyer. We'd meet Alphonso at the stadium.

On Monday morning, we boarded Amtrak's Maple Leaf express, hauling foam coolers full of beer, sandwiches, and sticks of pepperoni the size of police batons. A kid asked what was in the coolers, and Pudge, the pharmacist, barked, "Live rattlesnakes!" The kid's family fled. By Utica, the relentless *gooshing* sound of beer cans being opened rivaled Boxcar Willie's storied rhythms of the rails. By Albany, we were a gurgling, incoherent bunch — drunk on our limitless hilarity — which Amtrak personnel sought to quarantine, like the doomsday virus in a Bruce Willis movie.

At Penn Station, we bequeathed our coolers — beer, empties, leftovers — to the first homeless man we saw. Moose, the experienced traveler, deftly hailed a stranger and handed him a twenty-dollar bill to fetch us a cab. The fellow hustled off and, to this day, is probably still looking.

At the hotel, we changed into our road uniforms — acid-washed jeans, grunge plaids, and fluorescent suspenders—fashions too hip to wear in Syracuse without verbal abuse, and taxied to the tourism touchstone of the times: the Hard Rock Cafe.

"Don't expect to see any rock stars there," Moose observed, keenly. "They'll be elsewhere."

Moose chose not to say where. But he was right. Neither Bruce nor Mick was dining at the Hard Rock that night. Unfortunately, nearly every tourist in Manhattan seemed to be. We stood outside for twenty minutes, while Pudge, the pharmacist, regaled street crowds with accounts of an ongoing head lice infestation in Oswego. To the Big Apple scene, we brought a mirthful presence, posing for photographs and yelling, "Live, from New York, it's Saturday night!" Once inside, we ordered hamburger platters and supernachos, which we unanimously agreed tasted better than the hamburgers and super-nachos back in Syracuse—although at $25 per plate, maybe not *that* much better. We drank $4 beers, except for Steve, the Twins fan, who took this moment to disclose that he suffered intense migraines if his lips touched alcohol. I wondered what had possessed him to come. For the rest of the night, he watched us from a short distance, in rapt fascination, like Sigourney Weaver in a gorilla movie.

"Smart move, from a dollars-and-cents perspective," Moose observed, wisely. "One way to save money in New York: don't go drinking."

The next morning, we headed for the Church That Ruth Built.

Having finished last the previous season, the Yankees entered 1991 with modest expectations. Led by Stump Merrill, the most blue-collar manager in Yankee history (with due respect to Billy Martin), they had already played six road games and won two. Their starting pitcher, Scott Sanderson, was playing for his fourth major league team, and batting sixth was Jesse Barfield—still the epicenter of Alphonso's anger. Basically, the Yankees' season, which hadn't yet begun at home, was already over. But we didn't let it show.

"*Holy cow! I am in!*" Peyer shouted, as we found our seats during batting practice. We sat in an upper tier along the right-field line, so far from the field that the players looked like wriggling grains of salt. *"Hensley Meulens! I made it!"*

The forecast called for showers, so I had purchased a twenty-by-ten-foot plastic sheet to drape over us. Otherwise, we maintained our cool travel standards — sneakers, sweatshirts, Windbreakers, Yankee swag. We scorned the boots and heavy coats that would be standard wear in Syracuse.

"You don't want to look like rubes," Moose had said, sagely. "That's how you attract attention."

History records the game temperature that day as 38 degrees. That is a lie. It might have *touched* 38. Where we sat, the windchill — and being from Syracuse, we *knew* windchill — plunged into the teens. By game time, the drizzle had become sleet and then changed into the kind of heavy snow that upstaters describe as "good-packing." We unfurled our plastic sheet and tried to fit everyone underneath it, stomping our feet to stay warm, reminding ourselves that we were from Syracuse and this was balmy in comparison.

By the second inning, Peyer's lips had turned blue, and his teeth were clattering like maracas. Moose, wearing a fashionable denim shirt/jacket, yanked so hard on the plastic that it began to tear. Steve, the Twins fan, had moved to another section. We had stuffed our jackets full of napkins and debris. Now and then, you'd hear a horrible scream as an icy rivulet drained from the tarp down somebody's neck. By the third inning, the sheet had been pulled into strips, which we wrapped around our heads like turbans.

By the fourth, our section began chanting for the game to be called. Fans were streaming for the exits. We figured the game could not last more than five innings. With the Yankees leading by two, we needed six outs, and then we could go home.

"Six more outs!" we chanted. "Six more outs!"

Sanderson promptly served up a two-run homer to Chicago shortstop Scott Fletcher, tying the game. Worse, as the final out was recorded in the fifth, the rain seemed to halt. The umpires and managers huddled. Chants of "Call the game! . . . Call the game!" echoed across the stadium. Then the Yankees took the field.

The crowd poured toward the exits. Peyer and Moose said they could take no more; they'd watch the game on TV in a bar.

"Scattered showers — that's what you said!" Peyer shouted at me. *"Hensley Meulens! You lied!"*

For the next two innings, we huddled in the restroom — amid hundreds of sad, tormented men — like refugees in an air-raid shelter. Nobody spoke. We tracked the game on a restroom attendant's radio. Every paper towel and newspaper in the stadium had gone into a coat. I wore foam coffee cups around my arms and wrapped myself in shards of plastic tarp, which I'd confiscated from Peyer and Moose.

Chicago took a two-run lead into the ninth. With the end near, the restrooms let out, and waves of soggy hoboes staggered toward the empty seats down near the dugouts.

At the pit of every baseball player's memory, there lurks an unforgettable image of the first crowd that nearly drove him to quit the sport. It often occurs in a cold, empty ballpark late in a cold, empty game, when the good people have gone home, replaced by the hip-flask hordes from hell. It is as if the tide receded, exposing a shoreline of hypodermic needles. The ushers have fled. The children are in bed. What remains are beery humanoid creatures, their noses as red as the asses of baboons. They have spent eight innings in the cheap seats, the netherworld, and now they are bringing evil into the boxes of luxury.

Often such a scene represents the standard final inning of a game in Syracuse, or Scranton, or any minor league town that every player seeks to escape. That evening, we brought the minor league experience to Yankee Stadium.

"End this game, Steinbrenner!" Alphonso screamed, shaking his fist at the owner's box. "It's cold out here! We wanna go home!"

We stood behind the dugout, close enough to pound on the roof. Between chants about Steinbrenner, we shouted witticisms about Chicago closer Bobby Thigpen, which he surely had never heard before. Steve, the Twins fan, had joined us and, against doctor's orders, started taking hard swigs from Alphonso's flask.

"You gonna be okay with that stuff?" I asked.

"Thigpen, pigpen! Thigpen, pigpen!" he shouted, tottering on his heels.

As if to spite us, Thigpen walked the leadoff batter. We booed lustily.

Yankee pinch hitter Matt Nokes struck out, trudging back to the dugout to a chorus of "Thank you, Nokes!" That brought up Barfield.

"Al Leiter! Al Leiter! Al Leiter!" Alphonso yelled, waving his arms to rouse what little crowd remained. "Do the right thing, Barfield! Hit into a double play!"

Barfield eyed us coldly. He worked a walk and slowly marched to first base, sneering in our direction, as we booed.

Next, Yankee Mel Hall hit a double-play grounder to shortstop, but he hustled down the line and beat the relay to first.

One more out, and we could go home.

Outfielder Scott Lusader — yes, *the* Scott Lusader — singled to right, driving in a run and sending Hall to third.

Tying run at third.

Lieber's face fell into his hands. Suddenly, we confronted our worst fear: extra innings. We could not survive extra innings. We would die. Worse, we would miss our train home. We had to be at the train station by 7:30. It wasn't fair. We'd lasted nine horrible innings. It wasn't fair.

"We gotta go soon," Lieber said. "We can't stay for extra innings."

Next up, a kid named Leyritz.

"Who the hell are you?" Alphonso screamed. "End this fugging game, whoever you are!"

Leyritz drew a walk. Bases loaded.

Lieber poked my shoulder. "Base hit and we win," he said. "Base hit — *and we win!*"

We stared at each other. Alphonso turned to the crowd and began throwing imaginary confetti.

"Get up, everybody!" He swung his arms. "Base hit and we win! We are going to win this thing!"

Next batter, Steve Sax. The Yankee second baseman strode to the plate in a deluge of sound.

"Greatest Yankee comeback of all time!" Alphonso shouted, then spun to add. "Barfield, you still suck!"

"First-pitch ball!" I shouted. "First-pitch ball!"

"#%#@ you, Chicago, you $#@%, cheap #$@% bastards," Steve, the Twins fan, screamed. The rest of us stepped away from him.

Sax struck out on three pitches.

We were outside the stadium, running for the subway, before the second chorus of "New York, New York" had begun.

Later, Alphonso and I realized that we had witnessed an incredible phenomenon. For nine innings, we rooted for the Yankees — with no luck. As soon as we rooted *against* the Yankees, the team rallied. Then, when we again switched polarity and started cheering *for* them, the rally ended.

I mentioned my experience with Bill Buckner, back in Bonfatti's house. As soon as I began rooting for the Redsocks, they fell apart. We started piecing together anecdotes from throughout our lives as Yankee fans and scientifically analyzing the implications.

Was there another unknown force out there, an anecdotal counterbalance to Rizzutonic emissions? It made sense: for every action, there is a reaction; for every positive, a negative. Could we tap into this dark force? Had we been doing juju all wrong? And had we just uncovered a way to turn the Yankees around?

JUJU RULE 21

The Neg

In April 2008, the great Redsock slugger Manny Ramirez announced to the world that he had finally found the path to inner peace. It came in the pages of *The Secret*, Rhonda Byrne's best-selling New Age book, which preached the power of "positive energy."

The book, required reading for realtors, argues that positive energy is, well, *super!* And few people on the planet could use more upbeat vibes than Manny, who was known to refuse media interviews, wear sunglasses in discos, throw to the wrong base, jog out grounders, threaten team officials, use banned substances, and disappear inside the Green Monster to pee during pitching changes. "Manny being Manny," Redsock fans said dismissively. As long as he was hitting, no problem. Why take the cheese sandwich out of his pocket?

But now, with positive energy from *The Secret*, Boston could expect a new and improved Manny. The slugger's spiritual reawakening birthed a litter of happy news articles. "There's a lot that comes with Manny that's so good," Redsock manager Terry Francona told the *Boston Globe*, in a story that glowed like Lady Gaga (*Yankee fan, by the way*) in the presence of a klieg light.

Yeah, right.

By July, Redsock Nation wanted to hang Saint Manny from Fenway's Pesky Pole. Despite his newfound "positive energy," the slugger dropped fly balls, punched out the team's traveling secretary (what is it with traveling secretaries?), and called in sick with injuries that never showed up on MRIs. Then Manny committed the ultimate sin: he stopped hitting. Fed up, Boston dealt Ramirez to the Dodgers for a bucket of fried chicken, and that summer Manny was consigned to hell, three rings below the nuclear waste dump reserved for Yankees and serial killers. All this, just three months after he'd discovered *The Secret*.

Listen: If a book makes you happy, great. Be upbeat! Chant! Chirp! Meditate! Become a better human resources director. See the glass as half-full. (Or see two balls and one strike as a half-full count.) Make a groovier life for all.

But optimism wins no pennants.

Rule 21: In juju, never expect to win.

Never host a victory party. Never say the game is won. Never go to bed early. Never think your team will win.

Obviously, this is hardest for Yankee fans, who must dwell on negatives despite enjoying *thirteen extra wins per season.* Pessimism requires discipline.

Most Yankee fans are earnest, salt-of-the-infield lug nuts. They go to work every day, watch the game every night. They practice juju in the privacy of their homes, and they don't run around claiming to have struck out Josh Hamilton by doing squat thrusts. They are true Yankee heroes. Nevertheless, too many of them lap up YES Network Yankaganda like starving dogs around an overturned ice cream truck. Their "positive energy" costs us ballgames.

They do not understand Reverse Rizzutonic Juju Emissions, or RRJEs (pronounced *reh-jees*).

A pioneer of negative juju, Alphonso *never* speaks positively about the Yankees, regardless of the score. By "bringing the neg," he forms around the team a protective condom of impenetrable gloom. This verbal sheath provides a counterbalance to the oafs who think a John Mayberry will be reborn merely because the Yankees just assumed his bloated contract.

Alphonso's pessimistic rants on Yankee websites often rouse denunciations from fellow fans. They don't realize that when he calls for the Yankees to bench the previous night's hitting star, he is secretly expressing delight. Some question his Yankee allegiance. They do not understand that he is producing RRJEs.

Before *you* attempt RRJE negativity, some warnings:

1. Never use RRJEs around children or let anyone under age twenty-one use them.
2. Separate baseball negativity from pessimism in life. Be dour about your team but not about your spouse, family, or job.
3. Guard against hope. Don't let a few solid outings by a rookie pitcher destroy months of well-deserved negativity.
4. Be creative in your gloom. Always think, *What's worse than*

the worst-case scenario? Don't settle for a loss. Predict injuries and bad trades.

5. If the team *does* melt down, note that you predicted it.
6. Tell *everybody* how hopeless you feel. Be consistent. Don't debase A-Rod in one house, then go next door and sing his praises. The juju gods will know.
7. Concentrate your negativity on fellow fans. A twenty-minute A-Rod rant to an Armenian-speaking cabdriver does no good.
8. If you find yourself feeling positive, keep your mouth shut. Remember: *Nothing good comes from predicting a victory.*

The phenomenon of RRJEs extends back to ancient times. The Bible tells of prophets in wooden yokes who foresaw floods and plagues. They were condemned for their negativity. In fact, they were just working the umps. They knew that just because the world did not end today, that doesn't mean it won't end tomorrow.

Always predict a loss. Worst-case scenario: the team loses, and you're a prophet.

24

★

The Rizzutonic Verses

The next time I set foot in Yankee Stadium, I didn't have to worry about snow or sitting in the upper deck, barely in the same area code as the pitcher's mound. Instead, I sat behind home plate in a VIP section reserved for players' wives and hookups, and I prepared to appear on the New York Yankees television broadcast network as a special guest of the team.

This is not a literary metaphor or a dream. My fifteen minutes of fame had arrived.

For several years, Peyer and I had tried to make it as a humor-writing team. Once a week, we'd meet in his kitchen, churn out five hundred words on a topic, and send it off. We sold a few pieces to *National Lampoon,* but most submissions flew off into the void, never to be heard from again.

Thanks to Steinbrenner, we never lacked material. The hair, the weight, and the tantrums made George the Johnny Appleseed of punch lines. In fact, we enjoyed writing about him so much that sometimes we didn't even bother submitting pieces to magazines. We just sent out news releases. On October 3, 1989, this story appeared on the Associated Press wire service:

SYRACUSE, N.Y. Being manager of the New York Yankees is a tough job. So tough, in fact, that it's rare for one manager to make it through a whole season.

Recognizing that fact, two writers have come up with an award to honor one of the two or even three men "who serve as Yankee managers" each year.

The New York Yankee Manager Recognition Council, which consists of Hart Seely and Tom Peyer, has named Dallas Green 1989 Yankee Manager of the Year. Bucky Dent, who replaced Green when he was fired Aug. 18, was named first runner-up.

The award, given for the first time, will annually be given to the New York Yankee manager who "exemplified the conduct of a true Yankee manager," Seely and Peyer said.

"Every American child dreams of being—for at least one moment—Yankee manager," said Peyer, a writer for DC Comics. "Sadly, only a few per season can achieve this goal. We hope the award will encourage excellence and competition among those called up to serve in this noble—yet fleeting—capacity."

Our release ran on the sports pages in San Francisco, Chicago, and New York. We felt like giants of fandom, speaking truth to Yankee power.

But nothing George did could top the benders of alternative reality that Phil Rizzuto regularly uncorked on TV. Rather than rehash the most recent Yankee loss, we relived Phil's latest stories. He became our reason to watch Yankee games.

One day, I mentioned my idea from long ago: that Phil's words should be set in verse. Peyer couldn't grasp the concept, so I taped a game in Minnesota and showed him an example.

ALIENATION

I think my head shrinks a little
In this indoor stadium.

I am . . .
The mike is getting bigger
And I have to tighten it.

Peyer laughed so hard we grew depressed. It was funnier than any joke we ever wrote. But hardly anybody else would get it. We had fallen too deeply into Phil's reality. The poetry was a lost exercise, a waste of time. Nevertheless, a few days later, Peyer found one.

TO BE ALONE

Hey, White
You know where your loyalties are?
Right here.
The old pinstripes.
No.
You never wore them.
So you have a right to sing the blues.

We laughed ourselves into another funk. This was torture. Not only did the Rizzuto poems have no market, but they could get us sued. We tabled the idea. Whenever Phil spoke, however, we heard poetry.

In 1990, after the Yankees finished last, we sold a piece to the *National,* a sports daily run by Frank Deford. It was titled "Who Should Buy the Yankees?" We wrote thumbnails on six potential owners, including Steven Spielberg:

> **Club characteristics.** No final scores in sellout games, leaving sequel possibilities open. High-intensity spotlights, dry ice and low music every ninth inning. Bat boys decipher opponents' signals, save the day.

Deford asked for more stuff, but we had basically retired our cleats. After splitting the $100 freelance payment, we were earning less than a ten-year-old Korean seamstress on retainer for Kathie Lee Gifford. For lack of a better idea, we dug up a few Rizzuto poems and sent them.

Deford said he loved the concept, but it was too "New Yorky" for a national audience, which wouldn't know Phil Rizzuto from Phil Donahue. He suggested we try the alternative weekly the *Village Voice*. We changed the name on the cover letter and sent the poems off.

Days later, a *Voice* editor named Jeff Z. Klein called. He asked if he was too late — were the Rizzuto poems still available? We wondered if he was crazy. Two weeks later, *Voice* readers opened the Jockbeat section to see "O Holy Cow! The Verse of P. F. Rizzuto." It began this way:

> No sooner had leadoff hitter Steve Sax opened the Yankees 41st season on WPIX-TV than poetry began to issue forth from baseball's bard of the booth. With the count of one-and-one, Philip Francis Rizzuto began to compose the kind of spontaneous epos Carl Sandburg once called "the journal of a sea animal living on land, wanting to fly in the air."

The *Voice* printed six poems, including "Alienation." Best of all, Jeff said he wanted a weekly installment.

A steady gig. We were in heaven: being paid to watch Yankee games.

Then again, we wondered what Phil would think. We didn't picture Rizzuto as a devoted reader of the *Voice*, which focused on issues such as gay rights and nuclear power, and which printed page after page of steamy personals.

"Here's one Phil will like," Peyer said. "'Gay White Male, 33, 6'2, 220 pounds. Bearded, heavily tattooed. Seek straight-acting GWM for fun and friendship.'"

"We're gonna get sued," I said.

"Here's another. 'Gorgeous white male . . . pure muscle, no flab . . . herpes in total remission.' Maybe that's Don Mattingly."

"We're about to become the most reviled Yankee fans in history," I said. "We will be the only people on the planet who are hated by Phil Rizzuto."

By midseason, "The Verse of P. F. Rizzuto" had become a regular installment in the *Village Voice,* and no cease-and-desist letter had yet arrived. We just kept harvesting verses.

T-BONE

One ball, one strike
Two out, two on
The Yankees trail four to one
In the bottom of the seventh.
Michelle wants to say
"Happy Birthday to T-Bone."
That's his name: T-Bone.
The runners leading away . . .

Late that season, a small New Jersey publishing house called the Ecco Press phoned with an offer. The editors wanted a book of Rizzuto poetry, gleaned from the upcoming season. Again we wondered, *What about Phil?* It was one thing to publish goofy poems in an alternative weekly, another to sell a book based on his name. The editors sounded perplexed. They had assumed we had done everything with Phil's approval.

We made an offer: if Phil would bless the book, or just not denounce us in public, we would donate our royalties to charity. (*Note:* Ecco did pay a $5,000 advance, which Tom and I split.) This was no humanitarian gesture; we simply didn't want to be dragged from our beds and lynched from a batting cage. Besides, it was a poetry book. Nobody would even notice it.

Soon word filtered back from Ecco. Phil was onboard. Yogi had seen them, and Yogi had laughed.

Thus my most vivid memory of the following season: I am lying on the floor, eyes closed, listening to a VCR tape of a Yankee game from two weeks earlier. Whenever I detect Phil's voice, I try to visualize each word on a printed page. A stack of unwatched videocassettes sits in the corner. Each is a Yankee loss. I don't bother to go through victories, because in such games, Phil follows the action too closely. His best tangents occur during Yankee defeats. A blowout loss is the Saudi oil fields of Rizzuto poetry. When we fall far behind, Phil contemplates the hills, the things kids do with cardboard boxes: poetry.

So went the dreariest season of my Yankee life. Losses stacked upon losses. We came in fifth, twenty games out. Peyer had moved to New York City to work at DC Comics — another escapee from old *Sorry*cuse. We worked apart, which made it hard to compare ideas. The previous season, chasing Phil's poetry had been a weekly treasure hunt. Now it loomed as back pain and piles of losses. I stopped watching games live. I practiced no juju. From opening day on, the games moved into tedium.

I WALK WITH FEAR

Boy
I never forget
The first Dracula movie
I ever saw.
BELA LUGOSI!

Our conduit to Phil became a young, earnest Ecco editor named Bill Crager. He described visits to Rizzuto's house like trips back in time. Phil's wife, Cora, would set out a tray of coffee and pastries, and they'd retire to the sitting room. One topic would glide into another, and then another, and then suddenly the afternoon had passed with nothing accomplished.

"Maybe I'm going crazy," Crager said, "but whenever Phil speaks, I hear poetry."

Phil had asked where the poetry idea had come from. I told Crager about driving the back roads outside Sayre, listening to Phil and Bill White. I recalled that day listening to Phil discuss fishing. Crager pushed for more details. So I tweaked it: I said that I'd come to a bridge along the Susquehanna River where two boys — a black child and a white child — *were actually fishing,* and I thought, *Look! Eureka! Poetry!*

Later, Crager said that upon hearing the story of those two little boys, Phil wept.

I felt like a slimeball.

In September, we sent everything to our editor, Chris Kingsley. By January, we sensed a buzz. *New York* magazine wanted an interview. Roger Angell mentioned us in *The New Yorker.* George Vecsey called from the *New York Times.* And that spring, after a long conversation, Janice handed me the phone.

"CONGRATULATIONS! YOU AND GEORGE ARE THE NEW SYLVIA PLATH."

Glavin.

In the *New York Times Book Review,* Robert Pinsky — the future U.S. poet laureate — took time off from translating Dante's *Divine Comedy* to wax about our book, which he said "captures the slightly out-of-it, slightly mindless, amiable and unheroic state of confusion that takes up far more of any life than we who experience it may like to admit."

Pinsky knew the deal: you cannot put down a put-on, unless you are prepared to become the butt of it. We had stumbled onto the ultimate punch line, the inside joke, and anybody who didn't laugh would look like a fool. (Like book reviewers would look now, claiming that juju doesn't work, right? It's an inside joke, and anybody who doesn't appreciate it will look like a fool, right?) Pinsky was no fool. He climbed aboard.

Soon my phone was ringing off the hook with calls from people across the country wanting Phil to appear at their son's bar mitzvah or to wish their mom a happy birthday. Of course, Peyer and I had our own request: a gala book-release party, where we would cavort with Yankee greats, literary stars, and supermodels. Soon the date for that event was set: never.

At age seventy-five, Phil saw no reason to appear at some trendy bar to watch drunken dorks toast his words. And without Phil, who would come?

But late that summer, Crager phoned in a state of jubilation. We would appear with Phil on a televised Yankee game. We'd have an entire half inning to talk poetry and plug the book. The *publisher's* wildest dream had come true.

For weeks, I fantasized about my TV appearance. I would crack jokes, tell delightful stories, and, as the third out was recorded, be told by the hosts that I simply *had* to stay another inning. In this fantasy, Peyer was sick that night.

We made a game plan. Janice would keep the kids and videotape the game. Whenever I said "Mattingly," it would be secret code for "I love you." I would say it several times. I would travel to New York with Moose, drawing on his travel savvy. On the train ride, he would supply a few zingers. When Moose was in a funny mood, he could be Woody Allen (*Yankee fan, by the way*) in the body of Alec Baldwin (*Yankee fan, of course*). I would just relax, laugh, and write down his lines.

But that morning, Moose arrived at the Amtrak station with gunnysacks under his eyes. His girlfriend had dumped him. He said he was too depressed to go.

"Nonsense!" I said. "You'll be fine. We'll have a great time."

I told Moose to rejoice. He was a free man, about to be unleashed in the world capital of hot babes. His girlfriend had done him a favor.

She wasn't right for him. They had never been on the same level.

"What do you mean by that?" Moose said.

Nothing, I said. It was a figure of speech.

By Utica, Moose still hadn't spoken. I could steal more jokes riding with Elisabeth Kübler-Ross. By Troy, he had begun to ping-pong, his girlfriend going from "the greatest thing I ever had" to "really stank up the bathroom."

"All right," I said. "Let's focus on the game. I need a funny line that leads me to the word 'Mattingly.'"

"Mattingly says she can go to hell!"

At the stadium, we found Crager nervously watching Peyer roll a cigarette while cradling a beer in his free hand.

"You know, I would hold off on the beer," Crager said.

Peyer took a long, hard swig. Crager winced and marched off to the broadcast control center.

And then . . . *there he was!*

At first, I didn't recognize Phil. He looked so tanned, so cool, so spiffy in a powder-blue suit. Crager made the introductions, and Phil extended his hand. A crowd instantly formed. A lady pushed a magazine into Phil's face, demanding his autograph. He studied the page, saw a scantily clad model, and said, *"Hooooooo-leee cowwww!"* The crowd applauded. More were coming. Eyeing the surge, Phil said he'd see us later and dashed away quickly. I realized why they called him "Scooter."

Crager led us to seats behind home plate, where the rows were filled with the visiting team's groupies. One spoke at length about a particular infielder whose penis was the size of an adult dachshund. Moose—the bachelor—didn't even notice. He was drinking his fourth beer, one for each of the voices in his head.

It began to drizzle. For nostalgia's sake, Peyer chanted for a rainout and ordered another round of beers.

"You know, I really don't think that's a good idea," Crager said diplomatically. "Say, have you guys thought about what you're going to say to Phil?"

"I'm going to ask his opinion on the Catholic Church pedophilia scandal," Peyer said.

Crager pondered that for a moment.

"You know, I really don't think that's a good idea," he said.

He rubbed his hands together and decided to go check things in the WPIX booth.

At that point, the juju gods — or maybe an Uppercaser — intervened. The drizzle became droplets, the droplets turned to rain, and the rain turned to a fire hose. Lightning flashed from Old Testament clouds, and the ladies fled, soaked to their astonishing nipples. We scurried into a nearby tunnel to see Wade Boggs, dressed like a golfer, dash to an idling Range Rover and speed from the park. Moments later, Bob Sheppard's voice came over the public-address system to say the game was rained out.

We saw Crager trudging our way, stooped at the shoulders. He seemed to have aged ten years. Peyer handed him a beer, and he accepted it.

"Well, when do we come back?" Peyer asked.

Never, Crager said. WPIX had one home telecast left in the season. It would be stocked with celebrities. We missed the cut.

My last memory of the night is of Crager standing in an Irish bar near Peyer's office at DC. He is surrounded by a group of scruffy British comic book writers. They have heads the size of weather balloons, though not one weighs 120 pounds. Crager is glassy-eyed, tottering on his heels, in a heated dispute with one of the writers.

Crager says Swamp Thing has no superpowers. He is just Swamp Thing. A superpowered Swamp Thing could fly or see through objects. Swamp Thing can do neither. Thus, he has no superpowers. The scruffy comic book writer says being Swamp Thing means having superpowers. The guy says Crager doesn't know a goddamn thing about Swamp Thing. Crager says no, *the writer* doesn't know a goddamn thing about Swamp Thing.

Takeaway thought for the night: nobody knows a goddamn thing about Swamp Thing.

My fifteen minutes . . . rained out.

But the juju gods weren't done. Weeks later, a package arrived in the mail. It held a copy of *O Holy Cow!*

"To Hart . . . O Holy Cow!" Phil wrote. "Here's to poetry, and those two kids fishing."

JUJU RULE 22: COINCIDENCES

The Politics of Juju

In a 2007 Republican presidential candidate debate, former Massachusetts governor Mitt Romney identified the one issue that unites America: Hatred of the New York Yankees.

At the time, Romney was seeking the support of the GOP's anti-Yankee faction, the Curt Schilling Republicans. The group is named after the Boston pitcher who achieved fame in 2004 through the alleged "bloody sock," Redsock Nation's version of the Shroud of Turin. During the AL Championship Series, Schilling shut down the Yankees while allegedly bleeding from his ankle.

(*Note:* I use the phrase "allegedly bleeding" because, amazingly, no DNA analysis on the Schilling garment has ever been performed. Nor did Major League Baseball take immediate custody of the sock following the game. Despite all the hoopla, the footwear was whisked away to Schilling's private estate, where he had ample time to doctor the fabric with animal blood or that of his children.)

It is generally accepted that no living person hates the Yankees more than Curtis Montague Schilling. His Internet blog often criticizes Yankees, Yankee fans, Yankee blogs, and New Yorkers — that is, when it's not paying homage to America's eight years of peace and prosperity under President George W. Bush. Schilling may someday run for public office in Massachusetts behind the slogan, "Vote Curt: Because YANKEES SUCK!"

In early 2010, Schilling's anti-Yankee zealotry altered the course of U.S. history. At the time, Massachusetts attorney general Martha

Coakley seemed destined to win the U.S. Senate seat vacated by the death of Edward "Ted" Kennedy — a seat that had been held by a Democrat for forty-six years. Polls showed Coakley, a Democrat, leading Republican newcomer Scott Brown. Then Coakley made an incredible gaffe: she called Curt Schilling "a Yankees fan."

Coakley quickly retracted the comment. Too late. Massachusetts voters had witnessed an act of ignorance that could never be erased from public memory. Brown rolled to victory, which pundits hailed as a rejection of President Barack Obama's national health care program. From that point on, Obama never wielded the power of his 2008 election mandate. The so-called "public option" on health care disappeared, and the president accepted a watered-down set of reforms on the domestic issue that was most likely to define his legacy.

Once again, the Yankees were rerouting the nation's course.

Throughout history, the team has served as America's invisible Siamese twin: When we win, the nation wins. When the Yankees suck, America sucks.

You can look it up, during booms and busts.

Bust. World War I (1913–1920): *No Yankee pennants.*

Boom. Roaring Twenties (1921–1928): *Three Yankee world championships.*

Bust. Great Depression (1929–1931): *No pennants.*

Boom. New Deal (1932–1941): *Six championships.*

Bust. World War II (1942–1946): *One championship.*

Boom. Eisenhower/Camelot (1947–1964): *Ten championships.*

Bust. Vietnam War/Watergate (1964–1975): *Not even one fricking pennant.*

Boom. Bicentennial (1976–1981): *Three championships.*

Bust. Recession/Gulf War/S & L crisis (1982–1995): *No pennants. Nothing.*

Boom. Internet bubble (1996–2000): *Four championships.*

Bust. World Trade Center attacks/wars/mortgage meltdown (2001–2008): *No championships.*

Boom. Mini-recovery (2009): *One championship.*
Bust-Great Recession? (2010–?): *?*

In the summer of 2008, the U.S. economy collapsed, dropping property values in parts of the country to levels not seen since the early 1990s. Simultaneously, the Yankees folded and failed to make the playoffs for the first time since . . . the early 1990s.

That winter, Congress passed an unprecedented $152 billion stimulus package. The Yankees followed suit, spending $423 million to sign CC Sabathia, Mark Teixeira, and A. J. Burnett.

The economy briefly rebounded, and the Yankees won the 2009 World Series. The following year, both suffered setbacks.

Coincidences?

Rule 22: In juju, there are no coincidences.

This begs a question: if the two fates are intertwined, could Yankee juju also lift America?

Sadly, the answer is no.

No lotus position will ever provide shelter for a homeless child.

No torturing of an inanimate object, however well-intentioned, will push the hurricane out to sea.

American politics already has plenty of Reverse Rizzutonic negativity. And as for the Lookaway? Unfortunately, it is how we Americans deal with most of our problems.

Today, most Americans — on the right and left — believe they possess no juju in national politics. They have concluded that no matter how hard they try, they cannot change the system.

What the hell happened to us? Our great-grandparents seemed to hold such clout. But recent generations, much like the juju gods, have seen their powers shrinking.

In ancient times, the juju gods controlled weather systems, crop harvests, and entire economies. They were Big Shots, Uppercase Deities, and they starred in numerous oral traditions. Ah, glory days! Then the world changed. Fat old men in headdresses started sacrificing virgins, and jerks in flowing robes began burning people at stakes. Who wanted to be God at such events? And then came the missionaries with their killer germs, and the TV preachers, who flashed teeth the size of marshmallows. Today, being a headline God means handling the bearded clerics with the shining eyes and suicide-bomber vests — the unluckiest shirts ever worn. Who wants such work?

Once the Uppercasers took over, the juju gods were demoted to the bureaus and the sports desk, assigned to fix ballgames. It had to be a blow to their egos. Nevertheless, I suspect they were relieved. They must have been tired of dealing with wars, inhumanity, and the dictators who claimed to have their ears. I bet they're happier just watching ballgames and trying not to think about all the suffering in the world. (It works for me.)

So can Yankee juju affect the nation? No. The Yankees can only mirror America. We are the superpower. Everybody hates us. Everybody blames us for what goes wrong and takes for granted what good we do. We spend too much. We always face some crisis. We're always fretting over arms. We're always somebody's target. And be it friend or foe, everybody wishes they could be us: the Yankees, the United States of Baseball.

Still don't believe the Yankees' impact on the country? Let us consider a tale of two leaders.

In the summer of 1998, thousands of fans converged on a quaint village in upstate New York to celebrate the induction of one all-time great into the Hall of Fame. No, it wasn't the Dodgers' Don Sutton heading into Cooperstown. The crowd that day was celebrating First Lady Hillary Clinton's enshrinement in the National Women's Hall of Fame in Seneca Falls. Her speech electrified the throngs and, in essence, launched Hillary's candidacy for the U.S. Senate in New York.

Soon Hillary faced her own Buckner ground ball. Though known to be a lifelong Cubs supporter, Hillary donned a Yankee cap and proclaimed herself a Yankee fan. She might as well have put on a coonskin and claimed to be Daniel Boone. Republicans quickly accused her of pandering to the worst element of the American electorate: Yankee fans. One Hillary hater, Thomas Kuiper, titled his attack book *"I've Always Been a Yankees Fan."*

Outraged critics demanded that Hillary remove the sacred Yankee cap: she had not earned the right to wear it.

Lesser politicians would have punted. Not Hillary. She claimed to have loved Mickey Mantle as a child, and she scrounged up a photograph of herself in a Yankee cap, purportedly taken in 1992 (when we finished fourth). She never bailed, never renounced, and won the U.S. Senate election over Republican Rick Lazio (*Met fan, by the way*).

Hillary never pimped the Mets, Jets, Nets, Knicks, Islanders, Rangers, or even the Westminster Kennel Club. She didn't reminisce about Willis Reed or conjure up a teen crush on Frank Gifford. She targeted one fan base, only one, and she never loosened her bite on Derek Jeter's ankle, even after her boss in 2010 turned out to be a White Sox fan.

Thus, Hillary avoided the political quicksand that condemned Rudy Giuliani to a lifetime of FOX News all-star panels and jokes about the Hair Club for Men.

Throughout the 1990s, Rudy was a fixture at Yankee games, always sitting next to the dugout, in maximum photo op range. People loved or hated Rudy's politics, but no one denied his Yankee fan credibility—that is, until 2007.

That year, after the Yankees tumbled from the playoffs, Rudy—the GOP presidential front-runner—announced that he would root for *Boston* in the postseason.

The nation gasped. The hero of 9/11 had revealed himself to be a wobbler, a wuss, a wearer of crimson panties, and—to the Yankee power elite—not one to be entrusted with the nuclear football. The *New York Post* Photoshopped a Redsock cap onto Rudy's shiny head under the headline RED COAT. The *Daily News* cried TRAITOR! Topps later inserted Rudy into the Redsocks' 2007 World Series victory card: it shows Boston players celebrating, with Rudy leaping into the fray.

Giuliani attributed his secret fetish for red stockings to some previously unknown loyalty to the American League East. Nobody bought it. In fact, the harshest rebukes came in the dark glares from the Curt Schilling Republicans whom Rudy hoped to befriend. Even fans who appreciated Rudy's courage in coming out of the closet backed off publicly. He looked like a YINO: Yankee fan In Name Only.

Sensing an opening, Hillary pounced. She vowed to never — *absolutely never* — cheer for the Redsocks. She would rather be slathered in jalapeño oil and shot naked into the sun. That day, across the Yankiverse, she became Hillary Rodham *Winston Churchill* Clinton, a future U.S. secretary of state.

Rudy's presidential campaign tanked. The GOP selected John McCain, representing the Arizona Diamondbacks, as its candidate. But it was too late. Shaken by Rudy's show of weakness, the nation soured on Republicans, ensuring Obama's victory.

Your Yankee juju won't move the needle between times of boom and bust. But it might decide who controls that needle.

25

★

Yankee Incentive Rewards

Years ago, my aunt Connie found a grainy, black-and-white home movie that had been shot in the Seely family backyard in Waverly, probably during the 1940s. It shows a group of people standing in front of the garage, where I would someday win the World Series. Some are probably neighbors who dropped in that day to see the new gizmo.

Holding center square, looking regal and Rotarian, is my grandfather and namesake, the inimitable "Hart *I AM!*" He squints into the sun and poses like a statue, apparently not buying into this notion that you should move in front of a movie camera. Now and then, the people beside him wave to the lens. Clearly, this group has not honed its skills for reality TV.

Off to the far left stands one figure whose mannerisms are unmistakable. He appears to be in his late teens, hair slicked back and looking visibly bored. He slouches, shifts his weight, sinks his hands deep into his pockets, and then pulls them out to check his watch. He's in a hurry to be somewhere else.

The guy everybody thinks they recognize as me is, of course, my dad. I looked just like him as a teen, but I grew up vowing not to be him.

I would raise my kids as Yankee fans in a Yankee way of life. No hatred. No enemies. No drumming. Just Yankees.

Still, considering my roots, I could not trust DNA to supply the dominant Yankee fan gene. Thus, I decided to add established behavior modification techniques to my Yankee youth program.

If I had failed in teaching Peyer the true Yankee ways, it was only because he began too late in life, and the team stank for his first ten years. My children would know a better world.

"Hey, look, the game is on," I'd yell, coaxing the family toward the TV, as if it were the tree on Christmas morning. "Holy cow! We're playing the Redsocks!"

"We want *FernGully*!" Hart and Kyle would demand.

"No *FernGully* tonight," I'd say. "Roger Clemens is pitching, and that means bean balls will be flying!"

"Beam baws!" Maddy would shout.

Educators say the way to teach proper behavior is to mix praise with punishment, the carrot and the stick. Unfortunately, Janice — who grew up in St. Louis, a Cardinal fan — vetoed my use of the stick. She said no child would be punished for refusing to root for the Yankees. Our family would respect freedom of speech.

That was fine with me. The last thing I wanted to be was one of those domineering parents who tells his kids what to think. I would simply put out a menu of choices and then let each child decide for himself or herself which team to support.

Of course, as a caring parent, I wanted them to recognize the value of thirteen extra wins per year. Therefore, I instituted Yankee Incentive Rewards, loosely modeled on the sky miles programs offered by commercial airlines. Here's how it worked: if we won the World Series, I would buy each child a special gift.

A few parental know-it-alls have questioned Yankee Incentive Rewards, calling it "bribery" and "brainwashing." Nothing could be further from the truth. I would like to address this on several points.

1. I did not offer gifts for regular-season victories. Indeed, to pay for those wins would be overkill. I limited the rewards to Yankee world championships. Keep in mind: we had not won one since 1978. Who could have anticipated four in five years?
2. Yankee Incentive Rewards created teachable moments. The kids learned which chairs to avoid, the importance of not disturbing an adult while he was working, and the need for left-handed bullpen depth.
3. What the hell was I supposed to do, put a stupid gold star on their poster boards? Get real. Modern kids don't want a pat on the back. They want bling! They want cash on the barrelhead! It's a changing world. Get with it, bloated education bureaucracy!
4. I did not pay bling or cash on the barrelhead. There were no sleazy twenty-dollar handshakes or under-the-table payments. Everything was conducted out in the open. Nobody can say it was slimy.
5. I bought cheap gifts, under five dollars. I broke no family budget.

If Yankee Incentive Rewards failed, I personally blame point number 5: you cannot teach loyalty to the New York Yankees on a budget that belongs to the Seattle Mariners. If you expect the Steinbrenner family to shell out for free agents, shouldn't you shell out on behalf of your kids? Unfortunately, with Janice basically opting out of the program, I was required to keep costs at a minimum.

In its first year, 1996, Janice tolerated Yankee Incentive Rewards, and the kids loved it, even though they generally had no clue what was happening during games. Harty and Kyle would cheer the Yankees until bedtime, which usually arrived around the third inning. (On the

East Coast, World Series games start at 8:35 P.M., sadly putting them out of reach for children.) I would report the final scores the next morning at breakfast. That year, the Yankees won, and I bestowed on each child a dollar store coloring book and candy. They reacted like Sally Field accepting an Oscar.

By 1999, however, after the Yankees had won their third-straight world title, the coloring books were not cutting it. We now had three kids in the program, and the six-year age difference required a challenging range of gifts. Moreover, even if Harty and Kyle did not fully understand the famous "bullpen bridge to Mariano," they definitely recognized the World Series as the "bridge to Christmas." By 2000, they viewed Derek Jeter as their October Santa—and in divisive moments, due to our salary cap, they increasingly viewed him as their *cheap* October Santa.

As the 2000 postseason neared, grumbling emerged about the previous year's haul. Kyle even claimed—he still claims, by the way—that he never received his 1999 Yankee Incentive Rewards gift. That is simply not true. Unfortunately, Kyle had outgrown his Barney the dinosaur phase and had flung himself headlong into the Mighty Morphin Power Rangers. He received a Barney coloring book, which he wrongly perceived as an insult and made no secret of his disappointment. To the degree that he knew of Derek Jeter, he blamed the Yankee captain.

In 2000, the kids demanded to know in advance what the Yankees were going to bring them.

"Wait a minute," I said. "Let's not jinx the team. They haven't even won anything yet."

"We want a Nintendo GameCube," Harty said. As oldest, he had assumed the position of spokesman and chief negotiator.

"Nintendo GameCube!" Kyle chimed in.

"Tendo GabeCoob!" Maddy shouted.

"Well, this will be a tough series, and I guess if you all pooled your gifts—"

"Nobody's getting a GameCube," Janice said coldly. "That's a

Christmas gift from Santa. Get that out of your heads. Jolly old Saint Derek is not bringing anybody a GameCube."

The kids looked to their mom, then back to me.

"Your mom is right," I said diplomatically. "The Yankees cannot bring you a GameCube."

They looked to her, conferred a moment, and then turned back to me. "We want money," Harty said.

I glanced to Janice, whose eyes shook her head without moving it.

"I'm not doing cash," I said. "We're not going to put a price tag on a World Series. This isn't something that comes with a dollar amount attached. Absolutely not. But if we were thinking about it, what figure would you have in mind?"

They were in the ballpark of twenty dollars per kid, more if the Yankees swept. I looked to Janice. She mouthed the words "No way."

"I can't go twenty," I said.

They conferred. Again, Harty stepped forward.

"Fifteen, and we'll root."

I looked to Janice, who was gritting her teeth.

"We're not paying money," I said firmly. "No money, and no Nintendo GameCube. They're out."

The kids whispered a moment.

"Okay," Harty said. "Then we *don't* want the Yankees to win!"

"No Yankees!" Kyle chimed in.

"No Yang-geez!" Maddy shouted.

"Well, now that's a really bad idea," I said. "You start to play that game, and you know what? When the Yankees win, you'll get nothing! You understand? You'll get nothing!"

The kids conferred, then Kyle eyed me coldly.

"I didn't get anything last year."

I am not the kind of father who keeps sales receipts from the dollar store in order to prove that a Yankee Incentive Rewards gift was given. We had reached an impasse, and Janice was called in to mediate.

"Let's watch *FernGully,*" she said.

During the games, she would herd the kids into the proper chairs and keep them out of my base paths. They would be hypnotized by the sight of me on the floor, flopping like a circus seal, and she'd make sure nobody took a flipper to the head. At one point, Janice criticized me for attempting to dislodge the ball from an opposing infielder's mitt by throwing myself onto the floor at the precise moment of impact.

"That's it," she said. "Out! *Out!* Do you really think you're going to knock the ball out of a player's mitt? *Take it outside!*"

I tried to explain that, obviously, I was not trying to knock loose the ball. Everybody knows you can't knock a ball loose, but I was working on the next pi —

"Take it outside before you break the TV!"

I tried to explain that I would never hurt the TV, and —

"Take it outside!"

Soon I was walking the backyard, looking for places where I could soft toss a tennis ball against the garage wall. She had planted flowers, making it impossible. On Saturdays, she and Marge agreed to take both sets of kids so that Hank and I could watch the playoff and World Series games with the Secret Yankee Club without having to deal with them. The Yankee Incentive Rewards program was quietly discontinued.

Today, if given the choice, all of my kids prefer that the New York Yankees win. They know that, at least in the Seely home, life is slightly easier when that happens.

The reason? Their mom roots for the Yankees as her secondary team. God help me if we ever play a World Series against the Cardinals.

JUJU RULE 23

Stars

I believe we have entered the next phase of human evolution. Through selective hookups and Darwinian TV show competitions, society has begun breeding celebrities with celebrities, creating supercelebrities, the most amazing pieces of work to walk the planet since the age of reptiles.

Some fans believe that these beings will possess powers and abilities far beyond those of mortal men and that their juju will be able to turn a C. J. Nitkowski into a CC Sabathia. They believe the future will belong to the team that controls not just tomorrow's Dustin Pedroias but also its Sarah Jessica Parkers (*Yankee fan, by the way*).

They are completely wrong.

Rule 23: *Wealth and fame destroy juju.*

Yes, if you're a no-name shrub, you possess far more juju than the roundest Kardashian will ever know.

Why is this? The juju gods don't like big shots. Can you blame them? Every night, the Uppercasers get worshiped in churches, temples, and mosques (and at political fundraisers) — praised for whatever has happened lately, even if it's an obvious screwup. Meanwhile, the juju gods work late, finagling the West Coast scores. The Supreme Beings can do no wrong. For them, every human being is just a big brown nose. But the juju gods can't walk to the bus without catching a snide comment. Why didn't Ichiro's ball go fair? What do they have against the Twins?

So if Cameron Diaz (*Yankee fan, by the way* — at least while she was dating A-Rod) dons a rally cap, the paparazzi will take notice, but not the juju gods. They have enough divas up in the sky. They don't need any down here.

Nevertheless, celebrities can boost public juju in the way a speedy leadoff hitter improves his teammates' batting averages. If regular folks see Regis Philbin (*Yankee fan, by the way*) stand on a chair and windmill his arms, they'll follow suit. Thus, teams regularly welcome whatever *Page Six* beefcake/cheesecake sashays through the turnstile, be it today's Sexiest Person Alive or an ex–porn star whose lips have begun to leak.

Yankee fans can draw on the world's most powerful registry of celebrity contacts, outside the cell phone of Heidi Fleiss. Our roster includes renowned actors (Jack Nicholson, Denzel Washington, Robert De Niro), singers (Paul Simon, Paul McCartney, Jay-Z), and comics (Adam Sandler, Billy Crystal, Larry David). We dance with the stars.

Okay, enough about wealth and fame. I know what you're thinking: "If so many great celebrities are Yankee fans, why do so many people hate them? Why do I constantly hear about what pig-faced whores they are? Why do so many people think Yankee fans are mean and obnoxious?"

For starters, those people are fools.

That said, some Yankee fans believe their job is to pretend to be insufferable jerks. People expect it. If we don't put out cigarettes on their kitchen floor or mock their taste in dungarees, they're disappointed. They want someone to embody pure evil. And let's face it, in every James Bond film, the meatiest role always goes to the villain.

Nevertheless, it's hard playing a boar-headed lout, especially when it's the exact opposite of your true nature. Therefore, I often give tips to Yankee fans on ways to keep our "bad fan image" alive.

1. **Small-market = small brain.** Use the term "small-market" as if it means "stupid." Example: "I know you're small-market, Ed, but I'm asking you to try to understand the big picture." Or, "Yes, John is a small-market fan, but that doesn't make him a complete idiot!"
2. **Accent.** Do not talk like a New Yawker. If people think you're from New York City, they'll forgive you. What riles them is the notion that you root for the Yankees because they win (which is, of course, why). If possible, use a British accent and big words, preferably without meaning. Example: "That Curtis Granderson chap is absolutely scinnn-tillating!" Or, "Don't you agree that Joe Girardi can be profoundly titular?"
3. **Angry taxpayer.** Never hesitate to complain about the millions of dollars in luxury taxes that you — that is, the Yankees — pay annually to other teams. Act as if it comes out of *your* pocket. Remember: *You* are the taxpayer, and *they* are the

freeloaders and welfare moms. Example: "All we want is for Major League Baseball to get off our backs. These small teams, do they think our tax money grows on trees?"

4. **Shopping.** When the conversation turns to a player, inquire about his contract. Example: "Ah, yes, Albert Poo-hols. Do tell me, when does he come up for sale?"

5. **Appearance.** Wear a black eye patch. Grow a black beard and, if possible, metal jaws.

6. **Expenses.** Whine that big money is ruining the game. Example: "What's this league coming to when you can't even buy a utility infielder for four million dollars?"

7. **The tab.** After spending the entire dinner boasting about your Yankee wealth, leave 'em with the check.

Of course, small-market fans can be obnoxious in their own ways. They often corner me, looking for the latest gossip on Derek Jeter. I tell them they've come to the wrong fan. I tell them that Jeet ("I call him Jeet") has his own life, and it's none of their damn business. I couldn't care less whether he's with Jessica, Adriana, Vida, Jordana, Mariah, or Minka (the *Friday Night Lights* ex-cheerleader who may still have the inside track, according to the little birdies that chirp in my left ear). And I don't go around blabbing. That's how Jeet and I have stayed together so long. He doesn't gab about my private life, and I don't gab about his.

I try to greet small-market fans with a gracious smile, like Miss California visiting a high school. It means a lot to people when a Yankee fan is kind. They don't expect it. I ask about their players and feign interest in the team because it pleases them. I'll praise a Blue Jay pitcher without even mentioning that he'll soon be a free agent.

Now and then, you'll experience one of those moments that forever tugs at your heartstrings. A small-market fan, maybe a child, will mention his or her favorite player and ask sheepishly, "Are you guys going to sign him?"

My response is always the same: "Yes."

26

★

Bringing the Neg

Alphonso's last great Yankee hope was Brien Taylor, the top pick of the 1991 draft, which the Yankees earned for being baseball's worst team. Taylor's 98 mph fastball, plus an Oprah-like mom and the power agent Scott Boras, convinced the Yankees to pay an unprecedented $1.55 million signing bonus. Alphonso called it chump change. He said Brien Taylor was destined for Cooperstown.

Then the dice turned cold. Taylor's career collapsed in a bar fight, when he attempted to throw a 98 mph uppercut.

"CONGRATULATIONS," Glavin rejoiced. "YOU AND GEORGE HAVE THE HIGHEST-PAID BAR BOUNCER IN AMERICA."

"Five years, we're dead!" Alphonso raged. "What was I thinking? How could I have been so gullible? We're dead! *Dead!* Five years! *Ten!*"

In the early 1990s, I was turning forty, with a wife and three kids, living in Syracuse to stay, and still writing that damn novel. My main character was Eddie, a drifter who lived in his alternative Yankee reality and who planned to send the world a violent message. Every few months, I would hit the writing wall, lapse into my own Yankee reality, and rescramble the book from start to finish. I figured it was five years away, maybe ten . . . like Alphonso's Yankees.

But in 1993, a new ray of Yankee hope emerged: a young manager named Buck Showalter seemed to be channeling the fiery soul of
Billy Martin. Showalter would order a slugger to bunt or tell a tired
pitcher to just suck it up and throw, and his unorthodox moves usually worked. In 1995, he guided us to the playoffs for the first time in
thirteen years.

The last time my team played in mid-October, I was twenty-nine,
new to Syracuse, falling in love, and expecting to win every World
Series. Now Showalter's Yankees seemed overmatched against the
mighty Seattle Mariners, with Jay Buhner, Tino Martinez, and Randy
Johnson. But we battled Seattle to the final out. We lost an iconic five-
game series in the eleventh inning, as Ken Griffey Jr. slid into home. I
went to bed that Monday morning feeling we had restored the Yankee
name. We had kept our dignity, and I would wear my cap proudly.

Unfortunately, the loss did something to George Steinbrenner's
brain. He bullied Showalter into quitting and — to the horror of
Yankee fans everywhere — replaced him with a man whose name had
become synonymous with losing baseball teams.

"CONGRATULATIONS," Glavin rejoiced. "YOU AND GEORGE
CERTAINLY HAVE A BRIGHT FUTURE."

"It's a deathtrap, it's a suicide rap," the Dog Man said, calling from
somewhere.

We had hired Joe Torre, who in fourteen seasons managing the
Mets, Cardinals, and Braves had never won a pennant.

"Twenty years!" Alphonso roared. "*Thirty!* I won't live long
enough! We're done! You hear me? As of now, the Yankees are dead to
me! *Dead! From now on, they're all yours!*"

After I explained that I didn't want them, Alphonso issued a clarification: He would never again speak, write, or think a positive word
about the Yankees. He would never chat up a prospect, never approve
a trade, never believe in a hitter — never again swallow the troweled-
up crapola that was spewed by the team, the players, the coaches,
the announcers, the publicists, the sportswriters, the papers, the net-

works, the fans, the bloggers, or me. He would never again speak optimistically of the Yankees. Never again. Ever.

In the months that followed, Alphonso kept his promise with a vengeance. He mounted a daily e-mail smear campaign, in which he ripped the Yankees in ways that cannot be recounted here. His savage attacks violated not only both of our employers' e-mail policies but fundamental rules of human decency. Every morning, I would receive a message — usually several — full of capital letters, exclamation points, and dark conspiracy theories about trades the Yankees were considering. They went beyond most anti-Yankee screeds Glavin ever contemplated. I'd never seen anything like it from a brother fan.

Then a strange thing happened. *It worked.* The more Alphonso raged, the more we won.

He thundered pessimism about Torre's plan to hand the shortstop position to a rookie: *Derek Jeter.* He questioned the intensity of our new catcher: *Joe Girardi.* By July, it became clear that we had tapped into a source of incredible power.

Alphonso was unleashing Omnidirectional Reverse Rizzutonic Juju Emissions (ORRJEs, or "orgies"). I'd seen a variation of ORRJEs during the Buckner event, and we'd both witnessed it in the cold Yankee home opener. By pretending to be speaking to me, Alphonso could say things to the juju gods without fear of retribution. We staged our conversations, speaking in secret code, while Big Juju Brother listened, clueless to our real plans.

Now, every day, Alphonso "brought the neg." A Yankee victory, no matter how encouraging, just provoked harsher criticism of the team. He whined about Jeter. He ranted about David Cone. After every game, he called for someone's trade or demotion to Columbus. At times, it seemed as if Alphonso were snatching the bad ideas directly from Steinbrenner's brain, before they could hatch into the real world.

Alphonso's greatest ORRJE moment came in game three of the 1996 World Series. The Yankees had lost the first two games to

Atlanta in a demoralizing fashion, and we were losing the third by a score of 5–3. The Braves had brought in their fire-balling closer, Mark Wohlers, to put us out of our misery.

"We're dead!" Alphonso shouted on the phone. "I've turned off the TV! I'm going to bed! We lost! *It's over!*"

He slammed down the receiver, as if to show the objects around him what to expect if things didn't change. Moments later, the backup Yankee catcher, Jim Leyritz, homered, reversing the entire World Series.

(*Note:* I would love to take credit for Leyritz's shot, but when Leyritz came to bat, I was standing on the back porch feeling sorry for myself. I missed the pitch.)

(*Additional note:* I have subjected the porch to numerous juju tests over the years and never repeated the Leyritz success. I can categorically conclude that standing on the porch played no role.)

When Leyritz homered, I began screaming so loudly that Harty woke up and came downstairs. I kissed him and told him we'd get him a dog. (We did.) Immediately, the phone started ringing. Yankee fans were checking in. Conversations grew so involved that I even forgot to call Glavin and politely ask what was on TV tonight. Alphonso called again, restating that he had turned off the TV and gone to bed. He was likely summoning Mariano Rivera to close the game.

From then on, in key postseason games, Alphonso would call during the late innings to report his disgust.

"It's over," he would say. "We've lost, I've turned off the TV, and I'm going to bed."

And we would win.

After the 1996 World Series, Alphonso's bank sponsored a float in the Yankee victory parade down the Canyon of Heroes. Because of his love of the Yankees, he was selected by his employer to ride on it. He stood on a flatbed truck, as throngs of Yankee fans studied him, threw objects at him, and yelled, "Who the fuck are you?" Alphonso just smiled and waved, comfortable with his secret role in the team's success.

Now and then, Janice would ask how Alphonso was doing at work. I would throw up my hands. How would I know? We never discussed our lives. I didn't know what he did. Hell, I couldn't even name the bank where he worked. What kind of life did he lead? I didn't care.

Then one day, that changed.

JUJU RULE 24

ORRJEs

The story goes that Albert Einstein, standing beside a chalkboard full of incomprehensible equations, called on a student whose hand was in the air. "Dr. Einstein," the pupil said, "couldn't your formula be used to make an incredibly destructive bomb?" The renowned theoretical physicist replied by quickly erasing the board.

I considered erasing this chapter.

America doesn't need a nuclear bomb assembly kit posted on the Internet. Why put the Gino Castignolis and Vladimir Shpunts of the world a click away from the latest advancements in theoretical juju weaponry? But it's too late to wipe the blackboard clean. (Besides, the publisher paid in advance.)

Like it or not, humanity must confront the awesome anecdotal power of Omnidirectional Reverse Rizzutonic Juju Emissions. Through advanced capabilities of spin, reenactment, and computer-generated graphics, today's ORRJE anecdotes can be embellished thousands of times, creating the most terrifying juju forces ever known.

But to understand ORRJEs, we don't need Einstein's chalkboard of mumbo jumbo. The formula can be stated in nine words:

Rule 24: *When things are good, keep your damn mouth shut.*

The so-called jinx rule is hardly new to civilization. Its roots ex-

tend back to the first apelike grunts of human language. During the
Dark Ages, people understood that the mere mention of a demon's
name would call him to your doorstep, ready to poison your goat.
To speak about your good fortune required a defensive "knock on
wood," a knuckled Morse code for "Forces from hell, please don't kill
me."

Do you think our universal fear of jinxes merely evolved, without
cause?

Whether we believe in God or not, humanity has never quite shed
its paranoid sense that our phones are tapped, the walls have ears, and
the bugs are — well — *bugged,* and that whatever we say can *and will*
be used against us in the Last Judgment. The universe takes notes.
Little pitchers have big ears. Loose lips sink ships. Silence is golden.
Words can kill. Speak no evil. Watch what you say. STFU.

But who is listening on that omnipresent party line? God? Allah?
Satan? The government? All of the above? And if we're not blasphem-
ing, should we care? After all, everybody says stupid things. They
can't send us all to hell, or for that matter, Guantánamo Bay. Do the
math; there's not enough space. If God hasn't yet struck down Charlie
Sheen, should any of us worry? He's humanity's canary in the mine.
(*Note:* If at the date of this publication, Charlie Sheen is no longer
chirping, substitute Donald Trump.)

Nevertheless, this we know: the juju gods hear every word.

So watch what you say, especially about tomorrow's game. If you
laugh at an opposing player's slump, be prepared for him to burst out
of it. If you host a victory party, expect to lose the game. And if, before
the final out, you shout, "We've won!" . . . Well, just don't.

Before revealing the procedural tactics of ORRJEs, I have one final
disclaimer: Please . . . read no more. Burn this book. Forget baseball,
forget juju, build a tree house, take walks in gardens, read a book of
Jewel's poetry, fall in love. Stop here. Stop now. Erase the chalkboard.

Reader, this is not the Lookaway or the Snap-off. This is not phoning Rush Limbaugh to complain about Democrats or yapping with
the highway crew about the cleavage on last night's reality TV. Every

word, every intonation, every guttural bleat must achieve a perfect Zen equilibrium of righteousness and deceit.

Yes, you read correctly: deceit.

You must lie, bald-faced. We're talking about chicanery — a scam, a sting operation. You must *trick* the juju gods into intervening on your team's behalf, without them suspecting that they've been had.

Yes, we are talking about eyeball-to-eyeball, man vs. Fates dishonesty. And when mortals duel immortals, guess who usually wins? Legends tell of tragic fools who thought they could outsmart the forces that run the universe. Eve befriended the serpent. Faust sold his soul to Mephistopheles. George W. Bush asked Dick Cheney to find a vice president. It's always the same outcome. As they march to heaven in self-congratulation, they don't even wonder why Saint Peter has three heads.

(Ironically, the lone anecdotal victory by lowly mortals comes in the 1955 musical comedy *Damn Yankees,* in which a middle-aged slob cuts a deal with the devil to defeat the Bombers. Satan's harlot, the beautiful Lola, succumbs to the power of love, and the Yankee-hating fan limps home to his dumpy, Yankee-hate-filled life. This is supposed to masquerade as a happy ending. However, in the real world, the Yankees get screwed out of their rightful pennant, and a few years later, offstage, JFK gets shot.)

In our "private" discussions, Alphonso never speaks positively about the Yankees. Never. We both understand what will happen. So we go along with the fake conversation, speaking not to each other — but to the party line.

Constant negativity requires great discipline. Once, Alphonso berated David Cone through an entire perfect game — nine innings of sheer hell. After each batter, he projected a meltdown and called for Cone to be removed. With two outs in the ninth and New York leading by six, Alphonso still predicted Cone would cost us the game. After the final out, he never cracked a smile. He simply said we would lose tomorrow. It was a performance for the ages, and apparently the juju gods never even suspected what was happening.

Always predict defeat. Never speak optimistically. Accept the fact that we are fools, clowns, laughingstocks, that we know nothing about everything. Predict the worst. What are the odds that you'll be right?

Remember: You cannot appreciate what you have until you lose it. No one understands this more than Alphonso.

27

★

Alphonso

I remember Janice lying upstairs that morning, sick in bed with instructions from the doctor to rest, drink orange juice, and be waited on — the kind of orders she generally takes to heart. I stayed home from work, sparing her the usual four-alarm emergencies to make the school bus. The kids were gone. It was a day off. A mini-vacation.

I remember my own state of drunken anticipation. My great American novel, "Fireworks Night," which for twenty years had trampled my life like an occupying army, was done. It was polished, proofed, printed, and ready to hit a publisher: *done*. From now on, I could sit back and be discovered, appreciated, *validated*. I foresaw book tours, TV interviews, and publicists. Of course, I would resist the siren call of wealth and fame, staying true to my humble upstate roots — *for maybe two years*. Then *Hollywood Squares,* here I come! I'd skip to LA, buy a swimming pool on a hillside, and take up nose-candy Buddhism.

This was my baseball novel, the GED requirement for every literary bear. I could see the list inscribed at Cooperstown: Malamud, Roth, Coover, Sayles, Kinsella, Lardner . . . *Seely*. Moreover, this book would lift me out of that career cellar that was regularly summarized by ex-colleagues who, when returning to Syracuse, would say, "Seely, you're still *here*?" Yeah, I was still here. Reporters came and went, but not me. They padded their résumés. I padded my obit. I had become a newsroom fixture, an icon of old Syra*curse,* as fixed in place as the bronze plaques that commemorate the Erie Canal. I was whatshisname, that big Yankee fan, the one who stayed. *You're still here? What happened?*

But now it didn't matter. My book was done.

Its main character was "Eddie from Syracuse," a heavy-drinking drifter who inhabits the Yankee Matrix, a psychotic world where car alarms shout, "Mar-i-an-o, Mar-i-an-o," and robins chirp, "Paul-y-o-neel, Paul-y-o-neel." He roams the country, ranting about the Yankees to radio call-in shows. He meets a young woman who seeks revenge on her egomaniacal dad, the owner of a baseball team. To protest the corruption of the national pastime and America, they blow up baseball stadiums.

I remember e-mailing my daily Yankee screed to Alphonso. We had beaten Boston over the weekend, and I was cackling that my pet first baseman, Nick Johnson, finally had found his stroke. For months, I'd been predicting that Johnson would someday win a batting title. I announced that the Redsocks' season was over, and I began setting our rotation for the playoffs. We were, after all, reigning world champions.

In saying such things, I was throwing batting practice. Alphonso quickly would fire back a point-by-point tirade of negativity. Nick Johnson would break his wrist, Boston would go on a tear, and our bats would turn Syracuse cold. That's how we worked: I set the table; he brought the meat. We'd trade e-mails all morning, riding the juju train to another pennant. It had worked for most of five years. And when you're winning, why take the cheese sandwich out of your pocket?

I remember my computer dinged around ten o'clock, telling me I had an e-mail. I figured it was Alphonso's reply, which was overdue.

But this one came from the newspaper. An editor wanted to know if anyone had friends living or working near the attack.

I turned on the TV. It showed smoke billowing out of the New York City skyline. Something protruded from a building. It looked pretty comical, and I started laughing. But what caught my attention was the voice of Tom Brokaw. It had dropped an octave, deeper and darker than usual. It was like turning on a ballgame and knowing from John Sterling's tone that we were eight runs behind. I marched upstairs and plugged in a TV for Janice.

As we watched in horror, I remember wondering whether any Yankees could be in those towers. I couldn't think of friends — just ballplayers. Later, I would ponder dozens of friends who lived in New York City — *good grief, Alphonso, for starters!* — a long list of folks who might have been affected. But that morning, I thought only of the Yankees. Years later, when a similar tragedy actually *did* involve a Yankee — a pitcher named Cory Lidle crashed his plane into a building — I would recall a sense of shame and isolation: how shallow could I be, thinking of a sports team when the world was on fire? But that's what I did. I saw the smoke and thought, *No Yankees; nothing I need to worry about.*

Sometimes you'd give anything to take back even thoughts.

I remember standing there, dumbly watching TV, drinking coffee, and waiting for Alphonso's reply. I was ready to dash off another note, joking about the plane and wondering whether Jeter was okay. But Janice suggested otherwise.

"You ought to call him," she said. "Ask him if his daughter is safe. I think she works in the World Trade Center."

I remember my stomach clenching. I knew Alphonso had daughters from a previous marriage. I knew they were fully grown and out of college. And I knew he cherished them. After that, I knew nothing. Why would I? We never discussed our lives. *Who cared about our lives?* For twenty years, we'd talked about Mike Pagliarulo and David Cone, Jeter's women and Mattingly's soul. Family? Career?

None of that mattered. We enjoyed the perfect Yankee friendship —
all Yankees, all the time, like the YES Network. Nothing got in our
way.

Every day, we volleyed messages back and forth without an atom
of personal information, unless to note that one of us was going on
vacation and would be out of reach. Years earlier, Janice had mentioned that Alphonso's bank faced a takeover bid, and she was wondering how he was faring. It was news to me. She knew more about
him than I did.

I went downstairs and saw an e-mail message from him. His
daughter *was* in one of the towers. After the first plane hit, a few floors
above her, she phoned. She was going to leave the building. Minutes
later, she called from a stairwell. Alphonso could hear shouts in the
background. He begged her to hurry. She sounded frightened. He
said he loved her. Then everything went blank. He dialed her number
over and over. Nothing.

Alphonso said he was sure that his daughter was dead.

I knew exactly what he was doing. He was bringing the neg. He
was writing the absolute worst possibility in this world and sending it
to me . . . because that was how terrible things did not happen.

I e-mailed back to say she would be okay. Because that was how
we worked. That was how we won the World Series. That was how
we kept our players healthy. That was how we kept our Yankee world
spinning on its axis.

Alphonso wrote that he was leaving the office. He would try to
find answers. He didn't know where to go. He didn't know what to do.
He kept dialing her number. Nothing. She would have called by now.

I went upstairs to tell Janice. She was crying and staring at the TV.
The buildings were no longer there.

I didn't call for a while, because I knew Alphonso wanted the
line open. When I finally broke down and started phoning, I stu-
pidly dialed an old number, no longer in service, and kept getting a
busy signal. By midafternoon, Alphonso's wife had called Hank from
England, where she was attending a conference. Air travel had been

halted around the world. She could not get home. She feared her husband being alone that night.

Late that afternoon, Hank called to say he would drive to New York City after work. I said I would go with him.

Around 8:00 P.M., we set out on the four-hour ride, just as we had done two years earlier. On that occasion, Alphonso had secured tickets for a World Series game against the San Diego Padres. We sat in the upper deck along right field, near where Tino Martinez's pivotal home run landed. By the third inning, we developed a juju move against Kevin Brown, the San Diego starting pitcher. Whenever Brown went into his stretch, we shouted, *"First-pitch ball!"* And sure enough, Brown — famous for his pinpoint control — began throwing first-pitch balls. Then we yelled, *"Second-pitch ball!"* and it worked. Others joined in. Once, to start an inning, we forgot the juju, prompting an old guy to turn around and say, "Hey, you didn't yell!" On the next batter, the whole section screamed, *"First-pitch ball!"* We never stopped. We broke their ace. Tino hit his home run. From our far-flung section of the stadium, *we won that game.* It had been a glorious night.

Now, as we rolled through the Catskills, I started to tell Hank how my great American novel was officially kaput. Nobody was going to publish a book about lovable terrorists blowing up baseball stadiums. But I had to laugh. I couldn't feel sorry for myself, compared to what Alphonso was facing. We rode in silence.

We got lost near the Tappan Zee Bridge. Hank phoned for directions, and a family friend of Alphonso's answered. She asked us to hurry, because she needed to get home and she didn't want to leave him alone.

We arrived around 1:00 A.M. Police gumball machines flashed in the streets, and people stood on the sidewalks, staring at the smoky lights that flickered over Manhattan. When Alphonso opened the door, his eyes were full of clouds. He walked with a hump in his back, as if carrying a weight. He tried to smile, and we hugged.

He gave updates, attempting to sound analytical and detached, as if telling a story about somebody else's daughter. Midway through a thought, his voice would seize up, as if a trapdoor had opened and he'd fallen through.

On TV, with the volume muted, a psychic named Miss Cleo hawked her 99-cents-a-minute hotline.

"It's the only channel that's safe," Alphonso said. "I just can't watch that building fall again."

All day, he had worked the phones. He no longer had any hope. She would have called by now. His daughter was twenty-four, a beauty, just starting life. A good job. A network of friends. Loving parents. She would have called by now. Her roommates would have heard from her. He didn't know what to do. She would have called by now. He didn't know where to go. She would have called by now. He needed to keep the phone open, but what did it matter? *She would have called by now . . .*

The phone would ring, and he would leap to it. Hank and I would glance at each other. But it was never the voice he wanted to hear.

Around 3:00 A.M., as we sat dumbly on the couch, Alphonso turned to me and wiped his eyes. "So let me get this straight," he said. "You really believe Nick Johnson is a future batting champion?"

For the next few hours, the New York Yankees became our morphine drip. Whenever the pain grew too acute — and it did, again and again — we simply raised the name of some Yankee player, like a child picking up a toy, and we discussed him furiously, until each of us had nothing more to say.

Alphonso scrounged and found a VHS tape of the 1998 World Series game that we had attended. He pushed it into the TV, and we watched it from the beginning. We yelled, *"First-pitch ball!"* as Kevin Brown prepared to throw, and sure enough, his pitches missed the strike zone. We cheered Tino's home run, as if we didn't know it was coming. We laughed over the memory of that perfect night, and we drifted in and out of the horror of the previous day. Whenever we needed it, we just went to the morphine, full-tilt, no questions asked.

You really think Nick Johnson is for real? Yes, I do! And let me tell you why . . .

As the game wore on, I began combing my novel for material. I recited my character's Yankee rants almost verbatim. I told them of his moneymaking scheme: *Yogi Beer: You ain't drunk till you're drunk!* I did the riff on Cal Ripken, which I'd stolen from Peyer: *Some hero, Ripken! He beats a guy with a terminal disease! Big deal, consecutive games! You want to know what shows up for every single game? The dirt!* And when we heard car alarms in the distance, I said they were saying, *Mar-i-an-o, Mar-i-an-o*, and I got Alphonso laughing so hard that for a moment or two, I think he was in another place. We were drunk and tired to the point of delirium, but several times, for a few minutes, nothing else mattered; we talked Yankee baseball — *Yes, Nick Johnson is on the verge of a batting title!* — and we laughed until we cried.

I was Scheherazade, keeping him awake until dawn. I never ran out of material. After all, I had a whole novel to recite.

The book never went to a publisher. I spent the next fifteen months rewriting it, trying to make it fit the post-9/11 world. Each version was worse than the previous one. In the end, it became a fantastical mishmash. Friends read it and shook their heads.

I spent twenty years writing it, all for one night. I have no regrets.

JUJU RULE 25

Forgiving

On TV, fans often wave signs that say, "We believe!" These are not Yankee fans. Yankee fans do *not* believe. Yankee fans *know.*

This knowledge stems not from the bliss of thirteen extra wins per season, or a list of pennants that will overheat your bubble-jet printer, but from our sense that the universe long ago decided which baseball team to favor. On a daily basis, we give thanks for this secret executive order, offering our juju without fanfare or comment, much in the way that political lobbyists discreetly leave behind grocery bags filled with cash.

Some fans question why any respectable deity would allow itself to be linked to the Yankees. They see us as a cutthroat organization, a franchise that would trade the newly resurrected David Wells for the ever-darkening Roger Clemens, or that would sign Alex Rodriguez to a contract that made him not only forever wealthy but also forever marked. They view the Yankee lineup as they do the menu at Applebee's: start with the price and read leftward.

But money does not define the Yankees any more than it does the rest of America. What matters is the spirit, the juju. And the key to juju is one's heart.

Rule 25: Always forgive.

That shortstop who just let a ground ball shoot through his legs? Tonight you can demand his liver served with fava beans. But tomorrow he's your shortstop (or backup shortstop). Support him. Root for him. Forgive him.

I'm not suggesting that you be a "good sport." (If George Washington had been a good sport, this book might be about cricket. The passenger pigeon was a good sport.) But never blame a player because *your* juju fell short. It's not his fault, and it's not yours. If anybody screwed up, it's that scheming, mean-spirited recliner. Get rid of it. And forgive, always forgive.

In July 2010, my cell phone registered a call from Alphonso's number. I knew it was coming.

"We're done," he said. "Five years, maybe ten."

"Twenty," I said. "It will never be the same."

"I didn't think it could happen," he said.

Our great scourge and pariah, the man who'd traded away entire decades, George M. Steinbrenner III, had died.

"We'll never have another one like him," I said.

I have spent much of my life privately prosecuting George Steinbrenner's crimes against humanity. I've condemned his firing of managers, even when they needed to go. I've denounced his trading of prospects, even deals that worked. Yes, George could be a fool, a laughingstock, a clown. Yes, whenever some washed-up rust bucket came on the market, George *had* to sign him. And yes, whenever life was good, his turtlenecked jowls would suddenly appear on TV, as if beamed from hell, to announce the firing of a third-base coach, merely because he could.

But when my team lost, I knew I was never alone in punching the wall. Somewhere out there, George was making some poor stick of furniture wish it had never heard of the New York Yankees.

No owner ever loved his players more than George. At times, he loved them too much, the way fathers sometimes do their children.

They say George spent his life trying to impress his father. He always fell short. In 1978, to honor his dad, George built Henry G. Steinbrenner '27 Stadium at the Massachusetts Institute of Technology. His old man's reaction: "That's the only way you'd ever get into this school."

Listen: In juju and in life, all fathers and all sons must be forgiven. It is our only hope. *Always forgive.*

For nine years after his career ended, Roger Maris scorned invitations to Yankee Stadium. Then one day, he stood at home plate with tears in his eyes and fifty thousand fans chanting his name, and he forgave. That was 1977, and the Yankees won the World Series.

For fourteen years after George fired him, Yogi Berra refused to have anything to do with the Yankees. Then one afternoon in July 1999, he emerged from the dugout on Yogi Berra Day, while the capacity crowd went wild. A few minutes later, David Cone threw a perfect game.

Then there was Mickey Charles Mantle, born in the Dust Bowl of Oklahoma. At nineteen, he reached the majors. At twenty-four, he won the Triple Crown. At twenty-nine, he chased Ruth's home run record. At thirty-six, he could barely walk. At forty-five, he was a falling-down drunk. At sixty, he needed a liver. And at sixty-four, he begged forgiveness from every child and fan he had ever disappointed, because the great Mickey Mantle was not man enough to be a god. Days later, he died. At the next home game, they played his favorite song, "Over the Rainbow." Everyone stood and cheered. They forgave.

Five times, George fired Billy Martin. Five times, they forgave each other. That's how they worked their juju.

In early 2010, the Yankees reacquired Javier Vazquez. In essence, they forgave the man who had thrown the pitch that ended eighty-six years of global harmony.

Sadly, baseball does not always forgive — as Pete Rose and "Shoeless Joe" Jackson learned, and maybe Barry Bonds will yet discover. But most fans know better. They stand and cheer even for those who have failed us.

Some critics call this a sign of moral weakness and declining standards. They equate forgiveness with forgetfulness, and they go through life reliving each defeat, nurturing it like a seed planted inside them.

Avoid those people.

Up until now, that included *me*. Now, in the name of juju, I hereby forgive Sandy Koufax, Bob Gibson, George Brett, Tim McCarver, John Mayberry (who, damn it, was *never* going to hit for us!), Curtis Montague Schilling, and . . . George. And . . . yes . . . I do hereby forgive Javier Vazquez.

28

★

Apocalypse

On October 16, 2004, the New York Yankees defeated the Boston Redsocks by the lacrosse score of 19–8 to take an insurmountable three-games-to-oh lead in the American League Championship Series. I recall a night of cartoonish merriment — the kind of self-pleasure that, on a molecular level, could theoretically involve sex with everyone on the planet. In my younger days, I would have danced until dawn.

I luxuriated through most of what turned out to be the longest nine-inning game in postseason history — a ridiculously gratifying four hours and twenty minutes. Before it had ended, Alphonso and I were giggling on the phone like pie-eyed debutantes, marveling at our prowess, and planning an appropriate victory bash.

I floated off to bed before the final out.

Let me repeat that statement, for the judgment of eternity.

I . . . Hart I. Seely III . . . knowingly and without concern for my Yankee brothers and sisters, and for the juju gods they serve . . . *went to bed before the final out.*

What followed over the next five days was — to be charitable — the most disgraceful collapse of any organization, group, or human collective in history.

I won't sugarcoat this. If you have a pacemaker or are on heart medication, turn the page. Spare yourself and your laundry. As a professional journalist and truth teller, I will not hold back the scalding, unvarnished candor that must follow.

The 2004 Yankees — and we pink-potted ferns who trundled off in our shiny, silken pajamas — facilitated the most embarrassing, spirit-dissolving, soul-peeing, crap-ass, wussy choke in the history of this planet.

BIGGEST CRAP-ASS WUSSY CHOKES IN HISTORY

1. Yankees, ALCS vs. Boston, 2004
2. Spanish Armada, war vs. England, 1588
3. Goliath, bout vs. David, date uncertain
4. Montezuma and Aztec Empire, war vs. Hernán Cortés, 1520
5. Tie — People of Jerusalem, choice of Barabbas over Jesus Christ, ca. A.D. 30; Hootie & the Blowfish, second album, *Fairweather Johnson,* 1996

How did this happen? What brought us to this stygian darkness? How could we let ourselves be so forever soiled and humiliated?

Almost exactly twelve months earlier — on October 17, 2003 — Aaron Boone's ALCS-ending home run had vaulted us into the World Series and pushed Redsock Nation to the brink of self-immolation.

Seconds later, on that magical Boone night, Alphonso phoned, wailing in a state of human-animal euphoria. Neither of us could talk. No words would suffice. We just wept. For a week, I'd paced the house and shrieked at the kids for sitting in the wrong chairs. If I caught a stuffed bunny rabbit sitting on the floor, I kicked it hard in the groin. I watched one entire inning in a squat, giving aid to the gams of Jorge Posada. Each night, Alphonso phoned to state categorically that we had *lost* the game, it was *over*, he was *turning off the TV* and *going to bed* — a masterstroke of ORRJE that the juju gods swallowed hook, line, and sinkerball. The calls had become his signature move, like Pete Townshend smashing a guitar. We felt unbeatable. That night, with one swing of the bat, we believed we had defeated Boston for all eternity.

It had been a week of nonstop war, less a baseball series than the Friday-night card for WrestleMania. Their Manny Ramirez charged our Roger Clemens. Our Karim Garcia charged their Pedro Martinez. Their Fenway security guard charged our entire bullpen. I fought each battle at home, with hard jabs and wild uppercuts. I whipped my sons into wrestling frenzies, nearly knocking the TV askew and several times causing Janice to banish me from the house.

One Saturday, we gathered the Secret Yankee Club in a room roughly the size of a kiddie swimming pool. There were eight of us, so close our atoms practically intermingled. We sounded like a prison riot. In the most surreal moment of my life as a fan, we watched our seventy-two-year-old bench coach, Don Zimmer, bound from the Yankee dugout and charge Pedro Martinez on the mound. Pedro gave a matador side step, and the coach rolled like a pumpkin that had been hurled from the stands. I'll never forget the look on Pedro's face as the Yankees wrestled Zimmer back to the dugout and — hopefully — his medication. It was as if Pedro were watching the end of the world.

In that moment, if the juju gods had transported Pedro Martinez into our presence, we would have slaughtered him on the spot and fought over the honor of devouring his still-beating heart. We had turned into raging Yankee beasts, sweating testosterone and juju. Upon returning home, I hugged my children and told them they would all be receiving gifts.

"You guys missed one of the greatest games ever!" I roared. *"There must have been ten fights!"*

And now, one year later, there I was — fat, smug, and three games up — padding off to bed with pitches yet to throw.

My fellow Yankee fans . . . it happened on *my* watch. *I went to bed.*

The "Collapse of 2004" can never be erased from baseball's fossil record, nor should it be. Let my children and my children's children forever remember my failure, my shame, in leaving my post.

I went to bed.

Perhaps it was inevitable. For decades, we had brutalized Redsock fans, broken every rule of ORRJE. Seeing a Boston cap, I would ask, "Hey, what's that *B* for, Buckner?" Peyer would show off his Yankee swag and say, "Know how much I paid for that T-shirt? Nineteen eighteen."

So on the night of October 16, 2004, as we prepared to sweep Boston in game four, for the first time in my Yankee life, I felt a billion percent certain of victory. We had Jeet. We had A-Rod. We had Mariano. It was over . . . *over!* Boston knew it. Glavin had called to concede, and I'd cackled in triumph. The Redsocks were beaten, broken, sapped of hope, begging us to pull the plugs on their gurgling ventilators.

And we lost.

Of course, I was a juju has-been. I had sought to corrupt my kids by offering them bribes. I had equated the game to a series of mob muggings. I had reveled in every dark emotion that the national pastime, once a game played for fun, was originally supposed to suppress. Over the past seven Octobers, my kids had watched their father act more childishly than any child they knew.

And then, galloping in from the east, they came: the Four Yankee Losses of the Apocalypse.

I will not relive them in these pages; life is too short. But in my nightmares, I still hear (from the bathroom) Johnny Damon crush his game seven grand slam off Javier Vazquez. In that moment, the Curse of the Bambino, or the Curse of Shaughnessy, or whatever they call it, became clear for what it always was: The Curse of Hubris.

Friends, look at history. Whenever victory is assured — whenever the king says the uprising has been quashed, whenever the pharaoh says the locusts have been sprayed, whenever the president says the mission has been accomplished — run, for God's sake, *run!* The juju gods, or the Uppercasers, or the government, or whoever is running the show — they have picked up the dice, put them back into the shaker, and are going to reroll. *Run!*

On the morning after the collapse, I feared going into work. I thought of quitting my job and moving to rural China.

But something strange happened. My longtime Redsock enemies approached me with a kindness that would make Saint Francis of Assisi appear catty. They had every right to gloat. They could have coated my phone receiver with mayonnaise or danced on my desk with their trousers down. Instead, they moved slowly, carefully, not making loud noises. It wasn't weird — they didn't rub my back or anything — but they gently told me they understood. I will never forget their generosity.

Then again, there were the hotheads, the spiteful, anti-Yankee strain. They wanted my Yankee-capped head on a pike. They hovered, they pranced, they relived every pitch. They left newspaper clippings on my desk and forwarded e-mails from Denis Leary and Ben *"I would rather utter the words 'I worship you, Satan,' than 'My favorite baseball team is the New York Yankees'"* Affleck.

I couldn't blame them. Hadn't I done my share?

The Yankee-Redsock rivalry had become a mirror image of the political climate across America. The 2004 presidential election — George W. Bush vs. John Kerry — was days away, with the nation engaged in a cultural pie fight. The more our pundits and parties could polarize Americans, the higher their ratings, and the more they could charge for advertising.

So it had become with the Yankees and Redsocks. The rivalry was a commodity, a marketing angle, exploited by a media determined to promote anger. And we fans swallowed it. Instead of rooting for our players, we just booed theirs. Redsock fans hated the way Manny jogged to first, but they *really* hated A-Rod. I didn't like Roger Clemens shaving batters, but Pedro — he *really* pissed me off.

Everywhere, hate. And I couldn't understand why my kids didn't want to join the fun.

Game six of the 2004 American League Championship Series would end with an unprecedented sight in American sports: New York City police officers strung out along the foul lines in full riot gear. At one point, the Redsocks left the field because fans were throwing things. The umpires threatened to call a forfeit — *a forfeit in a league championship game.*

It's now part of Americana: When the Yankees play the Redsocks, gather the family around the TV! You don't want to miss it! Somebody might get killed!

Go to YouTube and search "Yankees Red Sox fans fight." Choose your preference. Want to watch Yankee fans beat up a Boston guy? Or would you rather see Redsock fans kick the brains out of a New Yorker?

In 2004, whenever the Yankees visited Fenway, they rightfully could have been charged with crossing state lines to incite a riot. And when Roger Clemens pitched — *remember:* he was run out of Boston to make way for Pedro — fans greeted him the way Italians hailed the upside-down corpse of Benito Mussolini. The hostility traumatized Clemens's wife, who vowed never to return to the city where his career began, where he had once been loved.

Riots occur, though the media disdain the r word. In 2003, following the Boone home run, students at the University of Massachusetts overturned cars. (They also rioted in 2001 after the Yankees lost the World Series.) Hours after the Redsocks beat the Yankees in 2004, Boston police fired pepper balls into an ongoing "disturbance," killing an Emerson College student named Victoria Snelgrove. Think about that: *a young woman died.*

Proud of your team? Be careful.

In October 2007, two Yankee fans in Yonkers beat the hell out of a thirty-year-old guy in a Boston T-shirt. He needed intensive care.

In March 2008, a Cambridge, Massachusetts, mob beat up a twenty-three-year-old guy in a Yankee cap. His girlfriend watched as they kicked him from all sides while he was lying on the ground.

In May 2008, a New Hampshire woman drove her car into a crowd and killed a twenty-nine-year-old man. The group had converged on her car because it had a Yankee bumper sticker. She freaked out and hit the gas.

In July 2008, a Cape Cod resident beat a man with a baseball bat. Why? He was a Yankee fan.

The nation was horrified in April 2011 when a Giants fan was beaten into a coma outside Dodger Stadium. The attackers, wearing Dodger swag, had taunted him.

Believe what you wish about the foolishness of juju. But when you kick a stuffed animal, it doesn't bleed.

And shortly after Boston beat us on that night in October 2004 — ending the "curse" and the world as we knew it — when the phone rang, I yelled, "It's Glavin! Don't answer! Let it ring! Don't touch it! Let it ring! Don't answer!"

Janice picked it up anyway. She spoke for a moment, smiled, and then handed the receiver to me.

"It's over," Alphonso said. "I've turned off the TV, and I'm going to bed."

JUJU RULE 26

Batting Seventh

In my life as a father and a son, I do not claim to have solved many great mysteries. I will never understand why the Fates reward some people and visit such sadness upon others. I will never know why one week Aaron Boone hits the most important home run of his life, and the next week he strikes out with the World Series in the balance. I will never figure out how one day I can feel so lucky and the next day so cursed.

There are times when every Yankee fan — even with *thirteen extra wins per season* — concludes that he or she can do nothing right, that the universe made a mistake in bringing us online.

We cannot hit. We cannot throw. We never could.

We wonder what we've accomplished, and we start thinking that we will never do anything that matters, other than watch others — the lucky ones, the gifted ones, those who earn more money and fame in an afternoon than we will in a year — pursue their greatness. That is the painful mentality of being a fan.

We cannot hit. We cannot throw. We never could.

All we have is juju — *if* we're willing to believe in it.

Listen: I claim no magical cure for slumps, or for the blues, or for the times in your life when every call to the bullpen backfires. Anyone who has ever paced a circle or screamed obscenities at a flock of birds knows what I mean. In the best of times, juju usually fails.

You can renounce your faith. You can quit your team. You can conclude that you're not Derek Jeter — that God did not give you the same ability — and that the cosmos put you here to take up time and space until somebody luckier comes along. But never forget:

Rule 26: Juju is always about the next pitch.

You're Billy, setting the table.

I believe that if we live long enough, all the juju we send to others comes back to us in one form or another.

True story: In the summer of 2001, I was walking with Harty and Kyle along the midway of the New York State Fair, when a sign caught my eye.

MEET CLETE BOYER
Member of the 1961 New York Yankees
"The Greatest Team of All Time"

We followed it to a card table under an awning, where an old man in a crewcut sat stoically over a pile of black-and-white glossies. A gum-chewing teenager with a thatch of Green Day hair stood over him, looking bored and on-the-clock. There was no line. We marched right up to them.

I bent to my sons and nodded to the old ballplayer seated low behind the table. "See this man?" I said. "Mr. Boyer, here, was your great-grandmother's all-time favorite Yankee. Nobody ever fielded third base like him. Not Brooks Robinson. Not Eddie Mathews. Not even his brother Ken. He was the best."

The old man beamed at my young sons, who had never heard of Brooks Robinson, Eddie Mathews, or — for that matter — their great-grandmother.

"He wasn't known for his bat," I continued, "but Mr. Boyer hit clutch home runs in the World Series. My grandmother used to tell me that nobody in our lineup — not Mickey, not Yogi, nobody — was a tougher out than Clete Boyer. In a key situation, she wanted to see him come to the plate. When he left the Yankees, she said it was a huge mistake. And she was right. He went to Atlanta, and he proved to everybody what he could do. He had almost one hundred RBIs!"

Their eyes widened at the man behind the table.

Clete Boyer glanced at each of them and leaned forward.

"While batting seventh," he said.

29

★

Iraq

In early 2005, I began covering Fort Drum, the sprawling U.S. Army post near Watertown, a ninety-minute drive from Syracuse. I wrote about soldiers coming home from Iraq and Afghanistan, and at times about the families whose loved ones did not come home. One day, I had just interviewed a group of young servicemen who had lost comrades in an attack near Baghdad. They looked like my sons. Afterward, I was decompressing, still trembling, when an Army official asked me if I wanted to go to Iraq.

The offer caught me off-guard. At the time, I was reeling, not just from the interviews, but from a sense that I would never again write anything of consequence. My novel was dead. So was my career. I was destined to be the eternal Syracuse print reporter, the byline that nobody remembered atop the story that nobody read, the guy who wrote the book that nobody would publish.

"How's that novel coming?" returning colleagues would ask, then see my face and try not to cringe. Folks no longer exclaimed, "Seely, you're still here?" Of course I was still here. I would always be here. This was *Seely*cuse. The local press club gave me a lifetime achievement award. That obit I'd been padding for twenty years? I sat in a banquet and heard it spoken aloud.

So when the Army guy asked if I would like to go to Iraq, I said yeah, sign me up. We shook on it.

On the drive back to Syracuse, this line kept repeating in my head: "I don't care if I *never* get back . . ."

"Whoa," my editor said upon hearing my plans. "Losing to Boston really *did* get to you."

Over the next six months, I convinced the Army, the newspaper, my family, and myself that I had to go. Then came the hard part: waiting. At first, I was to leave in August. Then it was September. By October, folks who had told me goodbye in August were now saying, "Seely, you're still here?" — a painful reminder that had I gone then, I would be home by now.

Every day, I swapped fiery e-mails with Alphonso, who was bringing unprecedented levels of neg — not for Rizzutonic impact, but because he truly had gone Jean-Paul Sartre on the Yankees. How could we express hope when our past tormentors, Gary Sheffield and Randy Johnson, now wore pinstripes? It was like dining with the cop who'd Tasered your mom. I couldn't do Lookaways for Randy Johnson. The juju gods would laugh at me.

Still, we soldiers of the Secret Yankee Club yearned for vengeance. We needed payback from the Angels, who had humiliated us in 2002 with a string of girlie-man singles. Then we could seek to pummel Boston back to the 1918 bird flu epidemic. If we could win, say, five quick world championships, I could heal from the pain of 2004 and move on with my fantasy life.

My anxieties diminished after we savaged Anaheim in game one of the AL Division Series. Alphonso didn't even need to burn an "I'm going to bed" call. Peyer was wearing a rapper necklace with dollar signs and a rhinestone "NY." In critical situations, he'd kiss it, reminding the juju gods just how visibly disturbing a Yankee defeat could be. Privately, we thought we had the Angels on the run. But in "monitored" conversations, we never expressed an iota of hope.

It didn't work. A-Rod booted game two, and Randy Johnson threw batting practice in game three. Meanwhile, Joe Torre could do noth-

ing right. In the 1990s, Joe couldn't botch a soufflé if he was cooking blindfolded with a blowtorch. Now every move backfired, as if
the International Bank of Juju had foreclosed. We had a $203 mil-
lion payroll but not one setup reliever who could throw strikes. Peyer
could kiss those rhinestones into a four-run rally, but why bother? We
couldn't hold a lead.

By now, my family recognized the Yankee Martial Law that went
into effect each October. Nobody flinched if he or she woke up in
bed to the sound of screaming downstairs. No one entered the TV
room to ask the score. Nobody interrupted Dad during his game. Nor
did anyone mention Yankee Incentive Rewards, which had withheld
dividends for four years. But the loudest unspoken topic sat in the
front hall, as silent as an Easter Island statue: the Army duffel bag
that I packed and unpacked every night. Was I going? Or was I gone?
Was this real or just another project, another novel I would write and
rewrite until nobody cared? Nobody knew. I certainly didn't.

Increasingly, Madeline would cry at bedtime. She'd ask why I was
going. I'd say I had to go. I would promise to return, but the words
came out in my "Yankees behind by six runs" voice, which everybody
in our house recognized. During game four, which we won, I chewed
my fingernails and knuckles so desperately that, next morning, Janice
vacuumed the floor where I had been pacing. In all our years, she'd
never done that.

Early in game five, our grab-bag center fielder, Bubba Crosby,
came to bat with a man on third. I locked in on Bubba. The pitch
came low and hard, but we swung together and slapped a single to
right, driving in the run. Jeter hit a sacrifice fly, and we led by two.

The phone rang. "Game-over-we-lost-TV-off-bed," Alphonso
blurted and hung up. Across town, Peyer was French-kissing his
necklace. In my lotus stance, I became the ball so intensely that I felt
Mike Mussina's nails digging into my ribs. We had that game.

And then we got screwed.

That night, the entire country saw Mussina strike out Angel center fielder Steve Finley. Everybody in the free world saw the ball catch the outside corner, saw Finley's eyes darken with the knowledge that he'd failed, saw a perfectly thrown strike three — everybody, that is, except home plate umpire Joe West. He saw ball four.

I collapsed. Ball four? Was this a hoax? A mass prank? How could he call it ball four? It had passed over the corner. Everybody had seen it. The whole world had seen it. The universe had seen it. How could this be allowed? This was America, not Russia or communist China. Millions of people had seen it. It had bisected the plate. Right down the middle. Strike three. Where were the juju gods? *Where was justice?*

I began screaming. Mussina glowered, Torre frowned, Finley jogged to first, and while the apathetic American viewing public chewed its cud, the FOX Sports announcers — Joe Buck and Tim McCarver, my lifelong anti-Yankee nemesis — pretended that *nothing had happened.*

I was still screaming when the next Angel batter hit a pop fly to right-center, giving baseball a chance to escape with its dignity. Crosby and Sheffield crashed into each other in the way that bugs smash into windshields, the ball dropped, three runs scored, and the juju gods — no doubt disillusioned with earthly events — called it a night.

I was still screaming when everyone fled upstairs.

The next day, Janice confronted me. Madeline had cried. Everybody was upset. Was I going to Iraq or not? And if so, why? Then she said something I'd never heard in all our time together.

"I'm glad the Yankees lost, because I can't take this anymore."

"Okay, look," I said. "Say the word, and I won't go. Just say the word, and I'll tell the Army it's over. Say the word, and *I won't go!*"

"Don't go," she said. "I'm saying the word. Don't go."

"I have to go."

"You *don't* have to go."

"Look, when this is over, we'll be glad I went."

She looked at me sadly and shook her head.

"This will never be over."

The following day, when the phone rang, I shouted to let it ring, not to answer it, because it was Glavin, calling to cackle.

It was the Army. My plane was leaving in twelve hours.

It took two days to reach Iraq. I sat in empty airports, nearly boarded a bus to the wrong country, spent a night chasing down luggage, then hooked up with the cast from a Quentin Tarantino movie in a predawn desert checkpoint that looked like the exact place in creation where God ran out of money. Through every wait, every coffee, and every delay, I was racked with guilt over what I had done: I had left my family, and for what? To chase a news story? To finally leave Syracuse? For eight months, I'd pursued this trip — going for the sake of going — and now I was gone, and what was the point?

I went to Iraq with a *Post-Standard* photographer named Li-Hua Lan, a woman with as much courage as any soldier I've ever met. On our first mission into Baghdad, while soldiers hugged the walls and eyed the rooftops, Li-Hua stood in the center of the street, framing a wide-angle shot. It's an image I will never forget. Minutes later, a sniper opened fire on our unit. I remember the sergeant pushing me toward the truck and yelling, *"Go, go, go!"* Trust me, I ran.

Each day, we traveled with a different unit of the Tenth Mountain Division. No two missions were alike. The day after the sniper fire, we were mobbed by adoring Iraqis in another section of Baghdad. In many ways, this was far more terrifying: little kids running at you, slapping your back, groping for candy. I ran inside the truck and stayed. So did Li-Hua.

Most missions were delightfully uneventful. We rode in big convoys, jabbering with the soldiers, waiting to get blown up. They would ask me how folks back home viewed the war. I had no answer. Later, the folks back home would ask me how the soldiers in Iraq viewed the war. No answer. Everywhere, I saw kids missing their families, while we rumbled around in a distant world, waiting to get blown up.

On the streets of Baghdad, I wore a forty-pound Kevlar vest, steel-toed boots, a helmet, safety goggles, and percussion earplugs. I felt like a scuba diver. I could hear myself breathe. Almost every day, we went on a "presence patrol." Basically, it meant maneuvering a convoy in and around dangerous neighborhoods, waiting to get blown up.

On those rides, the troops were supposed to stay constantly alert for improvised explosive devices (IEDs) that could be stashed along the road. But the entire city was a trash heap, the streets lined with garbage. We couldn't stop for every empty milk jug or plastic bag, so we just kept riding, waiting to get blown up.

(*Note:* When General David Petraeus took over Iraq War operations, he eliminated presence patrols.)

On the base, I wore a tattered Yankee cap that was older than most of the soldiers. I looked like a fool, a clown, a laughingstock — but it worked. Every day, somebody would confront me about the Yankees or denounce A-Rod for going 2-for-15 against the Angels. If I met a Redsock fan, we'd leap toward each other like magnets, launching into an argument that would blissfully transport us back home.

Generationally, I had crossed over: I was now the old guy, pleading to waste a young man's time. I was my dad, looking to escape Waverly for fifteen minutes.

After two weeks at Camp Liberty, Li-Hua and I moved to an outpost at the edge of Baghdad called Forward Operating Base Independence. We stayed with the 1-71 Cavalry, a unit of about seventy soldiers, in a football-field-size compound that was surrounded by concrete walls. From the guard towers, you could see into backyards and watch Iraqi versions of Homer Simpson tend their gardens. One old guy kept pigeons on a rooftop. They flew loops in the sky until he called them to roost. I would have given anything to talk with him, but in my scuba gear, that was impossible.

The unit's oldest soldier, Sergeant Evert Janson, was ten years younger than me. Every night, he chatted online with his wife and two little girls. Every morning, we walked the base perimeter together. He showed me the mortar-shell crater where a contractor had died recently, and bullet holes in the walls where families of birds now nested. He showed me his favorite place, near a graveyard of blown-up Humvees, where wild morning glories grew to the size of silver dollars.

"You wouldn't think something so beautiful could be here," Janson said.

We stayed at FOB Independence for four weeks. I remember moments of unbridled laughter, of riding in a Humvee (waiting to get blown up) and arguing over whether Richard Pryor was still alive. (I was right, damn it; he was! But he would die later that year.) I recall my knees buckling as I stood beside a sizzling, mangled hunk of metal, a car torn apart by an IED, as a crowd of Iraqis constricted around us. And I'll never forget my arrival.

As I walked into the mess hall, I felt the cold eyes of the entire troop on me. I stood at the coffee urn, searching for creamer. A huge guy pressed into my space. I ignored him. He nudged me. I moved away. He nudged harder. I was ready to melt down, and he handed me a carton of milk.

His name was Armer Burkart, and his smile that day brought me back down to earth. He came from Maryland. He was the type of kid who'd joined the Army to do right, to help people, not to play Rambo, not to run away.

Ten weeks before he was to come home to his wife, Armer was killed by an IED. The troop was devastated. The chaplain later told me that he'd never experienced anything like it. The toughest soldiers, the ones who joked about death, literally fell to the floor crying.

"One day, we will take our grandchildren to whatever memorial they build to honor this war," Captain Rob Duchaine said in Armer's eulogy. "We will find your name on it, along with our other brothers', and we will point to it and say, 'I knew that man; he was a hero.'"

Armer Burkart. I knew that man. He was a hero.

Listen: The Yankees are great athletes, great players, great competitors, maybe great men — I don't know. They are *not* heroes. That's not a knock. It's just the truth.

The day we left for home, the 1-71 Cavalry gave us a sendoff. The troop thanked us for coming and presented us with special coins and golden spurs. I was in tears. Li-Hua didn't want to leave. But the men had gotten it backward; *I* couldn't thank *them* enough. They had shown me what I had overlooked. They had taught me how much I missed my family, how much I needed to get home, to Syracuse, to the people and place where I belonged.

Our plane touched down in Syracuse around 1:00 A.M. on Thanksgiving Day. My family was waiting at the airport. Hank and Marge came, and Alphonso drove up from New York City. When I stepped into view, my kids cheered, and I hugged Janice until I nearly cracked my back.

"Welcome home," she said.

"Marry me," I said, and hugged her even harder.

"We watched some of the World Series," she said later. "But it just wasn't the same."

"Of course not. The Yankees weren't playing."

"No, *you* weren't playing."

I hugged her again.

"Do you know you are hopeless?" she said.

"The thought has occurred to me."

She laughed.

Janice laughed.

The next day, we drove to a nearby lake. It was freezing, but the November sun emerged. We walked the shoreline, and I told stories of my trip.

"You know what?" Alphonso said. "Someday you gotta write a book."

JUJU RULE 27

Trades

In Iraq, I found few soldiers who gave a whit about the 2005 World Series between the Astros and White Sox. Thanks to the unseeing eyes of Mr. Joe West, *I* certainly didn't.

But when not fighting on the battlefield, the U.S. Army lives for football, and the soldiers I met often pulled all-nighters to watch live satellite feeds of NFL games. One morning, well before dawn, I tried to help two Philadelphia Eagle fans — Robert Miller and Jerald Haffey — throw juju across the planet on behalf of their team.

Although it was only October, both soldiers assured me this game was absolutely critical. (See juju rule 12.) Their souls burned with the certainty that if Philly could beat Dallas, the Eagles would magically jell and begin their march to the Super Bowl. If they won this game, everything would fall into place.

In an otherwise empty mess hall, the two young men shouted, sack-danced, threw penalty flags (napkins), and deked imaginary tacklers for most of four quarters. Together, they willed the Eagles to a thirteen-point lead with four minutes remaining. To run out the clock, Philadelphia needed one more measly first down. Ten yards, and they would win the Super Bowl.

I'm no Eagle fan, but that morning, to support our troops, I mentally conveyed to the juju gods an unprecedented proposal. I offered to trade three future Yankee victories for one Philadelphia first down.

That's right: three Yankee wins for ten yards in a span of three plays. Crunch the numbers: that's just 3.33 yards per play — three plays — in exchange for three games to be named later. Magical threes.

Listen: That was a damn sweet offer. I wasn't trying to deal three George Zebers for one George Brett. *Three games for ten lousy yards.* Plus, the offer was made on humanitarian grounds: I was helping a team I didn't even like. I proposed the deal respectfully. I issued no ultimatum. I attempted no trickery. It was a damn square proposition.

Their response? Philadelphia quarterback Donovan McNabb threw a sideline interception, which Dallas ran back forty-six yards for a touchdown. Trying to make the tackle, McNabb tweaked something and limped off the field. The Eagles' backup quarterback threw like Téa Leoni (*Yankee fan, by the way*). Philly lost in the final seconds, and the two soldiers marched out that morning into a war zone, tired, beaten, and devoid of human hope.

I never felt worse about a loss that didn't involve the Yankees. And it was my fault.

Rule 27: Never try to cut deals with the juju gods.

Listen: They may not be wily John McGraw, but they're not the 1950s Kansas City Athletics either. They won't trade you Roger Maris, Bobby Shantz, Hector Lopez, Clete Boyer, Art Ditmar, and Ralph Terry for Jerry Lumpe.

Besides — and here's where I must be blunt — *you don't own a Jerry Lumpe.*

That day, I was trying to peddle three wins that I didn't possess. If the juju gods wanted three Yankee victories, all they had to do was put in the paperwork. Thus, Philadelphia lost. My friends lost. And one year later, almost exactly to the day, as if the juju gods were showing off, the Detroit Tigers skunked us in the American League Championship Series, rattling off three straight wins.

The juju gods don't negotiate with us for one fundamental reason: *we have nothing they want.*

I know what you're thinking: *What about our eternal souls? Don't deities collect eternal souls, sort of like* Star Wars *action figures?*

First, trading away your eternal soul is how Steinbrenner screwed up the team in the 1980s. He traded long-term prospects for a quick shot of Big John Mayberry or Jesse Barfield. Want a new car or a better shortstop? Don't even *think* about offering your immortal soul, unless you're ready to imagine an eternity of Rick Rhoden on the mound.

Second, the juju gods do not covet your eternal soul. They already have their own eternal souls. Besides, who needs a garage full of eternal souls? Each one lasts for eternity. It won't exactly wear out or spoil in the carton.

What about offering our unequivocal love? Doesn't every deity want to bathe in a warm, milky pool of human affection?

First, there's something icky about that image. Second, even though idolatry must be an ego boost, I believe the notion of juju gods watching you sit in your bedroom, lighting incense and praising their names, becomes astonishingly creepy after the first week. They get flashes of Jennifer Jason Leigh in the 1992 thriller *Single White Female*. There might even be juju god laws against romancing mortals. It's kind of like a six-hundred-year-old dating a ninth grader.

Save your immortal soul and eternal love for the Uppercase Deities. They're the rock stars. They know how to handle groupies.

And don't try to cut deals. *Remember:* This isn't an office fantasy league. This is baseball. This is juju. This is real. *This is life.*

30

★

Glavin

In the early winter of 2010, a friend called with terrible news. Glavin had been diagnosed with lung cancer. I hadn't heard from him in weeks but had given it little thought. I figured he was licking his wounds from the Yankees' World Series victory.

I grabbed my new world championship handkerchief — made in China from toxic fabric and featuring evil corporate logos — and drove to Glavin's house. I was determined to lift his spirits the only way I knew how: with a full-scale, in-his-face Yankee rant. Business as usual. I'd wave the hankie and assure him that he could never escape me, that sickness was no excuse to avoid my Yankee dance. Because those were the rules of engagement.

I stood on his stoop and pounded on the door.

"Hey, Glavin," I shouted, "I brought you something."

He cracked the door and peered outside. The wetness in his eyes, above the oxygen hose, turned my knees to wax. I couldn't talk. I just stood there.

"Congratulations," he said weakly, his voice a bucket of rocks. "You and George . . ."

He trailed off. He saw the hankie in my hand. I pushed it toward him.

"You and George must have run out of toilet paper," he said.

Chemotherapy didn't touch it. Glavin deteriorated quickly. The next time I visited, he grew tired so fast that I felt guilty for sapping his energy. Then two weeks later, a friend called to say it was now or never. If I wanted to see my friend again, I had to go immediately.

He had moved into hospice on the north side of Syracuse. I found him lying in bed. His face was bloated, his glasses no longer fit, and that booming voice had become a whisper. When he woke up, he couldn't lift himself, but he managed a smile, and he called me by my first name, which he almost never did.

"Okay, Glavin, you won," I said. "I figured the Yankees could outlast you. But you beat us. You not only won one World Series, but you won two."

"You got us with Bucky Dent," he said.

"Yeah, well you guys had Burleson," I said.

"Aaron Boone."

"Schilling."

"Guidry."

"Pedro."

"Munson."

"Fisk."

He smiled. The Yankees and Redsocks would be playing the next night.

"Gotta win it," Glavin said, and then abruptly drifted off to sleep.

He didn't make it to the game.

For the rest of my life, when the Yankees lose a tough one, or when we trade the next Doug Drabek or sign the new Ron Kittle, I will wait for a phone call that I know will never come.

Epilogue: The Yard

★

True story: Several years ago, the most magical ballpark I've ever known closed for business.

It was the true cathedral of baseball, one of a kind. None can replace it. None will come close. I was blessed to have it for so many years.

In it, my oldest son, Hart, hit home runs over the swing set in right field, and Kyle once leaped into the bushes along the third-base line to snare a foul, just like a certain Yankee captain. Madeline once smacked a line drive off the composter in left-center, and no one can forget the infamous "Mommy shift," instituted because a fearsome hitter named Janice happened to bat left-handed. In our backyard, Seely Stadium, every seat was a luxury box, and every game was the greatest ever played.

Out there, with my kids, the roster of Wiffle ball immortals included our neighbors — the Sheedys, who always wore their Redsock colors — and Marge and Hank's four children, best friends to ours. The yard hosted the greatest rivalry in sports: Kids vs. Parents. Here entire childhoods came one morning and disappeared by twilight. Here every game went down to the final out, and the pong of the bat

merged into shouts and pleas: *One more inning? . . . It's not that dark!
. . . We can still see! . . . One more inning . . . please?*

A few years ago, our stadium closed. Once, it seemed larger than
any major league park, and hitting a home run seemed an impossible
dream. Then one day, it shrank into a tiny patch of grass, too small for
even a game of catch. And suddenly its star players were gone, with
their own lives to live.

Kids grow up. Baseball careers fizzle out. Life goes on. Streaks
merge into slumps. But tomorrow always brings another game. And
even if we say we expect to lose, nobody really believes it — not when
you can count on *thirteen extra wins per season.*

This is the world as I know it.

Some physicists argue the existence of an infinite number of parallel universes, each one slightly different from the reality we know.
If they're correct, somewhere out there the Cubs own twenty-seven
world championships.

I've often wondered about the parallel universes of my life, the
dice rolls that could have changed my Little League pop-up into a
walk-off grand slam, or kept me in Norwich one Friday night rather
than driving to Syracuse. One flat tire, one five-minute rain delay,
one twist of fate, and somewhere out there Thurman Munson is still
alive, and I am still searching for the woman I love. You could go mad
thinking about such things (which may explain my condition).

I know for sure that one parallel universe exists, and I know exactly when it began.

I'm nestled in my mother's lap. We're sitting around the Admiral
TV, and let's say that it *is* Don Larsen pitching his perfect game. Mom
gives me a squeeze and says, "Harty, they want to know who you're
rooting for." I search my mind for what I am supposed to say, and this
time, I get it right.

"Anybody playing the Yankees!" I say.

They explode with laughter. It's hilarious, a showstopper. *Greatest.
Moment. Ever.* I take a bow. I stand proud. Dad hugs me. I own the
room.

Dad's universe, the one where I stick to the script, is out there somewhere. No ad-libbing. No confrontations. Maybe our lives move along a different path. Who knows, maybe I grow up and play for the Yankees.

But we don't get to roll the dice again, do we?

Early one morning in 2002, my sister, Virginia, called in a state of panic. She said that Mom had had a heart attack and was in the hospital. She told me to hurry. I drove like mad, yelling into the dashboard. I didn't make it.

I never told my mom goodbye. I never said thank you. I never got to ask her, *What was I supposed to say that day? Did I get my line right? Or did I blow it? All these years, was I making it up on the fly?*

These days, I tell people my two favorite cities in the world are Dallas and Los Angeles. When they ask why, I just say because they were my dad's favorites.

On that note, I am happy to declare that in this universe, the Seely family roots for the New York Yankees, who own more world championships than any other major league team. I am equally pleased to report that none of the Seely children fights lamps or flings himself or herself onto the floor during key game situations. They have other outlets for their juju, and their universes are just beginning to bloom.

As for me, every now and then, a surgical beam of energy from my living room chair in Syracuse, New York, merges with billions of similar Rizzutonic emissions from points around the globe, redirecting somebody's bat into the path of somebody else's pitch . . . propelling the ball into the right-field seats.

These days, I work several special moves, which are strictly my business. I may reveal them someday, after they cease to function or when we've simply won too many world championships, whichever comes first.

When the Yankees win the next big game, the Yankee Crier will have a new story to tell, and Jocko will spare a cap from some hideous torture. Even late at night, my phone will start to ring. Hank will call from the other side of Syracuse. Alphonso will report from downstate. I'll hear from Peyer, Moose, the Dog Man, Yankgers, Dodgints, even a Redsock aboriginal or two, from parts unknown.

"All hail the Yankees," the Duke will proclaim.

I will wake up the next morning in the same bed, with the same bills and the same car that needs the same new brake job. I will go to the same job in the same Golden Snowball Award city and deal with the same pains in the same butt. Juju won't buy me a new set of brakes. But I will have another imaginary World Series ring in my imaginary Yankee life.

I will remain true to the vows I made long ago on my mother's lap, at Bob and Zip's Hoosier Show Lounge, to the friends who are no longer with us, and to the Secret Yankee Club. I'm still standing, still changing chairs, still rolling the dice, still taking my placebos — which still work, as long as nobody spills the beans and tells me they're only sugar.

God willing, we'll win it again. We have the tradition. We have the money. We have the legends of A-Rod and Mariano. We have Bill O'Reilly *and* Keith Olbermann (*Yankee fans, by the way*). We have Alphonso bringing the neg, Peyer bringing the swag, and the collective force of a gazillion Rizzutons flowing across the universe every April through October.

I know what it's like to be Lou Gehrig, because I consider myself the luckiest man on the face of the earth. Somebody, somewhere, has always been shooting Rizzutons my way.

So here are my wishes:

May the inanimate objects in your home respect you.

May you find the right juju couch and, more important, the right person with whom to share it.

May you appreciate the children who never grow up and enjoy the elders who push your buttons, perhaps just to remember how it feels to be young.

And, of course, may you understand that I'm just kidding about all that juju stuff.

You do know that I'm kidding . . . right?

Remembering Lindsay

★

On September 11, 2001, "Alphonso's" twenty-four-year-old daughter, Lindsay, who worked for Keefe, Bruyette & Woods in the World Trade Center, was killed in the terrorist attacks on the United States. Just prior to her death, she was thrilled to be accepted as a mentor in the New York City Big Brothers Big Sisters program. To honor her memory and her commitment to this cause, her parents set up a college scholarship at Big Brothers Big Sisters to give deserving kids a chance for a better future. To make a donation online, go to www.bigsnyc.org/donate.php, or send your donation to the Lindsay Morehouse Memorial College Fund, Big Brothers Big Sisters of New York City, 223 East Thirtieth Street, New York, NY 10016.